THE
HISTORY OF
NIGERIA

ADVISORY BOARD

THE
HISTORY OF
NIGERIA

Toyin Falola

The Greenwood Histories of the Modern Nations
Frank W. Thackeray and John E. Findling, Series Editors

Greenwood Press
Westport, Connecticut • London

Library of Congress Cataloging-in-Publication Data

Falola, Toyin.
  The history of Nigeria / Toyin Falola.
    p. cm.—(The Greenwood histories of the modern nations,
  ISSN 1096–2905)
    Includes bibliographical references (p.) and index.
    ISBN 0–313–30682–6 (alk. paper)
    1. Nigeria—History.   I. Title.   II. Series.
  DT515.57.F35   1999
  966.9—dc21   99–17859

British Library Cataloguing in Publication Data is available.

Library of Congress Catalog Card Number: 99–17859
ISBN: 0–313–30682–6
ISSN: 1096–2905

First published in 1999

Greenwood Press, 88 Post Road West, Westport, CT 06881
An imprint of Greenwood Publishing Group, Inc.
www.greenwood.com

Printed in the United States of America

The paper used in this book complies with the
Permanent Paper Standard issued by the National
Information Standards Organization (Z39.48–1984).

10 9 8 7 6 5 4 3 2 1

To my wife, O'Bisi

Contents

Series Foreword

The Greenwood Histories of the Modern Nations series is intended to provide students and interested laypeople with up-to-date, concise, and analytical histories of many of the nations of the contemporary world. Not since the 1960s has there been a systematic attempt to publish a series of national histories, and, as series editors, we believe that this series will prove to be a valuable contribution to our understanding of other countries in our increasingly interdependent world.

Over thirty years ago, at the end of the 1960s, the Cold War was an accepted reality of global politics, the process of decolonization was still in progress, the idea of a unified Europe with a single currency was unheard of, the United States was mired in a war in Vietnam, and the economic boom of Asia was still years in the future. Richard Nixon was president of the United States, Mao Tse-tung (not yet Mao Zedong) ruled China, Leonid Brezhnev guided the Soviet Union, and Harold Wilson was prime minister of the United Kingdom. Authoritarian dictators still ruled most of Latin America, the Middle East was reeling in the wake of the Six-Day War, and Shah Reza Pahlavi was at the height of his power in Iran. Clearly, the past thirty years have been witness to a great deal of historical change, and it is to this change that this series is primarily addressed.

With the help of a distinguished advisory board, we have selected nations whose political, economic, and social affairs mark them as among the most important in the waning years of the twentieth century, and for each nation we have found an author who is recognized as a specialist in the history of that nation. These authors have worked most cooperatively with us and with Greenwood Press to produce volumes that reflect current research on their nation and that are interesting and informative to their prospective readers.

The importance of a series such as this cannot be underestimated. As a superpower whose influence is felt all over the world, the United States can claim a "special" relationship with almost every other nation. Yet many Americans know very little about the histories of the nations with which the United States relates. How did they get to be the way they are? What kind of political systems have evolved there? What kind of influence do they have in their own region? What are the dominant political, religious, and cultural forces that move their leaders? These and many other questions are answered in the volumes of this series.

The authors who have contributed to this series have written comprehensive histories of their nations, dating back to prehistoric times in some cases. Each of them, however, has devoted a significant portion of the book to events of the past thirty years, because the modern era has contributed the most to contemporary issues that have an impact on U.S. policy. Authors have made an effort to be as up-to-date as possible so that readers can benefit from the most recent scholarship and a narrative that includes very recent events.

In addition to the historical narrative, each volume in this series contains an introductory overview of the country's geography, political institutions, economic structure, and cultural attributes. This is designed to give readers a picture of the nation as it exists in the contemporary world. Each volume also contains additional chapters that add interesting and useful detail to the historical narrative. One chapter is a thorough chronology of important historical events, making it easy for readers to follow the flow of a particular nation's history. Another chapter features biographical sketches of the nation's most important figures in order to humanize some of the individuals who have contributed to the historical development of their nation. Each volume also contains a comprehensive bibliography, so that those readers whose interest has been sparked may find out more about the nation and its history. Finally, there is a carefully prepared topic and person index.

Readers of these volumes will find them fascinating to read and useful in understanding the contemporary world and the nations that comprise it. As series editors, it is our hope that this series will contribute to a heightened sense of global understanding as we enter a new century.

Frank W. Thackeray and John E. Findling
Indiana University Southeast

Preface and Acknowledgments

My focus is on the two interrelated themes of politics and economy that have defined the history of Nigeria during the twentieth century and that will continue to shape its future in the next millennium. Drawing on a large body of primary and secondary sources, this book analyzes the history of Nigeria from its early period to the present. All the major historical themes are covered, notably precolonial and indigenous state systems and societies, the penetration of Europeans that ended in colonial subjugation, nationalist struggles, and the various administrations since the country attained its independence in 1960. Nigeria is yet to emerge as a strong united nation, and its efforts at creating political stability and economic development have been disappointing. This book captures the history of lost opportunities and the mismanagement of a country with all the resources to become a world power.

I would not have undertaken to write this book but for the kind invitation of Professors Frank W. Thackeray and John E. Findling, the series editors of the Greenwood Histories of the Modern Nations. They along with Dr. Barbara A. Rader, the Executive Editor, shaped the format of the book. I am responsible for the contents, following the guidelines provided by the publishers on length, readership, and emphasis on the twentieth century.

Initial comments on the draft were made by a host of professors: Dr. Bayo Oyebade of Tennessee State University, Nashville; Dr. Wilson Ogbomo of Allegheny College, Meadville; Dr. John Lamphear of the University of Texas at Austin; Dr. A. G. Adebayo of Kennesaw State University, Kennesaw; Dr. Jeremiah Dibua of Morgan State University, Baltimore; Dr. Ann O'Hear, an independent scholar and expert on Nigerian economic history; and Dr. Axel Harneit-Sievers of the Center for Modern Oriental Studies, Berlin, Germany. I am most grateful for their suggestions and words of wisdom, not to mention their joy in revealing to me that the book will be well received. A revised edition also benefited from the comments of the series advisors and Dr. Rader. Bob Reppe prepared the maps, and Joel Tishken the index.

For other crucial forms of support, I wish to thank the members of my family: Olabisi, Bisola, Dolapo, and Toyin. The home is always filled with joy and eager anticipation of the future as the children proceed to college. I am also blessed by other relations, such as Dr. Ladi Olusola of Dallas and Eto Falola of Chicago, and a string of friends—Basil and Uju Ubanwa, Sade and Yemi Owo-Egbeleke, Vincent Thompson, Deji and Joke Fatunde, and Dr. Bunmi Adejumo, to mention a few. I regret the sudden death of Mrs. Afusatu Nike Olaniran, a Nigerian resident in Pflugerville, Texas. May her soul rest in perfect peace and may this book serve to immortalize her name and give joy to those she left behind— her husband Greg and two sons Greg and Tony.

As always, I have enjoyed the warm support of many outstanding colleagues in the university. Ever warm and wise, Dr. Sheila Walker ("The Spirit") remains a valuable ally. Members of my clan (Steve Ward ± Awo, Saheed Adejumobi, Rebecca Gamez, Joel Tishken, Vik Bahl, Jackie Woodfork, Andrew Clarno, Manuel Callahan, Christian Jennings and Steve Salm) continue to prosper. May the clan become a village!

Although these are troubling times for my country, I cannot but hope that the next millennium will bring the much anticipated progress to which all Nigerians, irrespective of religion, age, class, ethnicity, language, and gender, are entitled.

Timeline of Historical Events

12,000 B.C.	Stone Age evidence indicates the antiquity of various indigenous groups.
500 B.C.	An iron civilization emerged, with one major center at Nok. Technology was altered, with great consequences on farming, urbanization, and settlements.
200 A.D.	Evidence of a metal age became abundant, indicating the spread of cities and villages.
1000–1500 A.D.	Foundation of many kingdoms such as Benin, Oyo, Hausa states and Kanem-Borno.
1450–1850 A.D.	Contacts with Europe and the New World, dominated by the slave trade which had profound consequences on the people.
1804	An Islamic revolution took place in northern Nigeria. It created a huge caliphate and led to the spread of Islam.
1842	The beginning of success in the spread of Christianity. A new elite emerged and Christianity and Islam became the two dominant religions in the country.

1861	Establishment of a British consulate in Lagos, the beginning of a process that led to the conquest of Nigeria.
1886	Formation of the Royal Niger Company with a charter to trade and enter into treaties in the Niger basin and its environs. In the same year, a peace treaty ended a prolonged war among the Yoruba in the southwest.
1892	British attack on the Ijebu.
1893	Establishment by the British of a Protectorate over the Yoruba.
1897	Name "Nigeria" officially adopted.
1900	Establishment by the British of a protectorate in northern Nigeria.
1914	Amalgamation of the Northern and Southern Protectorates.
1929	Aba riot, a major protest by women against colonial taxation and other forms of injustice.
1936	Establishment of the Nigerian Youth Movement, a leading political association that demanded major reforms.
1946	Richards Constitution, with a central legislature and three Regional Houses of Assembly. This marked the beginning of constitutional reforms that led to independence.
1948	Establishment of the first university at Ibadan.
1954	Federal system of government introduced.
1957	Regional self-government proclaimed in the East and West, a major transfer of power from the British to Nigerians.
1959	Regional self-government in the North.
1960	Independence from Britain, October 1.
1963	Republic proclaimed. A Nigerian replaced the Queen as the symbolic head.
1966, January–July	The first military coup ended the First Republic, but created further political instability soon after.

1966–1975	Administration of General Yakubu Gowon presided over a war economy and later an economic boom.
1967	Beginning of the Nigerian civil war, July 3.
1967	Creation of twelve states to replace the existing four regions, but demands for more states continue as various groups see this as an opportunity to attain rapid development and benefit from federally distributed revenues.
1970	End of civil war, January 13. Nigeria embarked on a program of reconciliation and reconstruction, partly financed by oil revenues. While the East was reintegrated, secession demands by various groups have yet to end, while some outstanding issues of injustice during the war are yet to be resolved.
1973	OPEC oil-price increase led to an economic boom and prosperity for Nigeria. Development projects became grandiose.
1975–1979	Military regimes of Brigadiers Murtala Mohammed and Olusegun Obasanjo introduced far-reaching reforms in political institutions and became the first to transfer power to civilians.
1979–1983	The Second Republic, with Alhaji Shehu Shagari as president, was unable to create discipline among the ranks of the politicians and was ended by a military coup.
1983–1985	The military rule of General Muhammad Buhari was noted for firmness, investigations of political figures for corruption, and poor economic performance.
1985–1992	Nigeria under General Ibrahim Babangida, with both failed economic and political programs.
1991	A census put the country's population at 88.5 million, and this has since formed the basis of subsequent projections of population increase.
1993	Presidential election, won by Chief M. K. O. Abiola, annulled June 12. The country was thrown into a prolonged crisis thereafter.
1994	Short-lived Interim National Government, led by Chief E. Shonekan, characterized by chaos and public distrust.

1994–1998   Dictatorship of General Sanni Abacha, died June 8, 1998. Nigeria's image was battered and opposition forces were repressed.

1998–   General Abdulsalami Abubakar in power, the eighth general to assume power in twenty-eight years of military rule. He promised a successful transition to democracy to commence in May 1999.

THE
HISTORY OF
NIGERIA

1

Introduction: Nigeria in Perspective

Nigeria as a modern political entity was created in 1914 by the British, as part of the European partition of Africa that began in the last quarter of the nineteenth century. However, its peoples have a long history, with human habitation in some places dating back to before 500 B.C. The country has thirty-six administrative states, in addition to a federal capital territory at Abuja. Lagos was for many years the federal capital city, until 1991 when the government relocated to the inland city of Abuja. Lagos remains the main hub of diplomatic, media, commercial and banking activities. The army plays a prominent role in society, not for its ability to fight, but for its capacity to consume resources and prevent the growth of democratic politics. The armed forces stand at around 78,000 members, with 62,000 in the army, 10,000 in the air force, and 6,000 in the navy. The legal system is based on customary law, Islamic law, and English common law.

GEOGRAPHY

Nigeria is a big country bordering the Atlantic, occupying 336,669 square miles. It is twice the size of California and three times the size of the United Kingdom. The country stretches about 700 miles from east to

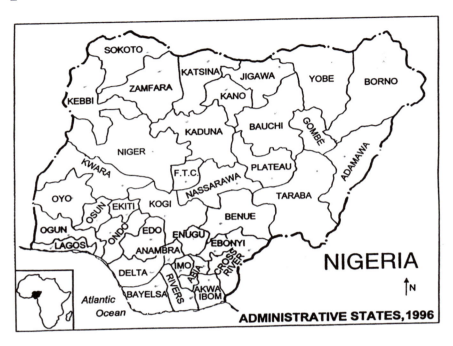

west and 650 miles from south to north. The country lies roughly between 3° and 15° E longitude and between 4° and 14° N latitude. Nigeria's neighbors to the west are the countries of Benin and Togo, to the
east is Cameroon, to the north are Niger and Chad. Nigeria is bounded
in the south by the Bights of Benin and Biafra. While relations with its
neighbors are generally peaceful, there has been a lingering border dispute with Cameroon over the Bakassi Peninsula.

The climate ranges from tropical to arid, from the mangrove swamps
and rain forests near the coast to the sahel savanna and semi-desert in
the north. There are two distinct seasons, wet and dry. In the south, the
rainy season lasts from May to October, and in the north from May to
September. Rainfall decreases from the south to the north, and temper-
atures are generally high. The dry season carries with it a dry north-
easterly cold wind, called the harmattan, which is most severe in the
north in January. The hottest months are March and April and the wet-
test are May, June, and October.

There are two vegetation types: the forest and the savanna. The former
is in the south where rainfall is heavy, while the latter is farther north.
Soils of good quality are abundant, although some areas suffer from
erosion, as in the east, or desert encroachment, as in the far north. So-

cieties in the savanna were exposed to ideas from North Africa and the Middle East, while those along the coast interacted with Europeans earlier than the others. Settlement patterns and cultures are partially affected by vegetation. In the coastal zone, including many creeks and the Niger Delta, fishing and farming cultures developed among such groups as the Ijo and the Kalabari, who exchanged salt and fish with their neighbors. Settlements tend to be smaller in the coastal zone because of the scarcity of extensive dry land. In the forest zone, home to such groups as the Yoruba, Igbo, Edo, and Ibibio, agriculture is the main occupation with emphasis on roots and tubers. States might be either small or large and included the two notable pre-colonial kingdoms of Oyo and Benin. In the savanna zone, livestock rearing is combined with farming (notably cereal) to produce a viable economy. The Hausa city-states and the Kanem-Borno empire emerged, sustained by a productive peasantry, powerful kings and highly developed commercial transactions, and the mobility provided by cavalry. Tsetse flies, the carriers of trypanosomiasis, are deadly to livestock. Where these flies are common, as in the rain forest, cattle and horse keeping has been difficult. Interaction between the zones is fairly common, including long distance trade to distribute products from various ecological areas.

The River Niger, the third longest river in Africa, runs for 730 miles within Nigeria. At Lokoja, its main tributary, the Benue, joins the Niger which continues to flow southward to the delta where it empties itself into the Atlantic Ocean. Other important tributaries of the Niger are the Sokoto, Kaduna, and Anambra rivers, while those of the Benue are the Donga, Katsina Ala, and Gongola rivers. These and other rivers serve as arteries of communications, especially during the rainy season. They have encouraged the establishment of many settlements along their banks. In recent years, dams have been constructed to supply water and electricity.

The geology is rich, with granites in the Middle Belt where tin, uranium, and columbite abound. A host of other minerals exist—coal, gold, lead, iron, salt, copper, and zinc. These have been worked at different periods in history, especially iron, which has enhanced the growth of agricultural communities and armies. Stories of abundant minerals generated European interests; a mining revolution occurred during British rule, while the country's railway network was designed partly to tap mineral resources. In such places as Jos and Enugu, mining has contributed to economic diversification and urbanization.

With a current population of over 100 million people, the largest in

Africa, Nigeria continues to record an annual growth rate of 2.83 percent. A quarter of the African population live in Nigeria. Nigeria prides itself as "the giant of Africa," no doubt with its population, size, and resources as the justification. There are three major population clusters: the Kano area in the north with a density of 100 persons per square mile; the Yoruba area in the southwest with a density of 140 persons per square mile; and the Igbo area in the southeast with an average density of 150 persons per square mile. Its population includes a high proportion of mobile youth—with an average age of seventeen—who seek opportunities within their country and, when they fail, try to migrate abroad. Children under fourteen years comprise 44.9 percent of the population while adults over sixty-five comprise 3.3 percent.

The country is experiencing a series of environmental problems, ranging from the encroachment of the Sahara Desert to soil erosion, slums in cities, oil pollution, and the illegal dumping along the sea coast of toxic waste from Europe. Ceaseless deforestation in the savanna leads to soil erosion, which in turn contributes to desertification. An estimate by the World Bank concluded that the country has lost 90 percent of its forest during this century and continues to lose 350,000 hectares of trees every year.[1] Another estimate put the encroachment of the Sahara Desert at two to three miles a year, leading to crop and fiscal losses and drought. The country has embarked on a number of afforestation projects, although these have been neither coordinated nor successful. In 1974 and 1976 over 200 miles of shelter belts were established. A tree planting campaign was launched in 1981, and the World Bank has supported more than thirty-five forestry programs to prevent further erosion and loss of soil fertility, and to increase crop yields and crop residues. The demand for fuelwoods and livestock fodder are great obstacles to these programs.

GOVERNMENT

The constitution stipulates a federal system headed by an executive president, and an independent legislature and judiciary. However, democracy has eluded Nigeria.

Except for a few years (1960–1965; 1979–1983) the military has controlled power since 1960. Military rule has been devastating, with its coups and counter-coups, lack of accountability, and anti-democratic orientation. Inter- and intra-ethnic violence, including the catastrophic civil war of 1967–1970, has become endemic to the system, and power holders at all levels are corrupt and authoritarian. Ethnic politics is both divisive and dangerous. The three leading ethnic groups, the Hausa, the Igbo and the Yoruba, have used their numbers to influence politics to their advantage. Ethnic-based political parties were formed after 1945; they have struggled with each other for power, and called for secession and the division of the country along ethnic lines. In the 1980s and 1990s divisions along religious lines have brought about conflicts between Muslims and Christians and debates as to whether the country should adopt the Shari'a law or remain secular. Thus far, no constitution has endured, while the military has stubbornly refused to engage in a genuine disengagement from politics. The country remains as one, not necessarily because the various ethnic groups desire it, but because of the use of force. In 1990 when a group of young military dissidents staged a violent coup, they decided to expel five northern states from the country, promising that their re-admission would be on the basis of negotiation; they condemned the northern political class for "internal colonization of the Nigerian state." Since 1992 the Yoruba have threatened to secede, and others continue to call for a national conference to discuss the future of the country.

SOCIAL AND CULTURAL SYSTEMS

Although the majority of the population lives in rural areas, urbanization has been growing at a fast pace throughout the twentieth century. Rural-urban migration, especially of youth, is also a common phenomenon, contributing in part to the decline in food production. Today, the rural-urban population ratio is 5.25/1 while 36 percent of the population live in 358 urban centers. Lacking modern means of communications, facilities for recreation and leisure, and occupations outside of agriculture, villages find it difficult to retain their youths. An aging population, dependent on traditional tools (hoes and machetes), takes grudgingly to farming.

Nigeria is a multi-ethnic nation with over 200 groups speaking over 250 languages. English is the official language, spoken side-by-side with widely-used indigenous languages such as Hausa, Igbo, Yoruba, Edo, Idoma, Fulfulde, Ibibio, and Efik. About 21 percent of the population are Hausa speakers, 20 percent are Yoruba, 17 percent Igbo, and 7 percent Fulani. A host of minority groups speak other languages. Pidgin, a combination of indigenous languages and English, is common, while the government under General Abacha promoted the use of French

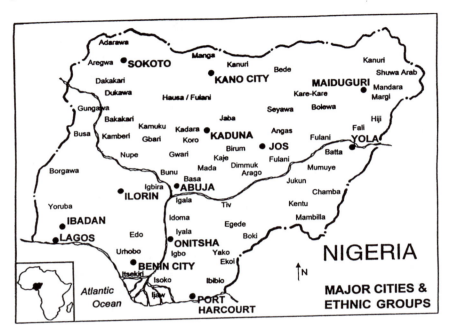

as another official language, largely for the political reason of creating better relations with France. While there has been a desire to choose an indigenous language as *lingua franca*, instability in politics has prevented such a decision as competing ethnic groups will interpret it as an attempt by one group to dominate the others.

The family is changing, reflecting more and more a nuclear arrangement of the man, his wife, and his children. However, the family is essentially patriarchal, connected to a large kin group, and remains large, with many children. The extended family is common, with a philosophy that everyone is his brother's keeper. Individualism is discouraged, and children are socialized to have respect for traditions and social ethics. Marriage is stable, although divorce is no longer exceptional; it is usually caused by childlessness and allegations of infidelity and irresponsible behavior. While there is evidence of arranged marriages, it is most common for the parties to court and agree to wed. Families are involved in the marriage, as bride wealth is paid to the bride's family for purposes of social approval rather than wealth redistribution. While monogamy is common among the educated elite, Muslims and traditionalists continue to practice polygyny. The ambition of many families is to encourage their children to acquire Western education up to the college level.

Religious life is equally diverse: Muslims are concentrated in the north and southwest, constituting about 50 percent of the population; Christians make up about 40 percent with a concentration in the south and the Middle Belt; the rest of the population practices one form of indigenous religion or another. As the leading representatives of either Islam or Christianity struggle to acquire political power, the role of religion in politics has become more visible, leading to controversy over whether the country should be secular or not, or whether it should integrate the Shari'a into its judicial system. Sectarian rivalries promote a number of conflicts. Many take religion very seriously, as evidenced by government-subsidized annual pilgrimages to Mecca or the Holy Land, daily worship, revivalism, and aggressive conversion.

Indigenous religions have been undermined by Islam and Christianity. In the precolonial era, religion provided the explanation for creation, the justification for authority, and the legitimation of power. Political power was regarded as sacred, held in trust by a king for his people. The supreme being and the gods were invested with attributes of creation, power, generosity, and benevolence. Even today, indigenous religions are not completely dead and in some areas, are vibrantly alive. Beliefs in various gods, witchcraft, magic, and charms remain strong among a number of people. In most communities age-old festivals are still performed, such as those celebrating the yam harvests among the Igbo. Ceremonies associated with rites of passage are still widely performed, especially funerals which consume many resources in many areas.

Traditional and modern cultures co-exist. Centers of creative cultural production in the past included Benin with its bronzes, many of which were looted during the colonial period, and Ile-Ife noted for wood carvings. In music, the country has a host of talents, including Fela Anikulapo Kuti who created the Afrobeat, and King Sunny Ade, the Juju superstar. Dance, music, and drama continue to thrive, influenced both locally and by many other cultures. There are many outstanding academics and literary giants such as Chinua Achebe, Wole Soyinka and Amos Tutuola. Nightlife is enriched by dancing pubs, and soccer is one of the daytime attractions of young men. In places where they still exist, traditional sports and recreations such as storytelling, moonlight plays, and wrestling are supplemented with radio and television programs that portray Western societies in an unrealistic and exaggerated manner. Although tourism is poorly developed, places and resources are abundant, comprising parks, ranches, beaches, wildlife, and indigenous festivals.

Survival skills and social values are transmitted in households and schools. Where Islam is practiced, Quranic schools exist side-by-side with the formal, Western-oriented ones, and both support the informal training provided by the family. In spite of modernization, contemporary culture retains many aspects of the past, such as respect for elders and seniors, proper greetings at all appropriate occasions, honesty, humility, and generosity. Society still respects those who are well-grounded in ancient lore and proverbs, and who can use them to entertain or settle disputes. The staple diets of the past are carried over to the present, notably yams, corn, beans, and millet.

ECONOMY

Economic and social indicators reveal both dynamism and underdevelopment. While Nigeria is still an agrarian society, the economy has been dependent on oil revenues since the 1970s. The country is rich in natural resources, including timber, fossil fuels (petroleum, coal, and lignite), metallic minerals (tin, columbite, tantaline, wolframite, molybdenite, lead, zinc, iron, gold), radioactive minerals (uranium, monazite, thorite, zircon), and non-metallic minerals (limestone, marble, industrial rocks and gravel, clay and shale, kaolin, and feldspar). Industrial activities revolve around the mining of coal, tin, and columbite, oil extraction and refining, natural gas production, and the processing of such export crops as cocoa, timber, rubber, and peanuts. Manufacturing activities include textile production, beer brewing, and the manufacture of building materials and cement. Agriculture is the mainstay of the peasantry; the majority of the population grow a variety of products, notably cotton, cocoa, rubber, cassava, millet, maize, rice, and yams, both for domestic consumption and for export. The informal sector—small companies of between one and ten workers—is highly developed and efficient, serving local needs for a host of services and repairs.

The economy grew during much of the twentieth century as it became transformed to a modern economy with cash crop production, mining, manufacturing, and banking. However, since the 1980s a decline has set in, the local currency, the Naira, has suffered massive devaluation, and inflation has been running at a high rate. International trade is crucial to Nigeria's survival: exports are worth over $15 billion and imports around $10 billion each year. Although in great decline, the transportation network is impressive with sixty-eight airports, 67,104 highway miles, and 2,178 miles of railroads. Thousands of dirt roads connect farms and villages to the towns. With over fifty newspapers, many radio and television stations, over a million telephones, and access to the internet, communication can be described as modern, although services are erratic and rural areas are excluded. As bad as the economy may appear, with a gross domestic product of around $35 billion, it is still the second largest in the continent, after South Africa.

EDUCATION AND HEALTH

Since the mid-nineteenth century, Western education has been important and sought after by the population. The adult literacy rate is now over 51 percent and perhaps much higher if we include the ability to read other languages such as Arabic. The intelligentsia is both articulate and highly trained in many fields, some having attained international stature in literature, history, geography, and medicine. For many years, university education was the major avenue for elite mobility, thus promoting the creation of many universities, even though their facilities may be grossly inadequate.

Modern health facilities are associated with Western education for the supply of medical personnel and new ideas. The ratio of doctors per population is 1 to 16,000, drugs are generally in short supply, and modern hospitals are few and far between, at a ratio of 900,000 persons per hospital bed. Life expectancy at birth is fifty-eight years for a female and fifty-four years for a male. Infant mortality remains high—one baby dies out of every twenty-one. The average caloric intake is 91 percent of the FAO minimum. Major diseases include river blindness, malaria, meningitis, and in recent times AIDS. Owing to the escalating cost of drugs and the scarcity of modern facilities, a large number of people continue to consult traditional healers or resort to Islamic and Christian preachers for solutions through prayer or charms. The country has a long way to go in educating its citizens about prevailing health problems and how to overcome them, providing adequate food, proper nutrition, essential drugs and safe water, ensuring basic sanitation, and maternal and child care, immunizing children against all major infectious diseases, and controlling common diseases.

HISTORY

Nigeria is composed of ethnic groups whose histories date to prehistoric times. Remains of ancient civilizations have been discovered in such locations as Ile-Ife in the southwest, Igbo-Ukwu in the east, and

Nok in the Middle Belt. By 1000 A.D., many groups with distinct political characteristics had evolved. Until the nineteenth century, many kingdoms rose and fell. Precolonial societies relied on agriculture, manufacturing, and trade. They produced consumer and commercial goods of high quality in ceramics, wood, and leather.

External contacts brought Islam, in addition to participation in the trans-Saharan trade. The legacy of Islam has endured, most notably in the creation of a caliphate in the nineteenth century and the widespread practice of Islam in modern Nigeria. From the fifteenth century onwards, Europeans began to make contacts with the Nigerian region. The slave trade was the enduring legacy of this contact, with Nigeria as one of the most affected areas in Africa, with part of Nigeria's shoreline being called "the slave coast."

During the nineteenth century, the slave trade was abolished, but this did not end Euro-Nigerian relations. The need to police slave traders brought the British naval squadrons to the shores of Nigeria. Liberia and Sierra Leone became homes to redeemed slaves, hundreds of whom later migrated back to Nigeria to form communities of returnees in Lagos and Abeokuta where they introduced Brazilian architecture and promoted the spread of Christianity and the English language. Trade with Europe continued, no longer in slaves but raw materials, notably palm oil and palm kernels.

From the middle of the nineteenth century, British interest began to move in the direction of colonization. In 1861 a consulate was established in Lagos. Forty years later, the British had established control over most of Nigeria, and were able to govern it for sixty years thereafter. The ethnic groups making up the Nigerian population did not develop into a strong nation during the colonial period. Indeed, a policy of divide and rule kept them apart. Western education grew faster in the south than in the north. The colonial economy relied mainly on exports, a trend that continues till today. Areas with valuable cash crops, such as the Yoruba area with cocoa and the north with peanuts, benefited immensely. Other groups, such as the Igbo, took to migration and became wage workers or artisans in different parts of the country.

Nigeria became independent on October 1, 1960. The country was divided into three big regions, North, West, and East, dominated by the Hausa-Fulani, Yoruba, and Igbo respectively. The three regions and their ethnicities competed as enemies. This was ended by a military a coup on January 16, 1966.

The coup, however, marked the beginning of a deeper crisis. Major

Nzeogwu who led the coup was unable to determine its outcome, and a fellow Igbo, Aguiyi Ironsi, emerged as head. The coup was interpreted by other groups as Igbo-inspired, thus leading to a counter coup in July 1966, bringing Yakubu Gowon, a northern officer from the Middle Belt, to power. Like the politicians, the soldiers too had their ethnic loyalties. Events degenerated further into chaos, leading to a general massacre of thousands of Igbo in the north, a declaration of secession by the Igbo, the creation of the Republic of Biafra by the Igbo in the former Eastern Region, and a civil war that lasted from 1967 to 1970.

The war years brought Nigeria to the world's attention, as some countries lent their support to Biafra and the others to Nigeria. The war consumed over a million lives, mostly on the Biafran side. In the crisis of the late 1960s, the Gowon regime broke up the regions into twelve states, partly to reduce the impact of regionalism. (Ever since, the creation of more new states has become frequent with the intention of satisfying various demands and gaining cheap political popularity.) Oil revenues began to accrue, helping the federal side to finance a costly war and to expand the size of the army far more than the country needed for its external defense. After the war, Gowon declared a policy of "no victor no vanquished," and the country achieved rapid national reconciliation. Oil revenues increased substantially and were used to finance a postwar reconstruction program. The federal government strengthened its control over the states, and federal civil servants became very powerful. When he reneged on a promise to hand over power to civilians, Gowon's popularity began to wane, and he was overthrown in a palace coup in 1975 which brought Murtala Mohammed (and later Olusegun Obasanjo) to power.

In 1979 the military disengaged itself from politics after thirteen years in power. The preparation for this had included the drafting of a new constitution and the formation of political parties. A presidential, American-style constitution replaced the British-style parliamentary one. The country's president was expected to be a popular national figure who should win at least a quarter of the votes in two-thirds of the states. Five political parties competed for power at the state and federal levels, and the National Party of Nigeria (NPN), a conservative party dominated by Northerners, won federal power and Shehu Shagari became president. The Second Republic turned out to be a disaster, as the politicians resorted to the same strategies that had destroyed the First Republic. When new national elections were held in August and September 1983, they were heavily rigged, and the party system lost its credibility once again. On December 31, 1983, the military staged a coup, bringing to power Major-General Muhammad Buhari. Although the society had clamored for democratic government in the 1970s, the people welcomed the military in 1983 because of the shoddy performance of the Shagari government, the massive electoral fraud that had brought the NPN to power, the abuse of power by the police and the judiciary, and large-scale corruption among the political elite.

The 1970s represented the peak of Nigeria's growth and pride during the twentieth century with a well-founded belief that it could be the most powerful and developed country in the Third World. Gowon declared in 1973 that money was not the country's problem, a boast which reflected the flow of substantial revenues from oil and projections that more were to follow. Murtala Mohammed promoted a radical foreign policy and championed the anti-apartheid cause, while the Obasanjo regime made history by successfully and voluntarily transferring power to the civilians. The level of economic growth was impressive. Hosting a Festival of African Arts and Culture (FESTAC) in 1977, the country advertised a credible achievement in human and cultural development. Hope was rekindled and the government made the country a regional power, the spokesperson for Africa in world bodies. Nigerians began to talk of developing nuclear power and creating an African high command. The economy was good, the middle class expanded, and luxury items such as cars, televisions, and videos became commonplace among the elite. Economic planners were confident of an even better future, although the opportunity was being destroyed by the political class who took to corruption, careless expenditure, and waste while an unnecessary large army consumed a large part of public expenditures. In the late 1970s, however, the end of military rule still encouraged a bright promise for the future with respect for the rule of law, protection of human rights, press freedom, and opportunities for state and local governments to develop along their own lines.

The government of Muhammad Buhari lasted two years. Its main goal was to restore discipline to public life, a worthwhile ambition given the decadence of the previous years. But the regime was overzealous, highly selective in punishing some politicians and sparing others, and revealed double standards. The Buhari regime paid little attention to public opinion and was involved in the abuse of human rights. The public cooperated because of coercion rather than patriotism.

In 1985 Major General Ibrahim Babangida overthrew the Buhari regime. To gain immediate support, he released political prisoners, abolished a decree that had victimized many journalists, and promised open government. While he had a more friendly disposition than Buhari, his ambition to hang on to power became his undoing. He survived two coup attempts in 1985 and 1991, the latter being very violent. His regime witnessed many protests by labor unions and university students, with the result that schools were closed for months on end. His period also witnessed intense inter- and intra-religious violence with thousands of people losing their lives. He harassed journalists, arresting many, and banning various publications as well as satellite monitoring of news from abroad. He used his promise to hand over to a democratic government as a means of manipulation in order to retain his own power. When in 1993, contrary to his wish, a presidential election led to the victory of Chief M. K. O. Abiola, he annulled the election. He himself then lost control and had to transfer power to an Interim National Government.

The Interim National Government (ING) presided over by Chief Ernest Shonekan, a notable business executive, lasted only eighty-two days; it was unable to generate trust and respect among Nigerians. Shonekan was regarded as Babangida's stooge; almost daily protests against his regime ensured its failure. A 600 percent fuel price increase further enraged an already bitter population. In the peculiar arrangement of the ING, General Abacha, for many years Chief of Defence Staff, was retained as the only senior military officer. Very quickly, Abacha began to dominate the scene, first removing fellow senior officers loyal to Babangida and later effortlessly overthrowing the ING and appointing himself as the president. Meanwhile, Abiola and his supporters continued to work for his possible inauguration and, for a while, they thought that Abacha would support them. When Abiola proclaimed himself as the president in June 1994, however, he was arrested and placed in indefinite detention until his death in 1998. Violence followed Abiola's arrest with many people injured or killed but with no positive results. Abacha manipulated ethnicity, the greed of civilian politicians, and brutal violence to stay in power against the popular will until his ignominious death on June 8, 1998. His successor, General Abubakar, embarked on initial steps towards reconciliation by holding discussions with various interest groups and releasing scores of political prisoners.

UNDERDEVELOPMENT AND POLITICAL PROBLEMS

Nigeria is noted for its lingering problems and its inability to use its enormous resources to overcome them. Poverty and political instability have plagued the country, without solutions in sight. During the 1950s, the last decade of British rule, hopes were high that the attainment of independence would bring rapid economic and political changes. Some changes occurred—expansion in schools, road networks, communications, and the modern-sector work force; the economy witnessed impressive growth, thanks to revenues from oil; and there were notable achievements in arts and cultures. However, Nigerians' hopes have been dashed, as the country has moved from one crisis to another.

Politics have been marred by gross instability dominated by the military. This political instability has ensured that economic problems will remain. The task in the early years of independence was to attain a rapid economic transformation. To this effect, the first national plan was published in 1962. This became a woeful failure, as there were not sufficient funds to execute the projects. Revenues from agriculture declined, external aids did not materialize as expected, and political competition diverted the focus away from planning. From 1965 to 1970 the concern of the country was to survive as a territorial unit, and development issues were pushed into the background.

The 1970s witnessed an oil boom. Nigeria became a leading member of the Organization of Petroleum Exporting Countries (OPEC), which was successful in bringing about a price increase in 1973. Enormous revenues rolled in, enabling the government to embark on massive public expenditure in education, communication, and industry. The number of universities increased from five in 1970 to twenty-one in 1983. In the late 1970s universal primary education was introduced. A comfortable middle class emerged, and, to curb their radicalism and meet the problems of inflation, government massively increased wages, paying huge arrears to thousands of people. By 1975 the oil boom was becoming less of a blessing. Many new millionaires arose, profiting not from legitimate economic enterprises but from access to public money. Agriculture and other non-oil related sectors were undermined as easy money came to the coffers of the government. High inflation undercut the peasantry who did not directly benefit from oil proceeds.

By 1979 however, when the NPN came to power, the economy was still doing well. The foreign debt was small and oil revenues increased substantially for a year. However, the regime squandered this opportunity. The concern of the NPN was to reward party members with contracts and import licenses. Grandiose projects, such as the rapid building of the new federal capital at Abuja, made this possible. Local production was severely damaged. The country had to import rice, vegetable oil, and other items to meet the local demand for food. Non-oil exports declined, the peasantry suffered, city dwellers found it hard to obtain cheap food, and smuggling of all sorts of commodities increased as the country banned some imports. The middle class, pampered in the mid 1970s, was now complaining loudly. Rural-urban migration intensified. In one case in 1980 such migration enabled a religious organization, the Maitatsine, to expand its membership and unleash an attack on the state condemning politicians for illegal accumulation of wealth. The Maitatsine clashed with the state, in a series of encounters that destroyed thousands of lives and an enormous amount of property. Organized labor staged its own protests with a major general strike in 1981.

The country had to take on more foreign loans as reserves declined. By 1983 the Gross Domestic Product (GDP) had shown signs of an impending decline. Industrial growth slowed down and oil wealth was not being fairly distributed to all social groups. The populist anger against the government encouraged the military to stage a comeback. In trying to repair the economy, Buhari focused on corruption, declaring a "War Against Indiscipline." Large-scale evidence of corruption was revealed at tribunals that tried former public office holders, and some were sentenced to long terms of imprisonment. But when the Buhari government extended its tough measures to innocent journalists, students, and trade union leaders, it began to incur the wrath of the public and its popularity waned.

The Babangida years witnessed economic reforms initiated under a Structural Adjustment Program (SAP). While initially rejecting loans from the International Monetary Fund (IMF), Babangida nevertheless implemented their austerity measures. In the famous 1986 budget that inaugurated the long years of SAP, the Naira was devalued, wages were pegged, spending was restricted, and state-run enterprises were to be privatized. Nigerians were promised a better future, if only they could wait a little while. The waiting only produced more suffering: inflation was on the rise; in 1988 the government lifted the so-called subsidies on oil, thus increasing transportation and related costs by almost 100 percent; and unemployment became much more common among educated youth. As if to say the generality of the public did not matter to him, Babangida concentrated on satisfying military officers and key political figures with opportunities to enrich themselves while the scale of corruption reached an unprecedented level.

Since 1993 the scene has been even more depressing. The Abacha regime lacked credibility both at home and abroad. The Naira lost its regional power and is badly devalued while inflation runs at over 70 percent. To purchase any item of substance, one requires caches of Naira. The standard of living is so low that Nigerians are among the poorest people in the world. Foreign investments come in trickles, external debts remain high, and many have taken to crime to survive. In 1997 the government approved a plan, Vision 2010, promising changes through policy and projects that would transform the country in a decade. Apart from the architects of the plan and their government allies, not many people put their trust and hope in this Vision. Throughout his regime, Abacha was challenged by domestic and international forces, sometimes even cajoled, but he showed an extraordinary callousness in dealing with poverty, inflation, and unemployment. His unambiguous message was that his own survival in power was far more important than the battered economy of his country.

In sum, the 1980s and 1990s have been trying times for the country. The economy has suffered a steady decline without any recovery in sight. The Naira is weak ($1-₦84), and the per capita income of $1,500 in the 1970s fell to $395 by 1993 and less than $300 by 1998. External debts remain very high, estimated at well over $30 billion. Foreign investors are scared of the country. Not a few "businessmen" make money through drug trafficking, money laundering, and other fraudulent practices. Oil earnings have been high but inconsistent, while oil has successfully displaced other sectors in significance, contributing 97 percent of export earnings, 75 percent of public revenues, and 20 percent of the GDP. As if to underscore daily the country's mismanagement and inefficiency, petroleum shortages have become a regular aspect of life, with the lowly paid forced to walk many miles to and from their workplaces. Agriculture is severely damaged and the peasantry impoverished far more than at any time in the country's history. As Nigeria enters the next millennium, it does so as a weakened nation with its economy in a shambles, its politics still unstable, its external image badly soiled, its people in great despair and agony, and violent protests and civil strife as routine occurrences. "The giant of Africa" is now listed by the World Bank as one of the twenty poorest countries in the world.

NOTE

1. Ma Xiufang, "Roundup: Africa in Battle with Deteriorating Environment," *Xinhua News Agency*, Nairobi, June 28, 1993.

2

Precolonial States and Societies

EARLIEST HISTORY

Brass items in Bida, brass and copper heads in Ile-Ife and Benin, bronze products in Igbo-Ukwu, terra cotta animals in Borno, terra cotta heads in Nok, and quartz, basalt, granite, and chalcedony tools dating to the Oldowan and Acheulian age scattered in different locations: all these are among the spectacular archaeological findings that have confirmed the evidence of indigenous societies in Nigeria during prehistoric times. The prehistoric period has been divided into two: the Stone Age and the Metal Age. There is evidence of Early Stone Age sites (notably in the Jos Plateau area), Middle Stone Age sites (in areas north of the Niger, Taraba, and Benue rivers, the Jos Plateau, and Okigwe) while evidence of Late Stone Age and Metal Age sites have been found all over the country.

The Stone Age was the period associated with hunter-gatherers who roamed the area for food and subsequently made the transition to agriculture. The use of microliths (small composite tools), bows, arrows, and spears defined the Late Stone Age during which human beings made better use of bone objects, engaged in rock painting, worked with ceramics, and polished stone axes. Evidence of Stone Age people in Nigeria dates back to about 12,000 B.C. with the existence of Neolithic humans in the forest engaged in agriculture, tending wild fruits, yams and palms, and in the north (for example, at a site in Daima) where people cultivated millet and sorghum and herded cattle, sheep, and goats.

The Metal Age began with iron, and later copper, brass, and bronze. The achievements of the Metal Age became pronounced in such places as Igbo-Ukwu in the ninth century A.D., Ile-Ife from the tenth to the twelfth centuries A.D., Benin from the thirteenth to the fourteenth centuries A.D. and other centers. The use of iron and other metals led to considerable improvement in agriculture and promoted the emergence of cities and centralized political systems such as those of Ile-Ife, the Hausa city-states, Benin and Kanem Borno. A major Iron Age civilization is that of Nok in the Middle Belt, which produced magnificent terracotta figurine sculpture. By the fourth century A.D., the knowledge of iron had spread to many places, thus transforming their agriculture and warfare.

All groups record the accounts of their past in creation myths and oral traditions, thus providing sources to complement archaeology and other evidence. Many traditions try to answer the question of origin by providing stories of migration either from within Nigeria or distant places such as Egypt and Palestine. Some traditions claim that their ancestors descended on a chain from heaven. Everywhere, there are stories of how ancestors and dynasties emerged, how wars were fought and won or lost, and how people traded and created a living. The stories may sound simple or incredible, but they generally reveal a number of points: that societies had existed for so long that tracing their beginning can be difficult; that societies had to cope with their environment and develop on the basis of their own initiatives; and that one group had to interact with others, as the migration stories point to important linkages. To illustrate these stories with one example, the Hausa who live in the north of Nigeria date their beginning to one Bayajidda, a prince of Baghdad who traveled to Daura in Hausaland to marry its queen. The prince and the queen gave birth to seven "true" Hausa city-states, known as the Hausa Bakwai—Biram, Katsina, Daura, Zaria, Rano, Kano, and Gobir. The legend also said that Bayajidda had another set of seven illegitimate children who founded the Banza Bakwai ("bastard") states of Zamfara, Gwari, Kebbi, Nupe, Yauri, "Yoruba," and Kwararafa. This is a legend of the migration of a powerful group transforming an autochthonous population. By the fifteenth century, these small city-states had grown into respectably-sized kingdoms, each with a principal city, the *birni*, serving as the center of power, commerce, culture, and the military.

STATES, POLITICS, AND ECONOMY

Pre-colonial Nigeria was made up of many states, small and large, with various forms of governments. To the north, in the northern savanna, was Kanem-Borno, located around Lake Chad. This empire had become powerful by the eighth century A.D., and was one of the earliest to benefit from links with North Africa. Controlled by the Sefawa dynasty until the nineteenth century, the empire was famous for its adoption of Islam, its commercial networks, and its military technology. The Sefawa kings, known as the *Mai*, were very powerful and they engaged in many wars of expansion and consolidation. Among the best known of the *Mai* was Idris Alooma (c. 1571–1603) who built a formidable army, including both infantry and cavalry, to subdue many areas and destroy pockets of resistance to his empire. Alooma was credited with the introduction of muskets to the region, in addition to paying for Turkish musketeers to train his army. He was a Muslim who promoted Islam among his people and forged productive diplomatic relations with Muslim rulers in North Africa. He undertook the pilgrimage to Mecca, introduced the Shari'a law, promoted Islamic learning, and built many mosques. His empire grew wealthy, due to established agriculture and long-distance trade. The ability of this empire and its dynasty to survive for so long (over a thousand years) owed much to the quality of its leadership, the efficiency of its political system, the rewarding participation in the trans-Saharan trade, the strength of its army, and the use of Islam to promote unity among its people and organize the administration.

By the thirteenth century, a host of Hausa kingdoms such as Gobir, Kebbi, Zaria, Kano, and Katsina had also emerged, thanks to a viable agriculture and trade. South of the Hausa states and Kanem-Borno is the area now known as the country's Middle Belt, sparsely populated and with many small states. However, the Middle Belt is a zone of ancient civilizations with advanced technologies and cultures. Here was the home of the Nok culture and the Jukun empire, and of riverain groups such as the Idoma, Igala, Tiv, Bussa, Ebira, Nupe, and Bariba, all of whom attained prominence. Around the Niger-Benue confluence there was a cluster of groups, Yoruba, Nupe, Tiv, and Igala, who interacted with one another to promote trade and diplomacy.

In the forest and the Niger Delta was a variety of great kingdoms and small states. The coastal area had a high population density, and some states in this area as well as the forest were politically fragmented, as in the case of the Igbo in the southeast. In the Niger Delta, such city-states as Bonny, Brass, and Calabar were famous for their control of the river and the coast, as well as for their trade with Europeans. Islam did not penetrate the forest region until very late. Valuable crops were produced, notably kola nuts, fish, and sea salt, all of which became part of long-distance trade. Trade routes also connected the forest with the savanna; they connected the Yoruba in the west with their northern neighbors, and the trading communities along the rivers Niger and Benue with each other.

The most powerful state in the south was the Yoruba empire of Oyo which was famous by the sixteenth century. Its early history goes back to an ancient period connected with Oduduwa, the progenitor of the Yoruba people. Oral history either says that Oduduwa descended from heaven to Ile-Ife or arrived there from the northeast. His descendants founded seven kingdoms, including Oyo, which became the most influential political power. Early rulers of Oyo laid the foundation of the kingdom by dominating their neighbors and establishing an effective monarchical system. One early ruler, Sango, was deified as a god of thunder and lightning. Oyo's rise to fame was due to a combination of factors. To start with, its geographical location between the River Niger and the northern edge of the forest enabled Oyo to control the leading Yoruba trade routes north to Hausaland and north-west to the Niger bend. It was able to play the role of a middleman to the Yoruba hinterland, and secure access to horses for itself. It was also successful in creating a formidable military machine, based on cavalry, and its administration was intelligently structured. Successful conquests brought in tribute and created a huge market for Oyo's goods. A strong system of administration was able to unite different groups and generate strong nationalism among the Yoruba living in the capital. At its peak during the eighteenth century, Oyo included a large area of Yorubaland, part of Nupeland, and parts of Borgu and what is now the Republic of Benin. The Aja and Ewe states to the southwest were forced to pay tribute to it. Oyo entered the eighteenth century as a strong power, the largest and most diverse in southern Nigeria. Troubles started in the second half of the century, and in spite of the prosperity during the 1770s, it never fully recovered.

Yet another great empire in southern Nigeria was Benin, one of the earliest to rise in the coastal area. It had become powerful by the fourteenth century. Created by the Edo group, Benin was highly centralized and its monarchy survived until its conquest by the British in 1897. Before c.1400, Benin's rulers were known as the *Ogiso*. Then, a dynasty was established by a certain Eweka who, according to tradition, was influenced by the Yoruba. He chose the title of *Oba* (king) and established the institution of seven kingmakers. In later years, powerful Obas emerged and assumed sacred characteristics. The idea of monarchy adopted by the Edo favored a centralized political system which unified divided groups. The monarchy controlled all key appointments, and was able to manage competing interests through a reward system which enabled the king to promote or give resources to those who were loyal to him. Benin profited from its association with its Yoruba neighbors, borrowing useful ideas from them to reform its politics and economy. It also enjoyed a long period of peace because many of its neighbors were small and militarily weak. Benin was well connected in terms of regional trade and was able thereby to acquire wealth to finance its army and administration. Benin reached the height of its power during the fifteenth and sixteenth centuries, with Oba Ewuare (c. 1440–1473) as the most prominent ruler of the era. Ewuare was able to end domestic political rivalries among members of the royal house and chiefs, add to the power of the king, rebuild the city and expand its defensive walls, and create a strong army. Other able successors added to these achievements, including Oba Ozolua, who reigned at the end of the fifteenth century. Ozolua, a warrior-king, expanded the empire and established its first contacts with the Portuguese. Trade began between the two, further promoted by diplomatic relations. In later years, the trade was expanded, allowing Benin to buy imported guns which served its interests in expansionist wars.

Centralized States

Irrespective of their locations, states can be classified into two types: the centralized and the non-centralized. A centralized state is a large political unit, its territory increasing and reducing on the basis of military strength. Such a state in pre-colonial Nigeria would be controlled by a powerful king and his chiefs, based in the capital city of the state where the palace and major market were located. In this capital, the king exercised direct control while allowing heads of kinship groups to govern their various wards. The state was divided into provinces, each administered by a chief loyal to the king. A province could have many villages and towns, and also many ethnic groups of people in the case of kingdoms like Oyo. The administration of a province tended to be indirect, to allow local authorities a say, and minimize tension with the central authority. The kings and their chiefs collected taxes, tribute, levies, and gifts to generate a public treasury, while provinces demonstrated their allegiance by regular payment. While the kings and chiefs could grow wealthy, the majority of the citizens engaged in small-scale agriculture. Examples of such states include the kingdoms of Benin, Oyo, and Kanem-Borno.

In the emergence of these powerful states, geography played a prominent role. The land was fertile enough to support agriculture, urbanization, and large population concentrations. Their locations encouraged participation in regional trade, so that they were able to generate wealth from commerce. An astute and strong leader would emerge to embark upon successful wars of conquest. The army was generally large, made up of able-bodied citizens. In the savanna where grazing land was available and the tsetse fly did not constitute a threat, strong cavalry forces developed.

The king was the central figure in politics. The empire-building king would create a dynasty which governed until its power was challenged by rivals or the kingdom collapsed. The empire-builder could be originally a clan head who grew powerful and subordinated other clan heads to his control. In some other cases, a powerful priest would use his control of supernatural power to acquire political authority. In yet other cases, a powerful warrior could suddenly emerge from a weak group and dominate it. Having established power, the empire-builder used an army to expand his territory to include other groups, important markets, and fertile land. His successors inherited the kingdom, and managed it to the extent permitted by customs, checks and balances, and strength of character.

One example of a centralized state in the north was Kanem-Borno. At the head of the administration was the *Mai*, a king chosen from the Sefawa ruling dynasty. Before Islam, his people regarded him as semi-divine, with the attributes of a god. With the introduction of Islam, he combined elements of semi-divine kingship with the attributes of a great Islamic leader. His power was supreme with the judicial right to impose capital punishment. In day-to-day administration, he listened to the advice of his counselors, a council of twelve, each with responsibility over a province. The councilors lived in the capital, and had to appoint junior officers to manage their affairs in the provinces. Women leaders were powerful, especially three of them: the *Mai's* mother (*Magira*), the *Mai's* senior sister (*Magara*), and the *Mai's* first wife (*Gumsu*). Not only was their advice important, they were major power brokers as well. The economic basis of power relied on harvest taxes collected from farmers, poll tax from many people, tolls and customs from traders, and gifts and tribute from the provinces.

In the south, Oyo was also centralized. It developed a political system based on checks and balances among the leading chiefs and the *Alaafin* (king). The empire was divided into two. The metropolis, Oyo city, was governed by the *Alaafin* and his leading chiefs. The provinces were administered indirectly; Oyo sent its officers (the *Ilari*) to supervise local rulers. In the center where power was concentrated, the *Alaafin* was selected from members of the royal family who descended from Oranyan, the founder of the kingdom. In theory, the *Alaafin* had absolute power and was regarded as next to the gods. In practice, his power was checked by other leading chiefs. When he died, several people, including his eldest son, were expected to die with him. He was wealthy and he lived in a huge palace. Next in rank to him were the *Oyomesi*, seven important chiefs, headed by the *Basorun*. These chiefs enjoyed enormous power, controlling the appointment of a new *Alaafin* and having the right to request a bad one to commit suicide. To resolve conflicts between the *Oyomesi* and the *Alaafin* and also to approve some decisions of the chiefs, there was a secret society called the *Ogboni*. There was an extensive bureaucracy, comprised of the *Ilari* who were based in the palace. As an expansionist empire, Oyo had a strong army based on an impressive use of horses under the control of warlords known as the *Eso*. The overall leader of the army, the *Are Ona Kakanfo*, was expected to win all his wars or commit suicide.

Non-centralized Societies

The second category of states in pre-colonial Nigeria was the non-centralized ones such as those of the Igbo, Isoko, Urhobo and Ibibio in eastern Nigeria and most states in the Middle Belt. These societies were small-scale in size, generally organized around a village or small town, or into chiefdoms, as among the Isoko and Urhobo. The exercise of power was distributed among elders and associations of young people. The government was decentralized, and there was no need to build strong armies for purposes of expansion. Interest groups within a region could be united by trade with members forming a trading association. The societies were orderly, regulated by sanctions, the power of religion, and the control exercised by clan heads.

A good example of non-centralized societies is provided by the Igbo, who were divided into many patrilineal clans, each with its own founding ancestor. Hundreds of villages existed, not as members of one Igbo kingdom, but as autonomous units, each with its own government. In a typical Igbo village, there was a Council of Elders (the *ama-ala*) comprising heads of different families and a village assembly where the majority of the public was allowed to engage in free speech and be involved in decision making. The administration of justice was democratic as elders and citizens discussed offenses and the nature of the punishment to be meted out. A secret society carried out a number of law-related activities, while an age-grade association took charge of public works. Providing a measure of unity to many villages, people worshipped similar gods and recognized the authority of a powerful oracle.

The states, whether centralized or not, shared many things in common. Their economy was dependent on agriculture, trade, mining, and manufacturing. Everywhere, people combined "factors of production"— tools, capital, land, and labor—to perform a variety of economic activities. The hoe and the machete were the most common tools used by farmers, while other occupations had their own specific requirements. As tools were manufactured locally, there was no dependence on external technology. As simple as they were, they made large-scale production possible, even well into the twentieth century. Finance was made available through family channels or local savings clubs.

The family was a unit of production. Members lived in the same compound and the head of the compound organized them for economic functions. Wages were not paid, but the basic needs of members were met. A large family was desirable in order to create more hands for work; hence, the practice of polygynous marriages. To secure additional labor, a family could team with others in a cooperative work group, known as the *gayya* among the Hausa, and *aaro* or *owe* among the Yoruba. To the wealthy and powerful, the use of slaves offered opportunities to expand their labor force and acquire more resources. Slaves were integrated into family units and were allowed to regain their freedom after meeting required criteria.

Land was essential to most occupations and the society ensured that all individuals had access to it. Land was a communal property, protected by the political class for the use of all. Every family in a community had its own share, from which it could not be dispossessed. Land could not be sold. As a most valuable asset, it was also sanctified, a way of using religious sanctions to maintain the laws preventing sale. Land was also regarded as belonging to the ancestors, the living, and the yet unborn, thus denying the living the right to part with family land. Strangers were accommodated either through adoption by a host family who would then allow them access to its own land or through land allocation by the ruler.

The main source of livelihood was farming. Agriculture provided a food supply and made possible population expansion and urbanization. In the savanna, pastoralism ensured the integration of large-scale cattle rearing with farming. Pastoralists were nomadic, in search of pasture and water. Due to limited grazing land and the tsetse fly, cattle herding was less common in the forest and coastal areas. Among the communities living along the coast and river banks, fishing was a major activity.

The economy was always diverse and included major mining and manufacturing industries. Producers relied on local resources, supplemented with raw materials obtained from regional trade. In a number of occupations, such as iron working, craftsworkers formed guilds to protect their secrets, ensure high quality, and protect their interests in relations with the political authorities. Mining was possible in areas with iron, gold, salt, tin, and copper. Iron was the most important metal because many tools and weapons depended on it. Where the ore was available, it gave rise to prestigious and sacred groups of miners and smelters. In other places, there were smiths to fashion iron into all kinds of implements. Salt was a major dietary requirement as well as a key commodity in regional trade. Sea salt was obtained in the coastal area by boiling sea water to obtain the salt sediment and in the semi-desert area by leaching saline soils. Gold was a luxury and lucrative item as well as a source of great wealth to political leaders. Tin occurred in shallow deposits in the Jos and Bauchi plateaus and was made into a variety of plates and utensils.

Manufacturing was dependent on different animal, mineral, and vegetable products. The most common manufactures were ceramic and leather objects, textiles, and foodstuffs. Where clay was abundant, skilled craftswomen and men turned it into kitchen utensils, decorative items, and ritual pots. Leather work produced a host of specialists in curing, tanning, and dyeing animal skins for others to turn into bags, cushions, saddle covers, and other valuable goods. The textile industry was wide-spread, including related occupations involving the production of cotton, yarns, and dyestuffs.

Trade was crucial to indigenous economies. It enabled them to dispose of surpluses, make specialized objects available to a wide range of consumers, and share products of different ecological origins. Widely circulated commodities included salt, iron tools, kola nuts, luxury items, and textiles. Within a community, producers were interdependent—the farmer relied on the blacksmith for tools, and the latter on the former for food. Between the regions, interdependence was also pronounced; for instance, the forest supplied kola nuts to the savanna and the latter supplied animal products in return. Widely circulating currencies and a network of roads ensured a distribution system, although the cost tended to be high. Cloth, metal objects, and cowries were the three major currencies. In Borno to the northeast, cotton strips served as money. In the Niger Delta, iron and copper rods circulated widely. The most common currency was the cowrie shell, favored for its small size, its durability, and the fact that it could not be counterfeited. The currencies enabled wealth to be stored over time, commodities to be priced, and a capital market—where lenders and creditors could negotiate—to emerge.

Transportation was either by land or water. The majority of the population traveled by land, carrying their goods with them. In the savanna, pack animals were used, notably the donkey, camel, mule, and ox. The most useful of these animals was the camel, well adapted to desert and semi-desert areas, and able to cope with shortages of water and food. Canoes were used where the sea and rivers provided the opportunity. Both by land and sea, road networks connected various locations and were maintained and protected by different communities.

The marketplace—a clearly demarcated open space with stalls—was the major site for transactions. Always large and full of diverse people, the market offered the best opportunity for members of society to interact: to trade, share information, and network. Political authorities also collected dues here to finance the government. A market could either be held on a daily or a periodic basis. Daily markets could be held in the morning or evening and they generally served the needs of people within a town or village and its environs. Periodic markets, on the other hand, were held at intervals of two or more days and they served primarily to collect, stock, and distribute regional products. The periodic markets in a region belonged to a ring, linked by a sequence of operation whereby different towns held markets on different days, thus allowing traders to different markets at different days.

A market could feed a local trading network and/or regional and international networks. The local network was concerned with transactions between town dwellers and the villages in the vicinity. The regional network linked many towns, separated even by great distances, while the international one connected different parts of the Nigerian area to markets elsewhere in the West African region and across the Sahara Desert. Long-distance traders, highly skilled, mobile, and enterprising, controlled the various networks. In many areas, they organized themselves into large caravans with many traders traveling at the same time, paying tolls, and eventually establishing trading colonies.

The various states interacted with one another for many reasons. By and large, most relations were promoted by trade. No state was self-sufficient in its needs either of basic items or of luxuries. This is largely a factor of ecological differences. Coastal communities had salt and fish to offer others. The forest had kola nuts traded to the north in exchange for rock salt, horses, and cattle products. Regional markets, with traders from various areas, emerged in many locations and they all served as zones of interaction. Trade routes cut across states, thus uniting many groups in their use and maintenance. The states were equally united by religious, social, and cultural agencies such as age-grade associations, secret societies, marriage ties, and oracle practices. Age-grade associations comprised young people who were born at the same time and initiated into an age set. There were many of those associations in an area, each with its own name and leadership. Membership cut across lineages and villages, thus promoting friendship and interaction, and a strong sense of loyalty. Secret societies members were also drawn from different towns and villages, with members united in secrecy. They had their codes and symbols which they used to forge a productive network in the service of friendship, power, and business. The oracle system was common in the southeast, an impartial judge consulted from far and wide with pronouncements sanctioned by the gods. Inter-group marriages were also common because most cultures prevented marriage within the kinship group. Through marriages, villages and towns were united and their offspring claimed relations in different areas. Through all the factors of inter-group relations, ideas spread, bonds were strengthened, regional trade flourished, and intermarriage was encouraged.

EXTERNAL CONTACTS: ISLAM AND THE
TRANS-SAHARAN TRADE

For centuries the Nigerian area maintained profitable contacts with the peoples of the Western Sudan, Sahara, North Africa, the Nile Valley and, indirectly, Europe. The most enduring of these contacts were through Islam and the trans-Saharan trade. Islamic missionaries from the Middle East and North Africa could, at the same time, be merchants, while the major commercial centers such as Kano were also colonies of Islamic preachers.

Conversion to Islam began as far back as the eleventh century A.D., in the northeast kingdom of Kanem-Borno. Through the activities of missionaries and Islamic traders from North Africa, Islam spread slowly in this area. Kanem-Borno kings were converted, and not a few became zealots, encouraging their people to convert and traveling to Mecca to perform the holy pilgrimage. Among the Hausa, Islam began to spread from the fourteenth century, with influences from neighbors to the west and from North Africa. Such cities as Kano, Katsina, and Zaria became famous Islamic centers. Over the centuries, Islam spread to other parts of northern and western Nigeria, but it did not become a mass religion until the nineteenth century. Among the Hausa and in Kanem-Borno, kings and chiefs accepted Islam. Some were very devout and contributed to spreading the religion. Whether devout or not, the rulers benefited from the opportunities associated with Islam: the wealth of the trans-Saharan trade, the spread of ideas from North Africa, and the ability to forge diplomatic relations with Muslim rulers elsewhere.

Islam was an agent of change. A new religion with its own practices, it altered the landscape with mosques and schools; it affected culture with its scholars, the Arabic language and Imams, fasting and the pilgrimage to Mecca. It contributed to the spread of literacy as Islamic schools multiplied in different cities and young men and women were encouraged to seek knowledge. The pilgrimage promoted the spread of material culture and knowledge, as pilgrims returned home with new ideas. Among the Hausa states and in Kanem-Borno, Islam encouraged a tendency towards the use of literate clerks, political centralization, and experimentation with Islamic laws, the Shari'a. A famous scholar and jurist, Shaikh Muhammad al-Maghili of Algeria, wrote a treatise for political rulers during the fifteenth century. Known as "The Obligations of the Princes," the book advocated a strong leadership, and an effective use of the army and clerics in administration.[1]

A number of rulers and people performed the pilgrimage. The rulers went with large entourages. Along the way they distributed gifts which displayed the products available in their areas, thus promoting commerce. On the return journey they were accompanied by traders, scholars, and craftsmen from the Middle East and North Africa, bringing new ideas and skills. In addition, the journey provided opportunities to enhance diplomatic practices and friendships.

The trans-Saharan trade was the major external trade for centuries, sustained by the use of the camel to cross the Sahara (the animal can endure the heat of the day and the cold at night, and limited water and food); the demand for West African gold in Europe, the Middle East and North Africa; and the enormous profits derived from trade by the key participants. Slaves, too, were valuable items, next to gold, and primarily used for labor and military service. Nigeria also supplied a wide array of luxury items, notably textiles and leather products, pepper, kola nuts, ivory, and ostrich feathers. In exchange, Nigeria obtained such luxury items as cloths, metalwork, spices and dates, glassware, beads, books, paper, and salt from Bilma and Taghaza in the desert. In addition, they bought horses to be used by the cavalry and as prestige items by rulers. The rulers in such centralized states as the Hausa cities and Borno profited greatly from the trade by participating as local merchants and collecting market levies. The southern termini of the trade, such as Kano, Gazargamu, and Katsina, were flourishing commercial centers. Some rulers established a monopoly over the trade in salt and slaves so that more wealth could accrue to them.

The trans-Saharan trade was complex because of the great distance (the journey took between seventy and ninety days, one-way from North Africa to West Africa), the desert that had to be crossed, and the multiplicity of groups along the way. Capital was necessary and this was largely provided by wealthy merchants and rulers in North Africa. The trade required the use of many agents—long-distance traders who procured the goods and took them to the Nigeria area, local agents who welcomed the foreign ones and acquired domestic goods for them, and a host of middlemen in various locations who procured goods and supplied current information. Traders had to be protected from raiders. Each state along the way tried to ensure security, while the caravans of traders, sometimes running into thousands of people, were accompanied by soldiers. Sandstorms and drought could cause great dangers to traders, so it was necessary to know the trade routes with reliable oases and to predict changes in weather. The use of experienced guides and guards to take care of camels and look after important matters such as water rationing was also part of caravan planning. Above all, the trade routes had to be carefully chosen on the basis of distance, the location of oases along the way, protection against raiders, and the availability of goods at the termini. One of the earliest routes was between the Chad Basin and Tripoli in North Africa. By the sixteenth century Kanem-Borno and the Hausa states were linked by important routes to Tripoli. Kano and Katsina became major entrepôt of trade during and after the seventeenth century. The trans-Saharan trade continued well into the nineteenth century, until it was threatened by the increasing European presence along the coast which shifted the direction of trade southwards.

This trade provided crucial inter-regional connections that allowed goods and ideas to circulate widely and over a long period of time. The trade allowed states in the savanna to improve their armies with imported horses. Kings and chiefs grew wealthy and were thus able to spend on the army, embark on territorial expansion, and maintain a grandiose lifestyle. Merchants, too, were able to prosper. The trade enabled the states in the Nigerian area to become better known to the outside world. Islam, new political and cultural ideas associated with Islam, and other aspects of Arabic civilization were able to spread to Nigeria, again as a result of extensive trade interactions.

EXTERNAL CONTACTS: EUROPE AND THE SLAVE TRADE

If the north had contacts with North Africa, the south had theirs with Europeans beginning in the late fifteenth century. European expansion benefited from improved techniques in navigation and shipbuilding and the desire to benefit from exploration. The Portuguese were the first to arrive around 1486 on the coast south of Benin. Motivated by a desire to trade, discover a sea-route to India, understand Africa's geography, and spread Christianity, the Portuguese established contacts with other coastal areas in the Niger Delta and with Lagos. Pepper, cloths, beads, and ivory were among the major items of trade which were exchanged for cheap European goods. The Portuguese had no territorial desire, and restricted themselves to fortified trading stations. In trade they were successful, but not in their attempts to convert people to Christianity.

Portuguese dominance was shattered in the sixteenth century as other European countries joined the trade, notably the British, French, and Dutch. The focus shifted to trade in slaves taken principally to the New World where successful plantation economies were created. The slave trade began in trickles, perhaps as early as 1480 when the Portuguese shipped out of the Niger Delta area two vessels loaded with four hundred slaves. During the sixteenth century, the demand for cheap labor in the Americas escalated the slave trade. From then on until the nineteenth century, the slave trade became the mainstay of Euro-Nigerian relations, as many millions of slaves were exported. This trade has been described as "triangular": European traders took manufactured goods to Nigeria in exchange for slaves; the slaves were taken to America; then European merchants bought America's raw materials (such as tobacco and sugar) to sell in Europe.

Demands for slaves were instigated by Europeans who went to the shores of Nigeria with ships to freight slaves. A number of European companies specialized in the slave trade, for instance the British-based Royal African Company and the Dutch West India Company. Societies along the Nigerian coastline responded to the incentive. Their chiefs and merchants found the slave trade to be lucrative and they became middlemen by obtaining slaves from the hinterland in exchange for imports, notably guns, metal bars, cloths, knives, liquor, and cheap jewelry. In the hinterland, kings and chiefs raided for slaves while they also perfected the means of disposing them to the coastal traders. In parts of eastern Nigeria, trading oligarchies emerged with regular slave fairs. Trade by barter was common with slaves being exchanged for textiles, iron bars, copper bracelets or manilas, glass beads, coral, and firearms.

The slave trade had major consequences. In the Niger Delta, as elsewhere along the coast, the trade promoted greater contacts with the hinterland to sell European goods and obtain local products. However, the trade in slaves dominated other types of trade, thus creating a narrow economy in which a small class of middlemen profited at the expense of others. The trade brought a population loss, as millions of people were exported, most notably the virile segment of society. As slaves were made in part by raiding expeditions and war booty, the scale of violence and inter-communal rivalries increased. From raiding expeditions, through the Middle Passage on the sea, to the plantations, slavery was dehumanizing—slaves were treated as inferior, regarded as property with no rights, and accorded little or no respect. Nigerian culture was affected: European languages were introduced to trading communities; pidgin, a combination of local and foreign languages developed; European clothes were adopted in some areas; the Portuguese brought Christianity to Benin and Warri; and new crops were introduced, including cassava, sweet potatoes, and maize, which changed food habits in positive ways. African culture was also exported to the New World, as seen in the case of the strong Yoruba influences in Brazil, Cuba, Trinidad, and Haiti.

The slave trade affected politics and state formation. Where states relied on revenues from it, the trade and its abolition affected their fortunes. Nowhere is this impact more noticeable than in the Niger Delta where the trade was intense. Before the fifteenth century, the Ijo settled in small fishing communities, smallish in size and population. A community was divided into wards or houses, a type of patrilineage headed by an elder, called the *amanyanabo*, who performed primarily ritual functions. There were age-grade and dancing societies, providing unity among members of different wards. Participation in the slave trade led to the transformation of fishing communities into trading states, most notably Bonny, Owome (New Calabar), Okrika, and Brass (Nembe). The Efik, another ethnic group, established Old Calabar at the mouth of the Cross River, also to benefit from the trade. In the era of the slave trade, the communities expanded in size, from a few hundred to about five thousand each. As more and more people acquired wealth from the trade, social and political relations became more complex. The determinants of status changed from old age and family history to wealth and economic standing. The *amanyanabo* was no longer a mere ritual leader, but a political leader and a wealthy merchant. A successful *amanyanabo* struggled to let his children inherit his title and wealth. The ward also became transformed into a trading community known as the "canoe house," a trading organization with rules and leaders. The leader of a "canoe house" was both powerful and wealthy, and each "house" was expanded by slaves. An ambitious slave could rise to the leadership of the "house." When a member became wealthy, he was allowed to create a new "house," holding allegiance to the parent "house." Competition was intense among the houses for the control of trade and power in the town.

REVOLUTIONS AND REFORMS

Pre-colonial societies closed their long histories during the nineteenth century with monumental changes. The events and issues revolved around trade, warfare, and Islam, as all of these affected politics and the economy. Societies and states were reorganized—some collapsed, other ones were born, some expanded in scale, all in reaction to profound internal changes and the impact of external factors.

Among the Yoruba in the southwest, the fall of their great empire of Oyo was accompanied by wars that lasted throughout the century. In the second half of the eighteenth century, Oyo had begun a process of decay. Power struggles became endemic, leading to constitutional breakdowns, the appointment of weak kings, and the decline of the army. So weakened was its army that some of its provinces became independent, while Oyo was unable to withstand an attack from the Nupe to the north and the rise of Dahomey to the west. The rise of the Nupe and political changes in the savanna interrupted operations on the trade routes that Oyo had benefited from, creating a partial economic decline. The crisis reached its peak in 1817 when the head of the army, Afonja, rebelled to carve out the autonomous kingdom of Ilorin. In the course of doing so, he involved Hausa Muslims living in Oyo, and allowed Islamic preachers, including the notable Fulani, Mallam Alimi, to settle at Ilorin. The Fulani Muslims turned against Alimi and killed him in 1823 to establish the only Islamic emirate among the Yoruba. With a better army, Ilorin successfully defeated Oyo causing its final downfall in the late 1830s. Refugees from the Old Oyo empire migrated in several directions, notably southwards, where they founded the new states of Ibadan and Ijaye. A series of wars ensued among the Yoruba in order to create new kingdoms, avoid domination by stronger powers, and control commerce, especially the routes to the coast where Europeans supplied firearms and other commodities. The successor states struggled among themselves and Ibadan emerged as the new power in 1840, building an empire that lasted until the 1880s. Two other Yoruba groups, the Egba and the Ijebu, resisted Ibadan's domination and were able to join its other enemies to begin a sixteen-year war in 1877. Making use of missionaries, the British successfully intervened in the war to bring about peace shortly before they embarked upon colonial conquest.

The various wars affected the Yoruba in profound ways. In the first forty years of the nineteenth century, thousands of refugees had to relocate to other places and cope with new conditions. Abeokuta, Oke-Odan, Ibadan, and Ijaye were new cities that started as refugee camps. In Ile-Ife, the Modakeke refugees were not successfully integrated, thus creating inter-communal clashes that have lasted until today. The population displacement enabled Oyo-Yoruba institutions to spread over a wider region, and new centers of urbanization to emerge. Politics were transformed in revolutionary ways, as warlords became prominent actors. At Ibadan a military republic was created, a rejection of the traditional Yoruba monarchy. In Ijaye, a state that collapsed in 1862, its leader

Kurunmi established an autocratic personal rule, the only one of its kind and scale. So successful did he become that his subjects began to fear him more than the gods. A federal political system was established in Abeokuta to incorporate the leading chiefs of the several wards in the city. The Yoruba economy was also affected. The need to service the war by procuring imported firearms, and to maintain the grandiose lifestyles of the warlords, promoted an extensive use of slaves in production both for domestic need and for the foreign trade in palm oil and kernels. The economy of the Yoruba hinterland was integrated with the coastal trade. The Ijebu and Egba who were close to the ports became middlemen, and their attempts to control the trade routes contributed to political instability and the intervention of the British on the coast in Lagos. In spite of the wishes and aspirations of their tiny educated intelligentsia, the Yoruba spent the nineteenth century competing with one another.

In other places in the south, competition for trade and state expansion were the two dominant themes. The Benin kingdom, the Yorubas' powerful neighbor, was governed during the nineteenth century by leaders who witnessed its decline and fall. Benin entered the century with signs of decay already visibly brought about by intense competition for the throne, weak rulers, civil wars, protests in the provinces, disruption of economic activities by wars and slave-raiding, and loss in revenue as control of trade passed to groups in the Niger Delta. In 1897 a British invasion put an end to Benin's independence.

In the Niger Delta where the economy had been re-oriented by the trans-Atlantic slave trade, the major concern was how to respond to the abolition of that trade after 1807 and the introduction of a new trade in palm produce. The transition to a new economy was successful, although it involved the interference of Europeans in local politics. Among the far-reaching consequences of the changes was the rise of a new class of merchants who made their money in the palm oil and palm kernel trade while those in Calabar also had palm plantations operated by slaves. The new class quickly used its wealth to acquire power, thus clashing with the old aristocracy for the control of the "houses." Unlike the situation in most other parts of the country, European merchants were intensely involved in the control of trade and domestic politics, thus creating a dimension of Euro-Nigerian trade rivalries. The Europeans involved themselves in various forms of intervention: the British navy policed the Atlantic ocean to halt the slave trade; the Courts of Equity in the area occasionally interfered in local judicial decisions; Europeans struggled to ensure that local economic and political decisions favored them; and

European firms resolved to penetrate the hinterland to reduce the control of local middlemen and increase their own profits. Such local leaders as Jaja of Opobo and Nana of Itsekiriland became heroes in the trade rivalries with Europeans. In the closing years of the century, the British took measures that would enable them to impose colonial control on the region.

North of the Niger Delta were the Igbo, who had to struggle with several small wars caused by disputes over land, price fixing, and debt recovery. Elsewhere, city-states emerged to create stability, but in Igboland a religious-cum-commercial organization, the Arochukwu, was the major force. The Aro used their network of trading colonies and their oracle to control many villages and towns. The end of the slave trade saw the decline of the Aro. Like their southern counterparts, the Igbo had to respond to the new "legitimate commerce," the penetration of missionaries, and the increasing European presence in general.

In the north the jihad led by Sheikh Uthman dan Fodio created the Sokoto Caliphate, the biggest state in West Africa in the nineteenth century. The background to the jihad was a crisis in the Hausa states, and Islamic leaders' resort to Islam to reform society. During the eighteenth century, Hausa society witnessed conflicts between one state and another, between Muslims and non-Muslims, between rich and poor. The states were heterogeneous and highly developed with established kingship, talented Islamic scholars and jurists. Succession disputes were endemic while ambition for political domination was common. Gobir in the northwest emerged as a dominant power, but not without costly and ruthless wars. Merchants and kings grew wealthy, and their ostentatious living displeased the poor and the devout Muslims. Methods of wealth accumulation involved corruption and unjust treatment of the poor. Taxes and levies could be excessive, demand for free labor ruinous, enslavement was common, and conscription for military service was indiscriminate. The practice of Islam was not always strict: many were Muslims only in name; traditional religion was synthesized with Islam in a way that displeased devout preachers; and only a small minority committed itself to spreading the religion.

Sheikh dan Fodio was able to bring together many disenfranchised and discontented groups into a powerful movement. He was a Fulani, a member of the ethnic group that initiated most of the Islamic movements in West Africa during the nineteenth century. His route to success was through an active missionary enterprise as a dedicated teacher and preacher. Born in 1754, he went to school early and started to preach at the age of twenty. With his base in the state of Gobir, he gathered many students and followers whom he inspired to become more devout. By 1788 he had become recognized by the king of Gobir as an influential preacher and was granted a number of concessions. However, this did not last, as a new king imposed severe sanctions on the Islamic community in 1802. Conversion to Islam was restricted, the wearing of turbans by men and veils by women was proscribed, and no new preachers were allowed. Relations between dan Fodio and the government degenerated to the point that the Sheikh was ordered to leave Degel, the town where he and his followers resided. By this time, dan Fodio had written many treatises to justify a jihad (holy war). Imitating the Prophet Mohammad, he performed the *hijra* to Gudu on February 21, 1804, a withdrawal to precede a war. The Sheikh became the *Amir al-muminin* (Commander of the Faithful), and attracted more followers. A punitive expedition by the king of Gobir triggered the war in 1804. Sheikh dan Fodio called for support across the land, issued flags to Islamic leaders in many parts of Hausaland to undertake the jihad, and within a few years was victorious.

From the point of view of the religious leaders, the jihad was brought about primarily by a desire to reform Islam and make it acceptable to more people, a mission to extend it to "pagan" areas, and a need to address issues of corruption and economic exploitation of the poor. Nevertheless, there were other related reasons. One was social: the jihad can be interpreted as a social movement of the poor against the oppressive taxation and high-handedness of the political class. The other was political; the highly educated Fulani felt excluded from power while others of their ethnicity complained of marginalization. As it turned out, in the execution of the jihad and the distribution of power that followed, the Fulani benefited a great deal.

The Islamic movement was able to capture a huge area—from Adar and Agades in the north to the northern frontiers of the Yoruba in the south; and from Macina in the west to Baghirmi in the east—because of a combination of factors. Uthman dan Fodio was a great leader who attracted thousands of followers, while many able scholars and warriors accepted his leadership. Many joined the Islamic army to overcome the oppression and exploitation they had suffered at the hands of the aristocracy. Thus the jihad encouraged a mass uprising by the poor against the state. Hausa kings failed to unite against the Muslims and were forced to fight defensive wars. For years before the jihad, the Hausa states had weakened themselves by inter-state wars and had become very distrustful of one another. The kings could not command the respect of their population, who chose instead to identify with the jihadists. The Muslims also won the propaganda war—the jihad would reform Islam, liberate the oppressed, and bring about the appearance of the Mahdi, the savior, before the world came to its end. The common soldiers even believed that death in the war was honorable and would secure them a place in paradise.

The jihad was accompanied by significant changes. The Hausa states collapsed and were incorporated into a unified theocracy, the Sokoto Caliphate. Old dynasties were replaced by new ones, mainly of Fulani emirs whose descendants govern till today. The caliphate was headed by a sultan, based at Sokoto, while the various emirates were governed by emirs whose appointments had to be ratified by the sultan. The emirs exercised the powers of kings, but were expected to show allegiance to Sokoto by sending tribute and gifts, and contributing to joint military expeditions against the enemies of the caliphate. All leading state officials were expected to contribute to the growth of Islam.

Islam witnessed a revival in many places: reforms were undertaken; new areas were added to the Islamic fold; learning received a boost; and some individuals learnt valuable lessons in the conduct of jihad, with men such as Seku Ahmadu and al-Hajj Umar initiating further successful jihads in the Western Sudan.

Politics in other areas were affected: as the jihad spread to the south, it contributed to the fall of the Oyo empire and the creation of the emirate of Ilorin. The jihad also spread to some parts of the Middle Belt. In the north east, it brought an end to the long-established Sefawa dynasty in Kanem-Borno, which was replaced by that of the al-Kanemi. Unable to control the army of the jihadists, the Sefawa turned to al-Kanemi, a notable leader and cleric, for protection. Al-Kanemi argued with the jihadists that their attack against another Islamic state was unjustified, he successfully withstood their military onslaught, used his victory to justify the usurpation of power, and was able to transfer the throne to his son, Umar, in 1837. Umar abolished the Sefawa dynasty in 1846 to inaugurate the al-Kanemi dynasty, but he made few changes to court ceremonials. His rule was long lasting until 1880. The empire declined in the last quarter of the nineteenth century as a result of the ability of some provinces to regain their independence, loss of control on the eastern Sudanase trans-Saharan trade routes, the invasion of Rabih Fadlalah from the Sudan, and the subsequent partition of the area by the British, German, and French.

In many parts of the north, population was dislocated or displaced, old towns grew in size and new ones were created. The economy expanded as plantations grew in size and many industries increased in scale. The caliphate was "a large market," boosting regional and long-distance trade. Islamic scholarship flourished in all the cities and great books were produced. The jihad contributed to the rapid spread of Islam, while the northern politicians of the twentieth century have been able to manipulate the unified structure of the caliphate to organize modern-day political parties to unite the large area of the north.

As all these events were unfolding, others associated with Europeans were also taking place. We shall turn to these other changes in the next chapter to complete the discussion of the foundations of modern Nigeria and the background to the twentieth century.

NOTE

1. *The Obligations of the Princes, An Essay on Muslim Kingship*, trans. from Arabic by T. H. Baldwin and cited in H. R. Palmer, *The Bornu, Sahara and Sudan*. London: Frank Cass, 1936.

3

European Penetration

Nigerian societies were affected by a steadily increasing European presence in the nineteenth century. The established pattern of staying mainly on the coast was changed as Europeans moved into the hinterland during the second half of the century, and the century ended with the imposition of colonial rule. European activities revolved around four major issues: exploration, Christianity, trade, and imperialism. All are ultimately related—explorers provided useful knowledge for others to use and encouraged the traders to move to the hinterland; missionaries served as the pathfinders for the colonialists; traders indicated the profits to be made from imperialism, and, together with the missionaries, pressured the British government to take over Nigeria. In this chapter, I shall examine the activities of explorers, missionaries, and traders as they affected the country.

EXPLORERS

Although Europeans had been in Africa for many years, their knowledge of the inland areas was limited until after the mid-eighteenth century. For instance, they had no accurate knowledge of the course of the River Niger or its relation with the Niger Delta. In 1787 the African

Association was founded in England to explore the course of the River Niger. Several British explorers—Mungo Park, Hugh Clapperton, and the Lander brothers—were leaders in the search to understand the Nigerian hinterland, especially the banks and course of the rivers Niger and Benue. Mungo Park traveled to Africa twice, collecting information on the course of the Niger. In the 1820s Clapperton and Denham traveled from North Africa to northern Nigeria. In the 1830s the Lander brothers traveled from Badagry in the south to Bussa in the north, from there to the Benue confluence, later to realize that the Niger flows into the Atlantic at the Oil Rivers.

While there was some interest in scientific knowledge, the desire to determine the commercial worth of the hinterland was a major factor promoting exploration missions. Reports were made available to commercial companies and traders who also contributed money to exploration projects. The impression that emerged from many reports was that of a country awaiting the exploitation of its resources by so-called "enlightened" foreigners. Interactions with the rulers in different societies were reported with some indications of how to relate to them. In some places, as in Borno and Oyo, rulers asked explorers for military and political assistance. Yet in some others, as in Sokoto, the rulers were cautious, doubting the motives of the explorers. The explorers presented their countries and peoples in the best possible light, as if preparing the minds of the rulers for receiving them.

MISSIONARIES

The spread of Christianity to many parts of Nigeria began in the mid-nineteenth century. Previous efforts were largely unsuccessful because of the dominance of the slave trade, the limited number of missionaries who spread themselves thinly, the inadequacy of money for mission work, the belief in influential Christian quarters that it was not necessary to convert Africans, the inability of missionaries to understand traditional religion, and limited cooperation and interest from African people and their rulers. In Europe and North America during the nineteenth century, Christian organizations were reorganized for a great missionary expansion. At the forefront were a number of Protestant missionary societies and Catholic organizations. Some among them, who had called for the abolition of the slave trade, argued that Christianity would aid in stamping out slavery and that the use of force was not enough to stop slave traders. A new set of converts would be morally equipped to avoid slavery and other unacceptable practices, and as alternatives, adopt new ethical codes drawn from Christianity. In addition, these converts would take to "legitimate commerce" either by cultivating cash crops or trading them. Thus was born the idea of the "Bible and the Plough," that is, a combination of conversion and commerce to produce a new class of Africans with a different worldview and set of moral standards. This class, it was hoped, would shelter itself from the so-called corrupting influences of their traditions. Moreover, they would become the recruits in the fight against Islam, which was condemned by European missionaries for causing evil among Africans and retarding the spread of Christianity. Between 1842 and 1892 many missions in Europe and America sent their missionaries to the Nigerian area.

A crop of morally upright and well-trained Africans was drafted for mission work as clergy and leaders to create among their people a "self-governing, self-supporting, self-propagating church."[1] While Europeans would go to Africa, they would do so as advisors and leaders and seek the means to transfer responsibility to Africans. This strategy, known as "native agency," was to reduce the cost of mission work, save European lives from tropical diseases, and use the locals to accelerate the creation of a new "Christian kingdom." Thanks to the abolition of the slave trade, there were many ex-slaves from Sierra Leone, Cuba, and Brazil who returned to Nigeria from the 1830s onwards. The European missions placed much hope in these people as "the cells of civilization from which the light would radiate to the regions around."[2] A number of them were eager to propagate Christianity, either as workers for the missions or even on their own. Men such as Samuel Ajayi Crowther, Thomas Birch Freeman, and J. C. Taylor distinguished themselves as tireless workers. Early converts also served in different capacities, either to spread Christianity or perform a host of education- or health-related duties.

An early expedition organized in Britain, known as the Niger Mission, arrived on the River Niger in the 1840s. The motives of the Niger Mission were a combination of religion, commerce, and politics; the Niger Mission would spread the gospel, establish a model farm, explore trade opportunities, and sign treaties of cooperation with indigenous rulers. It became one of the success stories of the Church Missionary Society (C.M.S.), providing strategies for evangelization and valuable lessons in the politics of race relations between the African clergy and their European counterparts. One of the heroes of the Niger Mission was Samuel Ajayi Crowther, a liberated slave of Egba origins, who rose to become the first African bishop of the C.M.S.

Various missions established themselves in different parts of southern Nigeria. The C.M.S. established considerable impact among the Yoruba (in Lagos, Abeokuta, Ibadan, and Ilesa) and in the Niger Delta area. This mission regarded Abeokuta as central to the spread of Christianity and initially concentrated much energy there. The Wesleyan Methodists also recorded great successes among the Yoruba, beginning as pioneers in Badagry in 1842. The Presbyterian Church was active in Calabar from 1840 to 1890. The Roman Catholic Church was similarly active, with strong foundations in Lagos, Abeokuta, Oyo, and Ibadan, all among the Yoruba, and also among the Igbo in the east.

The collaborative efforts of European and African missionaries yielded great results. For various reasons, indigenous rulers and people were receptive either to Christian teaching or to the presence of missionaries. For the Yoruba rulers, the expectation was that the missionaries would help them win their wars and procure arms and ammunition. To those in the Niger Delta, the hope was that the missionaries would facilitate greater trade and enhance the Delta traders' ability to master business relations with Europeans. When Bonny chiefs received the missionaries, they expressed the hope that they would "ensure their ability of gauging the oil casks, square up their accounts, read and write their letters."[3] A number of Delta kings requested the missionaries to establish schools for their people in order to produce a management class.

Christianity spread as a new religion in the south and gradually extended to the Middle Belt and northern Nigeria, although on a limited scale. It had to co-exist alongside Islam in the southwest and it failed woefully to "conquer" the Islamic north. It aggressively challenged indigenous religions, although these remained strong throughout the nineteenth century.

Christianity was associated with reforms and changes in many aspects of society. Its spread involved a strategy of political interactions between the missionaries and the indigenous rulers. The missionaries interfered in local politics, as in their call for the deposition of King Kosoko of Lagos. They served as peace mediators, as among the Yoruba, urging them to end their wars. Where they obtained the trust of kings and chiefs, they even performed the role of ambassadors. More generally, however, the missionaries wanted the imposition of British rule so that they could have greater scope to spread their religion. Thus, many among them became agents of imperialism.

The missionaries pioneered Western education. In many places, the church and the school went together. This aided conversion, as parents sent their children to the mission if only to secure education. Christianity and education produced a new elite that later dominated the country's politics, business, and professions. Many members of this elite imbibed aspects of Western culture and began to think of transforming Nigeria according to the Western model. The elite developed a notion of progress—the country would gradually abandon many of its traditions and move toward Westernization. In addition, the elite contributed to the study of many Nigerian languages, helping to reduce some of them, including Yoruba, to writing. Using either English or indigenous languages, they began to publish essays and books, thus pioneering a new tradition of scholarship.

This new elite was at the forefront of the nationalist activities which began in the early years of colonial rule and eventually led to the country's independence. The missionaries were successful in creating a new middle class much influenced by European ideas of nationalism and the nation state. The members of the elite were obviously divided as to the extent to which their society should be altered, but they were united in their ambition that they should provide the leadership and the ideas to govern a modern society. It was within Christianity itself that they began the process of asserting themselves. In the Niger Mission, Crowther and others were relieved of power in the early 1890s. The white missionaries who had arrived in the 1880s were unashamedly against the Nigerian elite, determined to see them in the church not as leaders but as mere converts. They also rejected the idea of an autonomous church administered by Africans. As notable a figure as James Johnson, a C.M.S. bishop, was humiliated, and the belief in white missionary circles was that their Nigerian counterparts were lacking in leadership qualities. The nationalistic response was to secede. For instance, the Native Baptist Church was created in the 1880s as a protest against the Southern Baptist mission which discriminated against Nigerians in the appointment of clergy. Many other indigenous churches, founded and controlled by Nigerians, were to follow with some among them supporting the institution of polygamy, contrary to the preachings of the mission churches.

The influence of the missionaries extended to the provision of health facilities, rudimentary in many places, but gradually upgraded. In addition, they encouraged economic activities as a way of supporting their members. They established model farms and plantations, although these were, in the end, unsuccessful. They had a better record in generating the interest of their converts in new crops and cash crop production and in developing tastes for European goods, thus promoting imports. They introduced such new crops as sugar cane and promoted the cultivation of cocoa which was to become a leading export commodity. New technical skills, such as carpentry, masonry, and printing were introduced, thus encouraging a number of people to set up small businesses of their own.

In the process of conversion, the missionaries had to condemn indigenous religions and cultures. To them, Christianity was superior to existing religions. Local gods and their priests were characterized as "pagan" and "evil," while the society itself was home to Satan. Where it was possible, the missionaries destroyed local temples and totems, and attacked practices such as polygamy. The extremists among them even criticized non-religious aspects of the culture such as singing, dancing, and story-telling. Where the missionaries were partially successful, they were able to undermine age-old values and cultures. New converts often joined in this crusade, thus creating divisions in their society. However, many Nigerian groups continued to hold on to their traditions well into the twentieth century.

Christianity during the nineteenth century did not attempt to indigenize itself. Missions were sponsored and controlled from abroad; the clergy was foreign. When European Christian practices conflicted with indigenous culture, the local was expected to give way to the foreign. Christian teachings, symbols, and rituals were essentially "alien." The task of making Christianity more meaningful to Nigerians became one of the challenges of the religion during the twentieth century.

TRADE RELATIONS

The abolition of the slave trade and the transition to trade in raw products—the so-called legitimate commerce—were the two defining aspects of Euro-Nigerian commercial relations during the nineteenth century. Trade brought more Europeans to the shores of Nigeria and led to major reorganization in various societies.

Changing economies, associated with the Industrial Revolution of the eighteenth century, made the use of slaves less necessary. The alternative and profitable trade in raw materials and manufactured goods called for changes in demand. In addition, positive humanistic values encouraged outspoken critics of the slave trade to call for its abolition. Many evangelical Christians attacked the slave trade as immoral. In 1807 the British parliament passed an act which made the slave trade illegal, and in 1833 its citizens were forbidden to own slaves. Although rather slowly, other nations joined Britain. France, next to Britain in the control of the slave trade, abolished the trade in 1815, and the Americans enacted a similar law earlier in 1807. Many nations enacted anti-slavery laws, while there was an agreement to police the seas and arrest slave dealers. The British established a naval squadron to patrol the sea off West Africa. In Freetown, Sierra Leone, illegal slavers, captured in the Bights of Benin and Biafra, were tried and their captives were released and re-settled in the Freetown colony. Patrolling the water was a rather difficult exercise not just for its sheer size but also due to the persistence of many European slave dealers. Between 1811 and 1870 over two million slaves were still captured, mainly from Nigeria and the Republic of Benin, many of them taken to Brazil and Cuba where demand was high. In the Niger Delta, the trade began to decline in the 1830s and the last ship left Brass in 1854. In Lagos and Badagry the trade continued until the 1840s, but suffered a major blow when the British captured Lagos, in 1851. By the 1860s many slave merchants had come to accept that the trade was over. In the United States, the enforcement of anti-slavery laws became stricter, while Brazil and Cuba stopped their imports.

The Industrial Revolution created the need for raw materials and markets in which to dispose of finished products. Nigeria had some of the raw materials demanded, while its people could also buy imported items. Abolition of the slave trade called for quick adjustments to this new economic demand. As to be expected, established slave dealers resisted abolition and, from the Nigerian end, they continued to supply slaves for as long as European ships were able to make their way to their shores. Political conflicts occurred among chiefs and merchants, divided as to whether to stop or continue the slave trade. Such conflicts drew the British closer to internal politics in Lagos, where they supported chiefs who opposed the slave trade. This was an era of treaties initiated by the British to end the slave trade and confer trading advantages to British companies. Violation of a treaty, in some cases, became the justification to interfere in local politics, although the British were themselves full of deceit and often failed to honor the provisions of a treaty.

While continuing to cooperate with European slave merchants until it became impossible to do so, some Nigerian groups, at the same time, began to expand the production of export crops to benefit from the trade shift. Slaves intended for foreign markets were diverted to domestic use, especially as farm workers. For the elite who previously profited from the slave trade, a lasting adjustment to abolition was to use slaves for large-scale production of export crops.

"Legitimate commerce" strengthened Euro-Nigerian relations. Many European companies established trade contacts with Nigeria, with trade representatives in such towns as Lagos, Calabar, and Bonny. A more direct control was taken by Britain to protect its commercial and political interests by establishing a consular authority in Lagos in 1861. The consul ensured that local rulers under his influence did not pursue policies detrimental to British economic interests. Where some powerful local middlemen controlled trade, as in the case of the Egbo of Old Calabar, the consul could seek the means to weaken them.

The European merchants traveled to the Nigerian ports along the shore. Before the last quarter of the century when they moved to the hinterland to establish stores, the merchants limited their stores and warehouses to the coastal cities. The European firms were mainly responsible for the imports, notably guns and gunpowder, beads, hardware, tobacco, salt, iron, textiles, and spirits. Salt, iron, textiles, and spirits comprised three-quarters of the total value of imports. As mass-produced items, they were cheaper than local products. From the Nigerian end, the exports included palm oil, palm kernel, rubber, coffee, indigo, pepper, peanuts, and cocoa. Vegetable oils, notably palm oil, were the leading products for most of the first half of the nineteenth century, since they were important ingredients in the manufacturing of candles and soap, and used as lubricants for machines until the 1850s. The Niger Delta was the leading producer, which was why European traders labeled it the Oil Rivers. In the second half of the century, peanuts and palm kernels also became major items, the former to make soap and oil and the latter for margarine and cattle feed.

Transactions were by cash or barter. In addition to existing currencies, new ones were added, such as British coins, Spanish dollars, and doubloons imported from Spain, Portugal, and the Americas. Credit trade, known as the trust system, was far more common with manufactured imports being exchanged for raw materials. The supercargoes (major European traders) would advance credit in goods to their Nigerian agents. The agents would, in turn, either sell the goods to buy local products or barter the European goods for the local ones. Months later, the agents would repay in raw materials the credit obtained from Europeans. To protect themselves, European traders requested agents to use local rulers as guarantors, while debtors could be dragged before European political agents such as the Consul.

While the trust system enabled Nigerian traders with limited capital to be active in business, it led to a number of problems, including many conflicts arising from betrayal and competition. To start with, the trust system ensured that European merchants controlled trade by compelling their agents to sell to them, even when it was not profitable for them to do so. Europeans abused the system by exploiting their African agents and even insisting on more supplies when initial contracts had been fulfilled. Once a local agent accepted credit, he was obliged to deliver the goods, even when prices had risen or another European merchant offered a better price. The so-called interlopers—new European merchants entering the trade with better deals such as selling imports at lower prices and buying exports at higher prices—sought agents who were ready to break previous contracts. Some agents also engaged in "double trusts" by collecting credit from two or more European agents. When they were unable to deliver, bitter conflicts ensued between the European trader and agent and among the European competitors. Moreover, agents were always in debt and uncompetitive, thus reducing possible profits and ability to accumulate wealth. So harmful were some of the outcomes of trust practice that some educated Nigerians began to call for its abolition by law. In one instance, a newspaper noticed that major credit recipients embarked upon immediate spending sprees:

> often, upon the receipt of large credits new modes of living are at once adopted; artificial wants rapidly increase; the luxuries, the expensive and perhaps not innocuous pleasures of European life, and the extravagance of foreign fashions become at once indispensable; large houses are built and furnished perhaps in very expensive style. . . . In some cases, harems grow rapidly in size, and are well furnished with inmates, and beyond jurisdiction, often slaves are quickly multiplied in addition. These people abuse the power of credit . . . and eventually bring themselves and others into a complication of miseries. Mushroom gentlemen, going down as quickly as they came up![4]

Despite the problems, the trade promoted the emergence of many local traders, some of whom grew wealthy. These merchants, based in coastal trading towns, were brokers and middlemen who exchanged products of the Nigerian hinterland for European imports. Great wealth accrued to the successful merchants. In the second half of the nineteenth century, when the use of steamships allowed many more to participate in trade, a new class of merchants—known as "the educated Africans"—also joined. Based in Lagos, they were liberated slaves, products of the mission schools, cultivating the lifestyles of Europeans. They reorganized their businesses, imitating the model of the European firms and performing as wholesalers and agents to diverse European companies. While many continued to receive credit from Europeans, a few struggled to engage in direct trade with Europe. Some Nigerian entrepreneurs were so wealthy and so successful that they began to rival the European firms.

Trade was always competitive, at various levels. Among Nigerians, those in the hinterland competed with their coastal counterparts who were accused of always cheating them. The ambition of hinterland merchants and traders was to have direct access to Europeans. Among the Yoruba, the Egba and Ijebu closest to the coast would close the trade routes to prevent such a penetration. In the Niger Delta, the quest to break the trading monopolies of coastal merchants led to many conflicts. One of the ways conflicts were restored was the establishment of the Courts of Equity in Bonny in 1854, a type of commercial or mercantile association with the authority to resolve disputes. Members comprised influential European and African traders, and the chair was "occupied by the white supercargoes in monthly rotation."[5] Although only an unofficial tribunal, the court was able to settle a number of disputes and regulate trade. It acquired legal recognition from the British government in 1872.

There was also competition among the European traders. While British firms took the lead in trade, there were others from France and Germany struggling to assert themselves. By the 1880s German traders had become far more influential than others because of their successful use of steamships, their ability to supply cheaper import items, notably liquor, and the large market for cattle feed in Germany. Traders from various countries competed for markets and agents. Resident traders combined against those who floated their wares. After 1852 steamships began a regular service, reducing freight costs and allowing many more merchants (without the means to own mail steamers) to participate in trade. Established firms clashed with aggressive new ones. And as explorers and missionaries penetrated the hinterland, they provided data for ambitious traders. In the 1880s increasing competition among European traders encouraged some companies to move to the hinterland in order to bypass the Nigerian middlemen and increase their profit margins. The intensity of competition eventually led to the establishment of a chartered company with a monopoly over trade—the Royal Niger Company (RNC)—which also became a successful agency of territorial acquisition.

THE ROYAL NIGER COMPANY

The hero of the RNC was Sir George Taubman Goldie, an aggressive British merchant and empire builder. He was one of the architects of the British conquest of Nigeria, primarily through his efforts to use his trading company to create an informal empire on the Niger, setting up a model for other chartered companies in Africa.

In 1877 Goldie's trading career brought him to the lower Niger at a time of intense trade rivalries among European merchants on the one hand and between them and the Nigerian merchants on the other. The Delta chiefs profited a great deal by collecting levies on those who used their waterways. Paying duties and maintaining a large number of agents and securing staff reduced the profit margins of European traders. Goldie's idea was to create a combine. In 1879 he brought all British trading parties together into a single company, the United Africa Company (UAC). Further competition with two French companies and the possible advance of the Germans from the Cameroons led Goldie to further reorganize the UAC. In 1882 he changed the company's name to the National African Company (NAC), increased the subscribed capital to £1 million from £200,000, and sold shares to the public. Unable to co-opt the two rival French firms, he skillfully undercut their prices by 24 percent, thus forcing them out of business. Playing on the threat of German and French colonial expansion into the area, he applied for a royal charter from the British government in order to control both trade and territory. The charter was granted in 1886, and the company acquired yet another name, the Royal Niger Company (RNC). Although the charter prevented the RNC from excluding other firms from the Niger area and transferring territory to other countries, it gave the company broad powers to govern areas where treaties of protection were signed, add new territories, collect taxes and duties to run its administration, and abolish slavery and the slave trade.

The charter enabled the RNC to operate like a government in the lower Niger until 1899, securing a significant presence for Britain. With its headquarters at Asaba on the River Niger, with an administration, a constabulary, and a High Court of Justice, the RNC not only established a strong control over trade, it began to govern as well. High duties were collected on imports and exports, companies operating in the area had to pay high charges, and firms from Germany and France were driven away. Goldie was able to sign about thirty-seven treaties with different chiefs which allowed him to interfere in local politics. A fleet of gunboats allowed the use of force when diplomacy failed, to punish towns and rulers that attacked the RNC's trading factories, and to assist indigenous rulers who collaborated with the company. The RNC also denied many Nigerians' participation in trade, leading to at least an attack on one of its stations. The RNC established control over the Niger Delta and parts of the Middle Belt. This "empire" benefited the public shareholders in Britain who reaped generous dividends and the government which eventually claimed control over the territories possessed by the company. Goldie was unapologetic about his racism, high-handedness, and excessive use of violence—the "natives" (as he called Nigerians) were useful as producers only as long as they cooperated with him.

TRADE, POLITICS, AND SOCIETY

The consequences of international trade were felt by critical segments of the Nigerian society. Unlike the slave trade of the preceding centuries, trade in raw materials generated production on a large-scale. If the slave trade depressed the economy, "legitimate commerce" set millions of people to work producing cash crops in addition to their regular food crops. Favorable conditions for farming, regular channels to dispose of the goods, and propaganda by missionaries and others insured production by peasants and slaves. Such products as palm oil and palm kernels had to be processed in tedious ways, thus again stimulating large-scale processing enterprises. Hundreds of people were traders as part of a long chain in the distribution system from the farms to the industries in Europe. As many participants required little capital outlay, many were able to join in the chain.

This enhanced economy had its implications on labor relations. People in areas where opportunities for large-scale production were not available were presented with the option of migration elsewhere. However, the labor that largely sustained production and trade was that of slaves. Rulers and wealthy merchants acquired slaves to work for them. They also had the opportunity to use pawns, that is, laborers who served as interest on loans, working for the creditor until the principal was fully paid.

The economy of Nigeria was oriented toward production for the external market. Where the production of export crops was rewarding, it could take priority over food production. Where imports were dominated by luxuries such as textiles and liquor, the gains of trade were more social than economic. As trade was characterized by fluctuations in price and volume, the incomes of producers and local traders were unpredictable. The rise of Nigerian merchants was associated with the trade. Where their number was significant, as in the case of Lagos, Abeokuta, and the city-states of the Niger Delta, the Nigerian merchants sought participation in politics, while some of them criticized local chiefs for their commitment to tradition, instead of responding to the opportunities.

The Niger Delta, the leading producer of palm oil, is the best place to illustrate most of these changes. A significant outcome of the opportunity to produce and trade was the acquisition of power and influence by former slaves and others of low status. Before this, a nobility deriving its wealth partly from the slave trade had controlled the five principal city-states of Calabar, Brass, Grand Bonny, Elem Kalabari, and Itsekiri. Slaves and commoners were able to take part in the palm oil industry and some among them accumulated great profits. They began to use their money to acquire status and authority in all the five cities. In Brass and Elem Kalabari, some of them, the "new men," became heads of "houses" while in Itsekiri, Nana, a commoner, made a bid for the throne although he was denied. In Calabar, there was a social revolution. Slaves and oppressed people established the Order of Blood Men, relocated to a separate community on the Qua Iboe River, and began to demand social justice and equal rights. Perhaps the most notable example was Bonny where the nobility competed with slaves for the throne. For thirty-six years (1830–1866) Alali, a former slave, was the head of the Anna Pepple house, and the most powerful person in the city. When he died, an Igbo slave, Jaja, succeeded him. When Jaja was attacked in 1868 by a rival house, he strategically relocated to Opobo where he was able to cut off Bonny from its trading contacts on the River Imo. Rather than return to Bonny, he established an autonomous city at Opobo, where he became king and leader of a thriving trading empire. Jaja's achievements, as well of those of his colleagues, were undermined by European penetration.

NOTES

1. Quoted in J. F. Ade Ajayi, "Henry Venn and the Policy of Development," in O. Kalu, ed., *The History of Christianity in West Africa* (London: Longman), 1980, p. 63.

2. Quoted in "Introduction," in *Ibid*, p. 2.

3. Church Missionary Society Archives, G3A3/1884/166, Pratt to Crowther, September 9, 1884.

4. *The Lagos Times and the Gold Coast Colony Advertiser*, August 10, 1881.

5. Quoted in K. O. Dike, *Trade and Politics in the Niger Delta, 1830–1885* (Oxford: Oxford University Press, 1959), p. 126.

4

British Conquest and Resistance

The conquest of Nigeria was the culmination of many years of contact between various European interests and Nigerian communities. By the mid-nineteenth century, the colonial take-over was not yet anticipated: the fear of tropical diseases and the high cost of expansion checked any ambitious imperial project, and educated Africans were able to hold influential positions in the church and civil service, suggesting that the future would be controlled by them. Nevertheless, the British did not withdraw from Nigeria. In 1849 they appointed John Beecroft as consul for the West African coast, to be stationed in Fernando Po, in order to regulate "legal trade."[1] In 1880 British colonies and influence were limited to Lagos and the Niger Delta, but by 1905 virtually the entire country was under British rule. With the exception of Liberia and Ethiopia, other African peoples had a similar experience of subjugation as part of the European partition of Africa and general scramble for colonies. The motives of colonial conquest included ensuring greater economic advantages for their countries, preventing rival powers from exercising control, and resolving political and diplomatic problems in Europe by using the competition for overseas territory.

As with the rest of Africa, the partition of Nigeria occurred in the last quarter of the nineteenth century. To minimize the tension arising from possible competing claims, Germany convened the Berlin Conference of 1884–1885 to discuss European incursions into Africa. An agreement establishing principles was followed by the frantic scramble for Africa, as competing European powers looked for evidence of "effective occupation" to convince one another that they could govern the areas that they had conquered or over which they had established a "sphere of influence." A protectorate declared over an area along the coast was assumed to extend to its hinterland, although rival powers contested this. However, Europeans were able to resolve their disputes through treaties and negotiations over boundaries, without consulting Nigerian political authorities.

France, Britain, Germany, Portugal, Belgium, Italy, and Spain participated in the scramble, each jealous of the others. To forestall one another, they all scrambled and sought the means to legitimize their claims. The British signed a treaty in the Niger Delta in 1884 to prevent the French and Germans from so doing. Consuls and governors regarded their contributions to imperial conquest as a way of attaining promotion and fulfilling other personal ambitions. European traders, such as those operating in Lagos and the Niger Delta, called for political control in order to establish trading monopolies. Enterprising merchants dreamt of gold and diamonds that could be obtained from unexplored mines, farms that would produce enormous raw materials, and markets that would consume manufactured products. European citizens saw the scramble as an expression of nationalism; a conquest showed the power of their country, even if the area was not necessarily economically productive. A colony was thus an object to boost national pride. Not a few people also expressed the racist opinion that a "superior race" had the right to dominate the "primitives" in order to uplift them.

The British conquest of Nigeria occurred in two stages: the southern phase from 1850 to 1897, and the northern phase from the turn of the century to 1914. Diplomacy and force were the key tools, with local leaders responding with similar tactics or merely surrendering to defeat. Many indigenous rulers understood the consequences of conquest and tried unsuccessfully to prevent it.

THE SOUTHERN PHASE

In 1851 Lagos signed a treaty surrendering its sovereignty after a British gunboat attack. The events leading to this revolved around the continuance of the slave trade, the desire of the missionaries to spread

Christianity, and complicated succession disputes in Lagos. Its ruler, Kosoko, was deposed for supporting the slave trade, while Akitoye, a so-called anti-slavery prince, was installed as the new king. A faction of Lagos chiefs refused to aid the abolition of the slave trade and denied cooperation to a number of British commercial interests and their allies. The missionaries, some of whom were based in the near-by city of Abeokuta, wanted to extend their work to Lagos. They painted the pro-slavery faction as the enemy and urged the British government to intervene. In addition, since 1811 various candidates had been fighting for the throne of Lagos. In the view of the ambitious contenders, the British and the missionaries could be manipulated for support. The British, too, were clever enough to exploit the dissension to their own advantage by throwing their weight behind Akitoye. In 1851 the British accused Kosoko of failure to sign a treaty to end the slave trade and assist the missionaries. On December 26, 1851, a British naval force attacked the city, forcing the king and his supporters to flee, while the new king was installed. Akitoye signed the treaty, promised to aid missionary work, and assured British firms of preferential treatment. In return the British offered security and protection to the king. This was an important inroad for the British in Lagos and its immediate neighborhood. From here, British officers were able to monitor events in the Yoruba hinterland. The consul in Lagos interfered in trade and politics in ways that favored his country, and the consul was involved in the selection of Akitoye's successor in 1853.

In 1861 the British annexed Lagos to make it its first Crown Colony in Nigeria, appointing a governor with the aim of further promoting trade. There was a discussion on the possibility of developing a road to link up with the River Niger through the Yoruba country in order to tap the products of this huge area. The missionaries were active in a number of cities, while British traders became firmly established in Lagos. The British took an interest in events in the hinterland. Although the Yoruba were passing through a period of civil war, the need to ensure that export goods reached the Lagos port was paramount to the governor. As control of trade routes became part of the diplomacy and strategy of warfare, the British sought the means to prevent permanent closure of routes. In addition, they mediated in the war, ensuring the signing of the peace treaty of 1886 which obligated Yoruba states to listen to the suggestions of the governor and allow uninterrupted trade.

The test of whether the Yoruba would respect the governor came a few years later at Ijebu Ode. Here, the assertive chiefs of Ijebu had denied access to the missionaries, blocked trade routes to the hinterland, curtailed the entry even of Yoruba traders to their markets, and refused to accept unfavorable offers from Governor Carter of the Lagos Colony who visited them in 1891. A year later, after accusing them of wanting to destroy trade, Carter ordered an attack on the Ijebu, who vigorously defended their sovereignty, although unsuccessfully. This was the major example of military resistance to imperialism among the Yoruba. Britain's successful attack subdued a major Yoruba power; indeed, the Ijebu not only accepted British rule, but many of them became very receptive to missionary teaching. The failure of the Ijebu weakened the resolve of other states such as Abeokuta and Ibadan to the extent that they did not even consider any military resistance to the British. It also prepared the ground for the final phase in the incorporation of the rest of Yorubaland into the British colony. In the months that followed, the British sent a Resident and a garrison of troops to Ibadan, extending their power to the most influential state in the hinterland. From here, the British extended their influence to other places where they obtained assurances of cooperation, except at Oyo, the capital of the Oyo kingdom, where force had to be used in 1895 to subdue the *Alaafin* and his chiefs. Abeokuta was temporarily granted a quasi-colonial status, but this privilege was later removed.

In the southeast intense British penetration led to the collapse of the Delta states of Opobo, Brass, Bonny, Elem Kalabari, and Okrika in the east, Itsekiri to the west, and the areas around the Bini River. The Delta was notorious for trade rivalries. In 1849 the British appointed John Beecroft as consul for the Bights of Benin and Biafra, thus establishing what would eventually become a permanent contact. During the last quarter of the nineteenth century, the British were eager to avoid possible rivalry with the Germans and French for the control of this area. As noted in the preceding chapter, the RNC established a commercial empire while Consul Hewett traveled around to sign so-called protection treaties. With a great deal of ruthlessness, the RNC used its military arm to dominate parts of the Delta and the lower Niger. In 1891 the British established a colonial jurisdiction, known as the "Protectorate of the Oil Rivers," with the implication that their resident officers would now be involved in the management of the area and their traders could expect few or no obstacles to trade. The British were also determined to keep the French and Germans out of this area. A consul general was appointed for the protectorate, based at Calabar, with a budget, staff, army, and deputies (vice consuls) in five other major towns.

Delta chiefs resisted this encroachment because they knew its implication for trade and sovereignty. Some were reluctant to sign any treaty, a document that was mistrusted and, as one chief rightly warned, could lead to the seizure of their country.[2] The first major clash occurred in 1887 at Opobo, led by Jaja of Opobo, merchant and king. Jaja had succeeded as a merchant, largely because of his ability as a middleman, his skill in forging alliances with other trading towns, and direct marketing with England. In 1885 the British had to negotiate with him, signing a treaty that guaranteed Opobo's sovereignty. However, the proclamation that followed threatened to undermine him. When British traders attempted to move to the hinterland, areas dominated by Jaja's network, a conflict ensued. Jaja blocked the access of British traders to lucrative supply sources, he punished any local trader who cooperated with them, and insisted on direct trade with Europe. All these provoked great resentment from British traders. In spite of Jaja's sending a delegation to the Secretary of State for the colonies in Britain, Consul H. H. Johnston insisted that he must allow uninterrupted access to his area and stop collecting "comey" (tolls) or face a military attack.

In a cunning device, the consul invited Jaja aboard a British ship to seek a peaceful means of resolving the conflicts. An unsuspecting Jaja cooperated, but was immediately seized and exiled to Accra, Gold Coast. Here, he was tried and found guilty of interfering with trade and failure to cooperate with the consul to administer justice and promote trade. He was deported to the West Indies. After being pardoned, he died in 1891 on his return journey. Like the attack on the Ijebu in the southwest, the humiliation of Jaja sent a signal to Bonny and Elem Kalabari that they must cooperate with the British. In 1891 the British administration of its Oil Rivers Protectorate commenced, with revenues derived from import duties. Additional territorial gains led in 1893 to the declaration of the Niger Coast Protectorate.

The occupation of the Itsekiri kingdom, west of the Delta, was also accompanied with great resistance. The British had to contend with Chief Nana, a wealthy merchant prince, and the Governor of the Bini River, as his title described him. The British wanted to add the Itsekiri to their protectorate, but Nana stood in the way. He was wealthy, powerful, and assertive. Nana understood the need to control the oil market and dictate the terms of trade, much to the annoyance of British traders. Not only was he accused of trade monopoly, but also of human sacrifice, both warranting a forceful attack. In August and September 1894, a military confrontation ensued after Nana refused to be tricked into a ship for a parley. An impressive British naval and military force, aided by a rival Itsekiri chief, subdued Nana. In Lagos, he was tried for obstruction to trade and progress, and his rival was appointed as a political agent. Other small wars were fought in four other locations in the Delta, and British expansion and conquest were successful there as well.

The conquest of the powerful and long-established kingdom of Benin in 1897 completed the take-over of the Oil Rivers. The British painted Benin as a land full of great resources in ivory, rubber, and palm oil, all waiting to be tapped if only its king would cooperate. Unlike the Delta states, Benin was not directly involved with trade with Europeans, but had managed to establish a trade monopoly in its area. However, Benin's trade with its neighbors, such as the Itsekiri and Yoruba, was extensive and affected by changes in the trade with Europeans. Benin's strength as a regional power was undermined in the nineteenth century, thus paving the way for British conquest. When a British consul visited Benin in 1862, he was unable to negotiate important trade deals, and his report presented the empire as barbaric for supporting human sacrifice and the slave trade. The British were able to persuade other advancing European nations to recognize Benin as part of their Oil Rivers Protectorate. In 1891 Consul Gallwey, assuming that Benin was under his control, visited the city for trade discussions, but the king refused to meet with him. In the following year another delegation presented Benin with a treaty that would ensure free trade and allow British officers to serve as advisors. The king refused to sign, but his chiefs did, which the British found sufficient. When the king refused to abide by this treaty, the British decided to attack Benin in 1897. In a first encounter led by Captain Phillips, Benin was able to rout the British force. In a second attack by a bigger force, Benin was itself routed after a heroic struggle, the palace was looted, and King Ovonramwen was captured and exiled until his death seventeen years later. Thus came to an end a famous empire.

East of Benin and north of the Delta groups were the Igbo and Ibibio who would experience their own incorporation into colonial Nigeria around the end of the century. Here, the British did not have to contend with kingdoms or city-states, but with the Aro trading oligarchy based on the oracle at the town of Arochukwu. The Aro were successful traders, using the power of their oracle, and sponsored armies to maintain their hold on their middleman position between the Igbo and Ibibio in the hinterland and the Europeans along the coast. To resist the British penetration, the Aro originally formed alliances with neighboring groups in the Cross River to organize resistance and attack pro-British elements.

In a carefully planned military expedition from November 1901 to March 1902, however, the British used their military force to subdue the Aro.

THE NORTHERN PHASE, 1900–1914

The Royal Niger Company had used its charter to penetrate the north. With its base at Asaba on the lower Niger, the RNC attacked and conquered Ilorin and Nupe in 1897 and signed treaties with the Sultan of Sokoto and the Emir of Gwandu. When the charter was abrogated in 1899, the British government immediately took measures to consolidate the gains of the company and further extend them, if necessary by force. The West African Frontier Force, a colonial army, was established with its headquarters at Jebba. Captain (later Lord) Frederick Lugard was appointed as the High Commissioner for northern Nigeria. On January 1, 1900, Lugard hoisted the Union Jack and proclaimed the area the RNC had controlled as the Protectorate of Northern Nigeria. When the sultan received the news of the proclamation in a letter to him, he expressed shock at a letter that "brought fear" and promised never to read another one.[3] With his base in the confluence town of Lokoja, Lugard had to extend northwards, conquering one emirate after the other. The emirates of Kontagora and Bida were violently attacked in 1901 after being accused of slave trading, and new kings, supporters of the British, were appointed for them. Next the emirates of Bauchi and Gombe fell, and the British established a provincial government in the area which had to deal with pockets of resistance until 1907. Kano fell in 1903 after gallant resistance.

Sokoto, the capital of the caliphate, put up the stiffest resistance, but it eventually lost in 1903. Here, Islam energized the resistance. Sultan Attahiru and his people were opposed to rule by those perceived as Christian infidels. Thousands of Muslims strongly believed that it was their religious duty to resist the British. Attahiru's reaction was to abandon the throne and undertake a *hijra*, a withdrawal. He was followed by hundreds of his subjects, but the British pursued him and halted his movement at Burmi. A war followed, with the British losing the first battle. He later opted to surrender and asked to be allowed to proceed to Mecca, but the British again attacked him, killing him and many of his followers. His son continued the resistance, fleeing with many followers to take refuge in the Sudan to the east.

In the Middle Belt the British engaged in a series of small wars with the Tiv from 1900 to 1901 and again from 1906 to 1908. In Borno to the northeast the British had to engage in bitter conflicts with the French and Rabih Fadlalah, a Sudanese military adventurer who had established control in this area in 1893. The French allied with the al-Kanemi dynasty while the British allied with the Rabihs. In April 1900 the French killed Rabih and installed Umar Sanda of the previous dynasty, while the British were able to strike back in 1902 to install their own supporter as king. After 1902 the British moved quickly to consolidate power by ordering the collection of tax, compelling the people to surrender their firearms to reduce the danger of violent protest, and creating a new capital at Kukawa, where Lugard presented the king with a staff of office after obtaining an oath of allegiance from him.

By agreements with the French and Germans, Nigerian territorial frontiers were established. As with other colonies, the boundaries were artificial creations which divided, for example, the Yoruba and Hausa into two different countries. In size, Nigeria became one of the biggest countries in Africa. However, its plural nature has never been turned to any great advantage as no solution has ever been found to enable its diverse people to create a strong united nation.

RESISTANCE AND ITS FAILURE

Indigenous authorities and their people had to respond to the colonial conquest. Astute leaders and those connected with other parts of the world understood what imperialism was all about. They knew that wars of colonial conquest were being fought in other regions, too. The Delta chiefs knew that the RNC and the British were undermining them. The military leaders of Ibadan lamented in the 1890s that their city that had for many years been posting residents to colonies was about to become a colony too. In 1903 the Emir of Kano described Lugard and his men as dogs who would "threaten to overcome" his people.[4]

The response took various forms. As indicated above, many places such as Sokoto, Benin, and Ijebu fought to defend their sovereignty. Whether small or big, centralized or segmented, many societies used whatever means they had to fight for their freedom. If kings and warriors led the attack, the peasants also joined. There were even cases where the peasants and other marginalized groups were more committed to protest than political leaders, as in the case of the Muslims in Satiru who were abandoned by the caliphate authorities or the Igbo cultivators, known as the Ekumeku, in western Igboland, who fought with good determination.

In the case of the Ekumeku, another pattern emerged. A group of small villages in western Igboland turned their male secret societies into a protest movement known as the Ekumeku that fought the British for a decade. In 1898 the Ekumeku successfully attacked the RNC, forcing its agents and staff to abandon the area. When in 1902 there was another fear of an Ekumeku uprising, the British moved fast to arrest their leaders and destroy many of their villages. Two years later the Ekumeku regrouped, but lost again. Of the almost three hundred prisoners who were captured, only a few survived incarceration. As if to pay homage to their fallen heroes, the Ekumeku rose again in 1909 with another round of fighting that lasted three months. In 1911 the British anticipated another uprising and arrested suspected Ekumeku leaders.

In northern Nigeria after the defeat of 1903, many turned to Islam for an eschatological response. The rallying force became the idea of the Mahdi, the Messiah, "a Rightly Guided Leader" who would come, as the last days approached, to reform the world. British invasions and other evidence of decadence were interpreted as the signs that the time was near for the Mahdi to appear. Some Islamic preachers predicted that the Mahdi would appear around Burmi where the Sokoto forces were defeated. A few people actually proclaimed themselves as the real Mahdi in Yelwa, Jebba, Nupe, and Mandara. In 1906 a Mahdist uprising broke out in Satiru, north of Sokoto. In the first attempt to crush the rebellion, government forces were routed. The Mahdists were encouraged and moved ahead to mobilize more forces, appealing to the sultan and other Islamic leaders for help. They were to be disappointed; the sultan and other political leaders, now acting as appointees of the British government, not only refused to cooperate, but they allowed their men to join with the British to attack Satiru. A reorganized government force attacked Satiru using maximum force, completely destroying the town. Those among the Mahdists who were captured alive were brutally treated as dangerous criminals.

Islam offered other ideological options. Should armed resistance fail, many were enjoined to accept conquest not with their "heart" but with their "mouth," that is, a diplomatic strategy of seeking accommodation while awaiting opportunities to rebel. Islam also advised that believers could emigrate to other areas, an option that Attahiru and his son chose. Migration was thus an option of resistance, rather than accommodation.

Islam was not the only source of mobilization. In many parts of the south, people turned to their gods and charm-makers for means to resist British challenges. Soldiers were encouraged by charms and sacrifices were offered to the gods for community protection. Stories of victories in the use of uncommon tactics—for example, conjuring diseases to destroy opposing armies—are common. Where a battle was won, as in the case of the Ekumeku against the RNC, credit was given to charm makers and soldiers. Losses were rationalized as either the failure of the gods to help or the superiority of the gods of the enemy.

Although their efforts were not very effective, a tiny elite used newspapers and pamphlets to condemn the British encroachment. Where the use of force was considered excessive, they complained, as in the case of the bombardment of Oyo in 1895, which compelled the *Lagos Weekly Record* to run anti-British reports.

Response was not only shaped by violence or protest. There were peoples and places that reconciled themselves to imperialism or surrendered to it. A number of elite members in the coastal town of Lagos interpreted British imperialism as an agency of modernization—they hoped that it would come with "benefits," that is, those aspects they associated with European civilization such as roads, industries, Western education, and Christianity. These members of the elite regarded Nigerian communities and their leaders who fought against the British as backward elements standing in the way of civilization. Cases of surrender were based on a rational consideration of the consequences of resistance in view of what other places and their rulers had suffered. Destroying towns, punishing chiefs who resisted, and sending kings into exile in great humiliation were events whose news spread across the land in a way that weakened the spirit of many people.

Why did the British succeed in their conquest mission and the Nigerians fail in their resistance efforts? Indeed, in a number of cases, resistance was doomed to failure from the beginning. By the 1880s when the partition got under way, a number of events had already worked in favor of the British. Due to the activities of missionaries and explorers, they had sufficient knowledge of the country to be able to plan military advances, establish bases of operations, and even set up administrative centers. Previous military and diplomatic encounters in the Niger Delta and Lagos had brought the British much respect, in addition to creating in the minds of many indigenous rulers the impression that they were dealing with a partner with access to superior weapons.

The British committed adequate resources to expansion. Losing a battle or retreating from one did not mean an end to the ambition to conquer but led to an allocation of more resources for a counterattack. On the other hand, a major loss by a Nigerian group could mean the end of their resistance due to limited resources or inability to reorganize. A large number of Africans were recruited into the British army, thus turning Africans against themselves, making them the real conquerors of their own people. The West African Frontier Force that subdued the north had many Hausa soldiers fighting against their own land. As big as Nigeria is, and as difficult as the task of expansion was, only a few British soldiers lost their lives. In addition to making use of Nigerians as soldiers, the British also used them as political agents for intelligence operations. These agents penetrated many areas, acting as spies to collect valuable information for the British. Many served as their interpreters, guides, companions, translators, and ambassadors. No doubt, many of these agents were motivated by selfish considerations—wages, stipends, closeness to power, and other opportunities. However, they became valuable collaborators in the conquest of Nigeria.

The Nigerian kingdoms and societies were conquered one after another, and many lacked the resources to engage in prolonged resistance wars. A tragic case was the Sokoto Caliphate, which failed to mobilize all its emirates to offer collective resistance. In this failure, the caliphate ignored the history of its own creation, whereby Uthman dan Fodio exploited the divisions among the Hausa states to destroy them. However, there were problems which negated possible collaboration efforts. Within the caliphate itself, there were pockets of resistance by those who did not want conversion to Islam or who rejected the domination of the new political class. The dissatisfied elements could not be expected to join in a mass uprising or collective resistance. There is the additional problem that the defense of the caliphate had been based on each emirate defending itself. At the time of the partition they again followed this arrangement, each emirate separately fighting the British army.

As in the case of the Itsekiri, one chief could be used against another to undermine collective resistance. Rivalries among the states played into European hands, as in the case of those Yoruba who were happy when the British invaded Ijebu in 1892. Leading Yoruba states such as Ijebu, Abeokuta, Ibadan, and Oyo had divergent interests which prevented them from uniting. And in such former colonies of Ibadan as the Ekiti and Ijesa towns further inland, the British were perceived by some political leaders as posing a lesser threat, a view shaped by the prevailing hostility and warfare. In the east, there were communities that sought the assistance of the British against their enemies or powerful neighbors, thus creating an alliance that ultimately led to their own subordination. In the Niger Delta inter-group rivalries and competition among the "houses" called for formation of alliances. In pursuing such a strategy some people regarded the British as valuable allies, not knowing that their interests were at variance.

There were cases where a region had weakened itself before the 1880s, thus preventing any strong resistance or collaboration. For instance, it would have been difficult for the Yoruba to unite, given their long-standing wars. In Benin, King Ovonramwen had antagonized a number of his own chiefs, again precluding a collective response. In some other states, including the Nupe, leaders could be divided into the "war party" and the "negotiation party," one favoring resistance, the other calling for collaboration, with the result that a concerted effort was impossible.

Those who resisted, in spite of the heroism of their soldiers, had severe military and technological limitations. Weapons were crude and firearms in short supply, faced with an opponent with modern weapons. Superior European weapons were decisive in the conquest process. Thanks to the industrial revolution, improvements in weapon technology had produced the Maxim and Gatling guns, capable of firing eleven bullets in a second, early machine guns that were unavailable to African societies. To societies still dependent on the traditional weapons of spears, bows, and arrows, there was obviously no answer to the devastation of machine guns. And those with firearms had old, slow muzzle-loading guns. Mud walls and massed cavalry were adapted to the old guns but not to the machine guns which could kill soldiers on horses before they had the opportunity to come close. Lugard, for instance, was able to defeat the strong army of the Nupe, turning their established defensive tactics against them. Where the country was open, as in the savanna, the invading army could move much faster and use their guns with greater efficiency. The invading army could be ruthless. For instance, the RNC's army massacred Nupe soldiers, destroyed half of Asaba, damaged hundreds of buildings, and destroyed Bida all to ensure that victory was decisive. The British army was more active, and perhaps better trained than the various forces it faced.

For the majority of the Nigerian groups, their armies were ad hoc, quickly trained to meet contingency situations, but lacking the tactics to withstand an invading army with modern guns and incapable of sustaining long periods of military actions. In a number of places, attempts were made to reform the military, but not with much success. The Ijebu and Opobo, for example, tried to obtain new rifles. However, they had limited opportunities to practice using them because ammunition could not be wasted. When war came, many of their soldiers lacked the training for accurate marksmanship. There were no generals to handle training in the use of new weapons or to change the old tactics of defending city walls and surprise cavalry charges.

Finally, realizing the futility of resistance after observing the humiliation and defeat of their neighbors, a number of places voluntarily surrendered. To cite two examples: after noting the defeat of Ijebu, many other Yoruba groups offered no resistance; and the emirate of Zaria surrendered in 1902 to prevent attack.

The conquest inaugurated a new political arrangement for Nigeria. Hundreds of diverse groups were brought together in one country, and a new administrative system was imposed upon them. New possibilities and problems were created in all aspects of life, as Nigeria moved into the twentieth century, the so-called modern era. We shall explore these great changes in the next chapter.

NOTES

1. Public Record Office (P.R.O.), London, FO 84/775, Draft of Beecroft's Appointment, June 30, 1849.

2. P.R.O., FO 84/1117, Hutchinson to Russell, February 12, 1860.

3. Quoted in D. J. M. Muffett, *Concerning Brave Captains* (London: Frank Cass, 1964), p. 39.

4. Quoted in Muffett, *Concerning Brave Captains*, p. 96.

5

Colonial Rule

Between 1900 and 1914 the British were preoccupied with consolidating their gains and establishing a new political system. They had to respond to a number of immediate problems. To start with, they had to cope with the people's protest and resistance to an alien authority by embarking on so-called pacification measures. There were uprisings among the Yoruba and Igbo during the First World War. The army and the police were used to destroy opposition forces in different parts of the country. In addition, when people were opposed to new policies or changes, they had to be forced to accept. The British needed to raise money to finance the administration without having to impose undue burdens on British taxpayers. The number of British personnel was not large enough for a country the size of Nigeria, and bringing more would exact a toll on public revenues. Personnel shortage was compounded by that of poor communications, both in infrastructure and language. There was a language barrier between Nigerians and their overlords. During the early years, the British had to participate in the First World War that further diminished available resources, but helped to affirm their grip on Nigeria. By the time of the First World War, the British had established a dual political system: a central administration to manage the entire country, and a local government format known as indirect rule. Between then and 1960 changes were made to correct problems and in response to various demands by Nigerians. The politics, economy, and culture of the Nigerian area were transformed.

AMALGAMATION

Areas separately conquered and administered were eventually amalgamated in 1914. Before then, there were three autonomous territories, two in the south and one in the north. Thus, there were "three Nigerias," an anomaly which generated a number of proposals. In 1906 the Lagos Colony and the Protectorate of Southern Nigeria were merged with a capital in Lagos, thus creating "two Nigerias." In 1912 Frederick Lugard was appointed the governor of the Colony and Protectorate of Southern Nigeria and of the Protectorate of Northern Nigeria. On January 1, 1914, he amalgamated the two into one country under a governor-general.

The primary reason for amalgamation was economic. The north was poor. Without a direct access to the sea, it could not generate sufficient revenues (by way of customs duties) while capital was being consumed by railway construction. The administration in the south and the Imperial Treasury in Britain had to render financial assistance to the north. Amalgamation would shift excess money generated in the south to the north. It was also reckoned that amalgamation would streamline a number of departments and thus reduce duplications. Senior officials in the different protectorates had clashed over policies and made divergent recommendations to the Colonial Office over a wide range of issues. With one official over all of them, it was reckoned that personality clashes would be minimized. More importantly, it was vital to unify the railway constructions being financed by the south and north. With the amalgamation, the governor-general received broad powers to manage the country. Lugard extended the system of indirect rule to the south, although this was greeted with opposition. A Supreme Court was established for the country.

A central administration emerged, based in Lagos. Legislation was initiated from Lagos by the Nigerian Council (later the Legislative Council) which was never fully representative of the country. Laws passed by this Council required the consent of the governor-general, who also enjoyed the power to issue proclamations in respect to northern Nigeria. The governor-general was in charge of departments dealing with the army, railways, treasury, forestry, posts and telegraphs, and public works. He presided over an Executive Council, made up mainly of British officials, which reviewed policies and recommendations from various departments. The governor-general reported directly to the Secretary of State for the Colonies in London. Lieutenant governors were appointed for the north and south, with their capitals in Kaduna and Enugu respectively. The two were under the authority of the governor-general who also approved their budgets, but they were allowed to run regional departments of police, agriculture, public works, forestry, education, mines, and prisons. Provinces were created in both regions, each under a Resident responsible to the lieutenant governor. A province was in turn broken into districts, each under a district officer. Public revenues were derived from direct taxes, and from indirect taxes on imports and exports.

Amalgamation did not, however, bring about a coherent integration of the country, as both the south and north continued to maintain many of their differences in aspects of governance and society. Lugard and his successors believed that the north was different from the south, and each should develop along autonomous lines. There was no central legislature in which the representatives of both regions would meet. It was not until the 1920s that a central secretariat emerged. Only a few departments were initially unified—the Treasury, Railways, Surveys, Post and Telegraph, and Audit.

In 1919 the Protectorate of Southern Nigeria was divided into nine provinces and in 1929 the Protectorate of Northern Nigeria was also divided into twelve. In 1939 the provinces in the south were divided into two regions, West and East, with the North forming the third region, a division that still existed at the time of independence in 1960. Regionalism became firmly established during the tenure of Governor Richards (1943–1947), with separate Houses of Assembly for the three regions. Each Assembly sent members to the Central Legislature in Lagos.

Although the central administration after 1914 made possible the coordination of various departmental activities, it was a weak institution in terms of bringing the country together. Until the 1940s the Central Legislature comprised only a few southerners. When it became broadened to include the north, representatives regarded themselves as defenders of regional interests. The British assumed that a plural society was difficult to unite. The central administration was also remote to the people; rather, what was close to them was their Native Administration, based on a policy of indirect rule.

INDIRECT RULE

Indirect rule was a system of local government that enabled the British to govern Nigeria through indigenous rulers and institutions. Colonial officials would advise local rulers and minimize direct contacts with the majority of the population. New regulations and instructions to the people would be announced through their chiefs and kings. Indigenous institutions would be retained, after purging them of their so-called excesses and inhumane practices. Indigenous laws not conducive to colonialism were to be abandoned.

The architect of indirect rule was Lugard who had observed how it worked in practice in India and the Sudan. Comparing the emirates in northern Nigeria with political institutions in the Sudan, he concluded that indirect rule was suitable for Nigeria. For Lugard and his successors, indirect rule was deployed to consolidate power and to overcome the various obstacles posed by communications and by limitations of personnel and finance. The ideological assumption was that the British and Nigerians were culturally different and the best way to govern them was through the institutions which they themselves had invented. These ideas and others were developed in Lugard's book, *The Dual Mandate in Tropical Africa*, a handbook on the justification and implementation of indirect rule. The policy of indirect rule was designed to secure the cooperation of indigenous rulers and their people. Approaching the people through their local leaders meant that opposition to British rule would become minimal. And by allowing local leaders to exercise power, the British could manipulate them to become "collaborators" of colonialism, rewarded with wages and emoluments. Their services would reduce the cost of administration and solve the problems of inadequate personnel. The cost of salaries, pensions, and home leave of British personnel was so high that the best option to reduce expenses was to curtail their number. Although the British believed that their culture was superior, they were in no rush to impose it because they were of the view that indigenous people were slow to adapt. Indirect rule would allow some preservation of traditions, but at the same time a gradual introduction of so-called advanced ideas.

Indirect rule was initiated in the north by Lugard to govern a vast region and control an Islamic population. There was already in place a long-established administrative structure with delineated hierarchies, civil servants, and administrative units. Identifying leaders and centers of power in such an indigenous system was thus easy. Also, there was an established system of public revenue based on tax and a judiciary based on the Shari'a and the *alkali* courts, presided over by learned Islamic jurists. Lugard carefully modified the indigenous system. He and other British officials would control the emirs, and the emirs would govern their people. The British would not interfere with Islam, so as not to provoke a mass uprising and to support the political structure that Islam had created. If the kings and chiefs led their people in wars of resistance against the British, indirect rule would turn them into friends and valuable allies. Old emirates became new divisions, each with a district officer (D.O.). The emirs assumed power in a unit called the Native Authority (NA) as the political head of the unit with a staff and power to collect tax and initiate new projects. The emir was in charge of the judiciary, as the head of the Native Court, and with a police unit under his command to enforce law and order. The Native Courts were allowed to administer Islamic laws with appeals directed at British officials. The emir was also a "financial manager," collecting tax, part of which he retained to run the local government. For the British, the system was very cheap and it assured them of stability and peace.

However, the emir owed his appointment to the government, he was under the supervision of a district officer, and laws had to be approved by the government. As most instructions to the people passed through the emirs, they had to take the blame for the unpopular ones, and had to join the government in overcoming protest. A commitment to the emirs and Native Authorities has been blamed for the slow development of Western education in the north, the argument being that the traditional elite showed little interest in many aspects of modernization. The district officer or Resident posted to the local government headquarters supervised the emirs, but were reluctant to make too many drastic changes or to modernize institutions at a pace that would displease local rulers. Indeed, not a few British officials regarded themselves as preservers of traditions, resisting changes and warning against influences that could create revolution.

From 1914 to 1916 Lugard extended the model of indirect rule from the north to the south, with the *obas* (kings) enjoying powers similar to those of the emirs. If the Yoruba kings and chiefs were happy about their enhanced status and power, their subjects were not. The Yoruba kings had never before exercised the same kind of power as the emirs. Under the new dispensation, they became authoritarian, ignoring the checks and balances in the traditional systems of kingship. Looking for the equivalent of the sultan, the British turned to the *Alaafin* of Oyo, thus ignoring Yoruba's history during the nineteenth century which had led to the breakdown of Oyo and the rise of Ibadan to supremacy. As taxation was part of indirect rule, the Yoruba reacted strongly as they had not been used to an imposed and regular form of taxation as in the emirates. There were anti-tax riots. Another source of tension came from the new educated elite who were sidelined by indirect rule. This elite had been pressuring for inclusion in the management of their towns, but indirect rule had no use for them. To press their claims, the elite had to attack the traditional rulers for their conservatism and loyalty to the British.

In the east, indirect rule ran into more serious problems as Lugard wanted to create paramount chiefs where none had previously existed and raise revenues from taxation among people who were not used to the idea. In societies with a largely fragmented political system, with a village constituting the largest political unit, and without any powerful leader, indirect rule became a disaster. The British deliberately created new powerful chiefs, invested with authority not based in tradition. Known as the "Warrant Chiefs," they were more like strangers to their people. Indeed, some of these chiefs were inconsequential people who could not command respect and trust. The chiefs became notorious for unpopular decisions and violating well-established customs. When direct taxation was to be introduced, and a suspicion spread that it would also be extended to women, the Aba Women's Riot of 1929 ensued and forced the British to democratize the local government in the region and involve the elders.

Indirect rule had severe limitations. To start with the co-optation of indigenous rulers, it should be emphasized that the British interfered in the appointments of many new leaders, created many laws that the leaders had to implement, and paid them wages which could be withheld if they failed to cooperate. The so-called advice that British officers gave was no less than commands that local rulers often had to obey. Those who disobeyed the commands or resisted the changes in the early years were deposed, exiled, and imprisoned. Indirect rule assumed that all Nigerian societies were traditionally governed by powerful kings and chiefs when in fact some did not have them, and other groups (like the Yoruba) had restricted their power.

Indirect rule increased the power of chiefs far more than tradition allowed, thus promoting abuse of power and tyranny. Unpopular kings and chiefs could not be removed by their people. Since they owed their appointments and income to the government, they knew that pleasing the British was more important than satisfying their own people. Cases of abuse were reported, for instance of corrupt and extortionate rulers, but the government ignored them in order not to antagonize their partners.

The staff to support the Native Authorities—court clerks, messengers, followers of kings and chiefs—created enormous problems for the administration. These people interpreted their role as that of power wielders, rather than that of public servants. They demanded respect, collected bribes, and offered services as favors. The most notorious were the court clerks, who recorded and translated proceedings from local languages to English in ways that influenced justice in favor of whichever party had greased their palms. Except in the north where officials endeavored to learn the Hausa language, the British essentially relied on translators to communicate with the people they governed. Clerks and others who understood English converted it to their advantage, manipulating their intermediary role for power and material benefits. The clerks, police, and other government staff aspired to imitate the lifestyles of the British officers—spacious houses with stewards, gardeners, cars, and formal dress habits. As their salaries could not meet these excessive demands, they resorted to corrupt practices.

In the north where indirect rule was most successful, it generated minimum progress as colonial officers believed that traditions and society were static. Retardation was particularly noticeable in the provision of Western education as missionaries were prevented from aggressive expansion while the government did very little. The emirs and their subordinates, benefiting from the system, were also prominent defenders of tradition. In the words of one contemporary observer, the emirates became "medieval monarchies" in a modern state, difficult to develop.[1]

All over the country, indirect rule showed preference for chiefs instead of the new educated elite. Many among them were even despised for their alleged arrogance and excessive demands for reforms. In the north, the British preferred to identify more with the Islamic intelligentsia who, according to them, were better behaved and more respectful of authority than the Western educated elite. Some officers even recommended the suppression of the educated people in order to curtail their so-called excesses, arrogant claims to equality with whites, and "vanity, trickery, and litigiousness."[2] Western-trained lawyers were not allowed to practice in native courts, thereby leaving chiefs without legal education to administer justice. As the chiefs identified with the colonial government, there was little incentive for them to align with the educated elite to fight for independence.

Taxation was the most resented of all the changes. It generated protests in many areas and lasting bitterness among a majority of the population. Taxation forced many to work, even in unpleasant tasks, to obtain the money to pay tax. Armed guards were used to enforce payment, further presenting the government as callous and unsympathetic to the people, especially the poor. The chiefs were turned into tax collectors, destroying their standing among their own people. What the government did with the money was never clear to many groups who did not see amenities or industries in their communities.

Both the central administration and local governments contributed to division and inter-ethnic hostility in Nigeria. The south and north were kept separated as much as possible. The pace of change was not the same all over the country, thus creating an imbalance that ultimately provoked conflicts. Native authorities fostered ethnic consciousness; the colonial government regarded every group (such as the Tiv) as a distinct corporate entity, when such a perception had not previously existed among the people. One ethnic group competed with another for amenities and revenues.

ECONOMIC CHANGES

The economic objectives of British rule were to make Nigeria financially self-sufficient, produce raw materials, and consume imported manufactured goods. The fulfillment of these objectives was far more important than satisfying the aspirations of Nigerians for rapid development. To protect British industries, competitive ones would not be created in Nigeria; the peasantry had to produce more export crops than food for local needs; new changes must promote external trade; and foreign merchants must be allowed to operate without much restriction. Capital investment in the economy and long-term planning did not even begin until the 1940s.

Essential to the attainment of all objectives was modernized transportation (harbors, roads, and railways) and communication services (telegraphic and postal). Railway lines, running from south to the north, were built to connect production sites with harbors to facilitate raw material extraction. Between 1907 and 1911 the Lagos-Kano lines were built to pass through the extensive cocoa and peanut belts. In 1911 the rails were extended from Zaria to Jos to transport tin ore. When coal was discovered in Enugu, the rail lines followed. Thus, railways were primarily for the evacuation of raw materials. As important as Nigeria was within the region, not a single railway line connected it with other African countries.

Roads were built to link the railways, cities, and farms. As the railways terminated in the port cities of Lagos and Port-Harcourt, the harbors, too, were upgraded. Post and telegraph services were expanded at the same time as many towns and cities were connected to Lagos by telegraph. In addition, new money, notably portable coins and notes of various denominations were introduced to replace indigenous currencies.

The new transportation and communication systems brought changes of revolutionary proportions. The railways and roads increased the mobility of goods, people, and ideas. Production of raw materials increased. The distribution of imported items was facilitated with rural markets connected to the urban centers and the port cities. New currencies promoted the growth of wage income and increased trade transactions. The roads and railways promoted inter-group interaction and aided massive population movements from the villages to the cities. Paid for with money generated from customs duties and taxes and cheap labor, the construction of railways and roads was also one of the earliest ways of drawing Nigerians into wage employment. A new class of wage earners developed new tastes and lifestyles, a blend of European and traditional.

Agriculture was the bedrock of the colonial economy, primarily geared towards the production of export crops. Communication networks were designed to transport farm products to travel to the ports. Food crops and other items needed for internal consumption received limited interest from the government. In the east, the emphases were on palm oil and palm kernels, in the west on cocoa and rubber, and in the north on peanuts, cotton, and shea products. Many farmers had to produce these to obtain money to meet such compulsory demands as taxation, basic needs of survival, and to train their children in the new Western schools. Agricultural technology was not altered in any important way and production techniques were still based on indigenous knowledge. Domestic markets responded to external needs, as many became leading collection centers for export crops. Where production for export became successful, not much effort was made to diversify the economy with the result that the lives of millions of people depended on price fluctuations.

Industrial activities were primarily based on extracting minerals for export. Mining of tin began in the Jos Plateau in 1904, growing into a lucrative industry. Coal mining started in 1911, and its product was used locally for the railway, tin mines, steamers, and steamships and exported to the Gold Coast. Other minerals included gold, tantalite, lead, zinc, wolfram, and columbite. Foreign firms controlled the mining sector, making substantial profits without being asked to pay tax. For instance, the United Africa Company, a British firm, monopolized mineral rights in northern Nigeria. Low wages and bad working conditions led to the formation of unions and to strikes among mine workers.

Manufacturing was slow to develop, not beginning until after 1945, apparently to avoid competition with European industries. In the early years, the preference was for the processing of exports. The manufacturing of bread, soft drinks, and beer and a few other consumer goods followed. The technology had to be imported, sometimes at high cost, and without the technical know-how to maintain it.

Steps were taken to expand Anglo-Nigerian trade. External trade witnessed a rapid growth, while domestic markets also expanded. Shipping, banking, and the export-import trade were all dominated by large European companies, notably the John Holt and Company, United Africa Company formed in 1929, and two French firms, the Compagnie Francaise de l'Afrique Occidentale (C.F.A.O.) and Societe Commerciale de l'Ouest Africain (S.C.O.A.). The firms offered low prices to producers and engaged in price-fixing, thereby avoiding competition which would have led to higher prices. In retail trade, Nigerians had to compete with Lebanese traders, many of whom became successful to the extent that they were able to forestall challenges from aspiring Nigerian merchants.

The colonial economy was basically exploitative. A focus on exports was a mechanism for wealth transfer from Nigeria to Europe. Revenues derived from exports were spent to maintain the administration and kept as reserves in Britain, especially when the British currency became weak during the Second World War. European and Asian firms made substantial profits, which were not necessarily invested in Nigeria. Indigenous technologies were not markedly transformed, while modern ones were slow in arriving. In general, Nigeria was integrated into the international system as a producer of raw materials and a recipient of finished products. Its fortunes were affected by external demands—it enjoyed prosperity in the 1920s, suffered from the depressions of the 1930s, and was affected by the two World Wars. After the Second World War, development planning was initiated, with wide-ranging discussions on how various sectors of the society could be transformed. Limited funding, however, ensured that results were not as far-reaching as anticipated in the plans. During the same period, the state increasingly intervened in the economy, laying the foundations of the socio-economic order in later years.

SOCIAL CHANGES: WESTERN EDUCATION, HEALTH SERVICE, AND URBANIZATION

The Christian missionaries pioneered education and dominated its growth during the colonial period. Missionary schools focused on writing, reading and arithmetic, and the production of an elite to service the colonial society. During the early years, the colonial government displayed little enthusiasm for educational expansion. In the north for instance, Lugard was of the view that Islamic education should be strengthened and protected from the "corrupting influence" of Western education. Even missionaries were curtailed from creating new schools in the Islamic north. In the south, the missionaries continued to expand their facilities and establish new schools. The colonial education policy was to build a few primary and secondary schools and provide the guidelines for mission schools. Grants were offered to private agencies if they met a number of standards, thus reducing the cost that the government had to bear. Most of the government schools were located in urban areas and centers of administration. More clerks were produced than technicians. In general, the education system was not tailored to producing any large number of professionals to manage an industrial, technological society.

Demands for education at all levels became part of the expression of nationalism. Agitation led the government to establish the first institution of higher learning, the Yaba Higher College, in 1934. Even then, it was not a degree-awarding college, and student intake was low in its first ten years. Following the great changes in the years after the Second World War, the first university was established at Ibadan in 1948. Throughout the colonial period, enterprising Nigerians struggled to go abroad for higher education.

Western education, despite its limitations, was a powerful agency of social change. An elite was created, the vanguard of change in modern Nigeria. Not only were members of this elite united by their ability to use the English language, they also gradually became committed to an anti-colonial agenda. The schools enabled this elite to come together, thus overcoming some of the barriers created by ethnic and regional divisions. Students were able to interact and form lasting friendships which they later exploited to form political parties. A working class also emerged, located in the public service sector and elsewhere. Many among them were able to form trade union movements which also contributed to the nationalist struggles.

Through education, aspects of Western culture, generally perceived as "civilization," began to spread. This can be noted in the use of the English language for communication and prestige. European material culture, especially manners and clothes, was important as a measure of social standing and refinement. To travel to Europe became the ultimate achievement for an elite seeking assimilation into the Western world. British officials and missionaries encouraged this desire by saying that the principal objective of imperialism was the civilization of "backward" people.

The south benefited more than the north, creating an educational imbalance that became difficult to redress. The southern elite was, for the duration of the colonial era, able to dominate the civil service and other sectors that demanded formal educational training. As wage incomes became more and more important, education provided access to money and comfortable living standards. Formal education also proved an advantage in raising loans from the banks, providing funds to start or consolidate new business.

Western health services spread. From seventeen hospitals in the country in 1917, the number grew to 157 by 1951 and over 300 by 1960. The colonial government, to take care of its staff and others, built hospitals, clinics, dispensaries, and maternity homes. In addition, vigorous attempts were made to administer vaccination against smallpox, leprosy and measles, and to improve sanitation. The hospitals were never enough and they were concentrated in areas convenient to colonial agents and Europeans. The missionaries continued to make their impact felt, meeting some of the health needs of their converts. Facilities and personnel were inadequate and training schools were few, but in spite of these limitations, the foundation of modern medicine was successfully laid.

Urbanization was yet another remarkable change. Older cities such as Ibadan and Lagos were greatly expanded. Many cities were of new creations, notably Enugu, Port-Harcourt, and Kaduna, as administrative headquarters. Railway stations, such as Kafanchan, grew into cities because they attracted hundreds of traders, buyers, and settlers. Centrally located towns, such as Aba, were able to benefit from access to both the railway and highway. Port towns (such as Lagos) or mining areas (like Jos and Enugu) grew very rapidly. In the east, not noted for large cities, no town exceeded a population of 26,000 in 1931. By 1952 four cities had grown beyond 50,000 and the growth rate of towns between 1921 and 1952 was close to 70 percent.

Rural-urban migration became widespread, largely caused by the search for employment opportunities in colonial and commercial institutions located in the cities. Self-employment was also possible in the large informal sector in the city—as craftsmen, barbers, tailors, food vendors, and repairmen. Paid employment and trade offered faster means to make a living, compared to the drudgery of farm work. The rural areas lost their attraction. Important economic and political events took place in the cities. Opportunities for profit and leisure were more abundant in the cities than the villages. Modern amenities such as pipe-borne water and electricity were located in the cities, giving the rural areas the label of "primitive." Many young men and women sought the means to shed this characterization by relocating to cities. As the rural areas were abandoned, they began a process of decline from which many have yet to recover.

As heterogeneous places, the cities allowed members of different ethnicities to interact, both for economic and social reasons. To help one another and take care of new migrants, unions emerged as powerful representatives of towns, religions, and other interests. Some of the unions described themselves as "progressive," to indicate that members were dedicated to modernity and were expected to fulfill certain obligations to the people or the community they represented.

The cities were also avenues of conflict. There were tensions between strangers and indigenes over land allocation. Land belonging to native populations was sold or given to strangers in a way that promoted competition. As amenities were never adequate, attempts to distribute them always created rifts. Jobs were insufficient, creating an army of unemployed, some of whom took to crime. To cope with the difficulties of city life, many people had to abandon the members of their extended families, thus opting for a more individualistic lifestyle.

In cities and elsewhere, those who lived during the colonial period experienced rapid changes and tension. Many were upset by the use of forced labor, the greed for money that pushed young men out of villages or into criminality, the increasing rate of divorce, fast-paced living, and taxation. But their contemporaries were also impressed by the new amenities such as pipe-borne water, electricity, modern hospitals, and schools. They wanted more of these, and of course the opportunity to exercise power, a desire that fueled nationalism.

NOTES

1. W. R. Crocker, *Nigeria: A Critique of British Colonial Administration* (London: Allen and Unwin, 1936), pp. 216–217.

2. Crocker, *Nigeria*, p. 22.

6

Nationalism and Independence

No one, not even the most far-sighted, ever thought that British rule would last for only sixty years. In the early years of colonial rule, the idea of an independent Nigeria within so short a time would have sounded ridiculous. "The whiteman has come to stay as long as men lived," boasted an official in 1919.[1] Nevertheless, nationalism started early, instigated by the need to respond to conquest and new policies. The radical phase came during and after the Second World War, subsequently leading to independence. Although the ultimate goal of nationalism was to secure the country's independence, it had other interrelated dimensions: the "new Nigeria" would be governed by a Westernized elite, working, through the agency of political parties and Western political ideas, to create a united and developed country. If the British took over power from a traditional elite, nationalism and modernization forced them to hand it over to an educated elite.

THE GROWTH OF NATIONALISM

Nationalism had a nineteenth-century origin. The wars of resistance in various places were later to provide inspiration to the nationalists of the twentieth century. The first generation of modern black thinkers, notably Edward Wilmot Blyden, reflected on Africa and race matters, calling for progress, the understanding of Africa's contribution to civilization, and pride in the black race. In the last years of the century, there was a secessionist movement within the Church, an expression of protest against domination. Edward Blyden, for instance, called on Africans to establish their own independent churches. Some members of the new churches became prominent members of the anti-colonial movement. Nationalism in the early years was expressed mainly as a feeling of national consciousness and an awareness that Africans were members of one race. As the colonial era began, an awareness of being residents of the same country became important and a desire for freedom from colonial rule was a paramount expression of nationalism. Nationalists wanted to work within the new state of Nigeria, not within their older indigenous nations such as those of the Yoruba or Ibibio. Nationalism was accelerated by colonial rule, whether those forces merely demanded corrections to abuses in the system or were the more radical forces seeking self-rule.

Colonial policies generated discontent among the people, especially the elite who originally demanded reforms, and later on, independence. Among the issues that displeased the people were racism and the damage to traditional values during European rule. Nigerians in the civil service complained of racial discrimination in appointments and promotions. The aspiring ones among them were envious of the status and privileges enjoyed by white officials. Among those who complained about excessive changes, nationalism was expressed in cultural ways, that is, in deliberate efforts to promote Nigerian food, names, forms of dress, languages, and even religions. The Christians among them tried to reform Christianity to suit local values, such as large families and polygamy, and to draw from it ideas of liberty, equality, and justice. To the majority of the population, the Native Authorities were both oppressive and corrupt. Many Nigerians believed that they could overcome the problems of low prices for raw materials and expatriate control of the economy only if they had the power to determine their own destiny. To the Nigerian businesswomen and men who saw themselves driven out of trade by foreign companies and combines, an identification with anti-colonial movement became a strategy of regaining control.

The economic depression of the late 1920s and 1930s brought economic hardship, unemployment, and retrenchment. Bad times enabled nationalists to criticize and condemn the British and to use these demands to stimulate national consciousness. For instance, Michael Imoudu, a distinguished trade union leader, led the strike by railway workers in 1931 to demand better wages. Unemployment and discrimination generated discontentment with colonial rule and enabled nationalist leaders to enjoy a mass following.

Some of the notable changes of the era—urbanization, Western education, and transportation—contributed to the growth of nationalist activities. With cities acting as centers of interaction and acculturation, urbanization contributed to the development of national feelings. Newspapers, magazines, and other information circulated to influence opinions. Political and nationalist ideas grew and spread in the cities. Urban dwellers carried many of these ideas to their villages and ethnic communities, thus connecting the city with the countryside. The new infrastructure aided easier movement of people and integration of different parts of the country. Thousands of Yoruba and Igbo moved to the north, with many of them becoming members of political parties outside their own home areas. The spread of Western education, especially in the south, created a population segment that could read and write and follow the discourse on nationalism and development. Education produced leaders with new ideas, visions, and ambitions.

A growing local media devoted space to nationalist issues, raising consciousness to a high level in editorials and special columns devoted to anti-colonial issues. One of the early heroes in this area was John Payne Jackson, originally a Liberian, who lived in Lagos from 1890 to 1918. His newspaper, the *Lagos Weekly Record*, supported demands for reforms and called for unity among Nigerians to fight the British. The press had an ally among the Nigerian students abroad who established organizations to unite and protest. The best known of these organizations was the West African Students' Union (WASU) founded in London in 1925 with the objectives of, among others, fostering national consciousness, racial pride, self-help, unity, and cooperation among Africans. WASU called for cooperation among the chiefs and elite, lobbied British politicians to initiate reforms, and used its monthly journal to serve the nationalist cause.

Political associations emerged very quickly and ultimately became the key platform from which to express nationalism and contest elections. The early leaders sought changes in the system rather than independence. The earliest associations were protest movements, such as the People's Union established in 1908 to protest the introduction of water rate in Lagos. Yet another was the Reform Club, established in Lagos in 1920 to oppose direct taxation. Far more successful was the National

Congress of British West Africa (the Congress), established in 1920 to fight against discrimination, unite the West African elite, and achieve self-government. At its first meeting held in Accra, Ghana, the Congress resolved to call on the British to let half the membership of the Legislative Council be educated Africans, establish a university, introduce compulsory education, and eliminate racial discrimination. These were all demands to empower the elite. In September 1920 to March 1921 the Congress sent a delegation to London to press its demands, but it was refused a hearing by the Secretary of State for the Colonies. This was a resounding failure caused by the deep hostility of the colonial administration which regarded members of the Congress as self-appointed leaders who wanted to destroy indigenous institutions for selfish interests. The chiefs were equally opposed to the Congress, because they were afraid that their power would be usurped. The Congress ceased to exist in 1923 but not without recording some successes: several senior posts were created for Africans in the civil service; an elective principle was introduced in 1922; and the West African Court of Appeals was reconstituted in 1922.

In 1920 a branch of the Garvey Movement (the Universal Negro Improvement Association) was established in Lagos. Militant and race-conscious, this movement was established by Marcus Garvey, a Jamaican, to unite all blacks into one organization that would establish an independent country. He moved to the United States in 1916 where he created a mass organization and held conventions attended by delegates from Africa. He established the Black Star shipping line (operating to Africa) to encourage blacks in the Americas to return home to fight for freedom. His journal, the *Negro World*, was eagerly awaited and read in Nigeria. The conventions worked on a plan to create a Negro State of Africa and chose Garvey as the provisional president of Africa, in addition to choosing a flag and an anthem. To Garvey, Africa's independence was not negotiable, even if violence had to be used. His movement collapsed, he was jailed and subsequently deported, but his political philosophy was not without dedicated converts. His ideas influenced a number of Nigerians, including prominent nationalists such as Ernest Ikoli and Nnamdi Azikiwe.

The most successful of the early parties was the Nigerian National Democratic Party (NNDP) established in June 1923 by Herbert Macaulay in response to a constitutional reform in 1922. A new Legislative Council was empowered to legislate for the Colony of Lagos and Southern Nigeria. The Council had forty-six members, nineteen of them unofficial and twenty-seven official. Of the nineteen, four had to be elected in the municipalities of Lagos and Calabar, the only two towns where the educated elite was allowed to use the franchise. The NNDP was founded to contest these elections. The NNDP published the first elaborate manifesto, with an important preamble:

> To secure the safety and welfare of the Colony and the Protectorate of Nigeria as an integral part of the British Imperial Commonwealth and to carry the banner of "Right, Truth, Liberty and Justice" to the empyrean of democracy until the realization of its ambitious goal of government of the people by the people for the people.[2]

The party was opposed to forced labor, land appropriation, plantation estates, and harsh laws. It called for municipal self-government for Lagos, compulsory education for all, a West African Court of Appeal, and the Africanization of the civil service. The party won all the elective seats in the Lagos Town Council between 1925 and 1938, and the Lagos seats in the Legislative Council in 1923, 1928, 1933, and 1943. The party was able to involve local chiefs, trade guilds, and market women, thus mobilizing critical segments of the population. Also, its newspaper, the *Lagos Weekly Record*, served to announce the activities of the party and to criticize the government. The party confined its activities to Lagos, understandably, because Lagos had a concentration of elite, but its members in the Council also asked questions on other parts of the country. The NNDP did not challenge British rule, but only sought the means to be empowered within it. It hoped that the transfer of power would come as a gradual process. With just a few members in the Legislative Council, the voice of the party and the elite it represented was easily subdued.

The need to respond to the inadequacies of Yaba College, the first institution of higher learning in the country, led to the formation of the Nigerian Youth Movement (NYM) in 1934. Yaba was established in 1934 to train students to work in the civil service, with diplomas in arts, economics, agriculture, engineering, and medicine. It was not affiliated with any British university. The Nigerian elite was dissatisfied with this school on the ground that its diplomas were inferior to that of a British university and would not be recognized outside of the country. They read a racial motive into its limitations: graduates of Yaba would be permanently subordinated to British officials and would never rise to leadership positions.

The NYM was able to transform itself into the first national, multi-ethnic organization. It organized a mass rally in 1933 to protest the decision on Yaba. The government failed to respond, but the NYM broadened its agenda to include anti-imperial measures, economic exploitation, and social inequality. It published a comprehensive manifesto with the objectives of enhancement of the standard of living of Nigerians and the political advancement of the country. The manifesto demanded mass education, equal economic opportunities for everybody, transfer of power to Nigerians, and universal suffrage for everybody over twenty-one. In 1938 its candidates won elections to the Lagos Town Council and the three Lagos seats in the Legislative Council. This victory marked the end of the monopoly of the NNDP. The NYM created branches all over the country with a total membership of almost 20,000. The branches in the north were composed mainly of resident southerners, giving rise to criticism from the British, who regarded them as a nuisance polluting a conservative environment. As a "national" party, it got involved in condemning many issues outside of Lagos, using its newspaper, the *Daily Service*, as its main organ. However, as many of the members of the NYM were political moderates, they did not seek any immediate end to colonial rule. In 1941 the party split along ethnic lines over the candidates it would sponsor to the Legislative Council. It never recovered from this crisis.

A prominent member of the NYM was Nnamdi Azikiwe. When he joined in 1937, he was elected into its Central Executive Council. In the same year he established the *West African Pilot*, which became an instant success with a wide circulation and an unapologetically anti-colonial stance. The paper's editorials focused on the themes of colonial injustice, exploitation, and racism. With Lagos as his base, Azikiwe was the first prominent nationalist from eastern Nigeria and he was able to mobilize the Igbo elite in Lagos in support of the NYM. Azikiwe energized the nationalist movement in West Africa from 1934 to 1949, becoming the best known anti-colonial crusader and journalist. Articulate and indefatigable, Zik, as he was called by thousands of his admirers, employed oratory and complex diction to great effect. He himself experienced the dramatic changes of the colonial period. As a young boy, he grew up in an urban heterogeneous setting. He disliked the treatment of his father in the Nigerian Regiment, and of himself as a clerk from 1923 to 1925. He struggled to reach the United States where he attended a predominantly black college as a poor student and observed racial discrimination and protests by African-American organizations. Even with two degrees, he could not secure a civil service job in his own country and had to go to the Gold Coast (now Ghana) to establish the *Accra Morning Post* and publish his first book, *Renascent Africa*. In 1937 his newspaper published an essay by a labor leader, I. T. A. Wallace-Johnson, entitled "Has the African a God?" that criticized the colonial government in a way that it found libelous. Azikiwe was convicted, but later acquitted on appeal. He returned to Nigeria, where he became both a journalist and a nationalist.

Azikiwe contributed to the rise of militant nationalism and combative journalism. Drawing on his experience in the United States, he saw the struggles in Nigeria as between blacks and whites and called for a united front against the British. His newspaper was modeled after American yellow journalism and expressed a deep commitment to race matters. Using a highly provocative style that shocked colonial officers, he lambasted the British constantly. He popularized journalism by establishing provincial dailies and using a wide variety of outlets for distribution which enabled nationalist ideas to spread to the hinterland.

Internal developments benefited from events and ideas from the outside. The viability of the independent states of Ethiopia and Liberia was used as evidence by other Africans as an example that they could govern themselves. Pan-African movements, founded by notable black leaders in the United States such as Garvey and W. E. B. Du Bois, encouraged black militancy and cooperation. The rise of the Soviet Union and the growing influence of socialism and communism supplied ideas on freedom and emancipation to African leaders. The independence of India in 1947 was an inspiration to them. The Second World War also provided conditions which intensified local demands and reshaped the nature of international politics.

THE SECOND WORLD WAR AND ITS AFTERMATH

Until 1930 political parties were largely elitist, urban-based, and focused on demands for reforms rather than independence. In the 1940s and beyond, nationalism witnessed an upsurge: the anti-colonial movement was expanded beyond Lagos to other cities and even to villages, and vigorous demands were made for independence by the media and front-line nationalists. In the preceding years, the atmosphere had become charged by the invasion of Ethiopia by Italy in 1935. Many Africans were enraged by this attack on an independent African country, rich in history and culture, and they began to call for self-government.

The Second World War had its impact on nationalism. About 100,000

Nigerians were recruited to fight. Many were exposed to wartime propaganda on liberty, equality, and freedom. After their discharge, many of them joined political parties. The allied propaganda in favor of freedom and against exploitation was used against the British. The interactions between Nigerian soldiers and their white counterparts, and the contacts with white soldiers stationed in Nigeria, diminished the respect which many Nigerians had for whites in general, further emboldening them to make demands. Many of those who served abroad enjoyed a higher standard of living, which they could not maintain when the war ended, and they came to associate an end to colonial rule with better living standards.

When the war spread to North Africa, the Middle East, and India, Nigeria became of strategic importance to Britain and its allies as a staging-post for troops and for the organization of supplies to these places. Military camps, airports, and roads to connect them were rapidly constructed in or around such towns as Ibadan, Lagos, Kano, Enugu, Maiduguri, and Jos. Over 100,000 troops passed through West Africa. Many cities benefited and the wage-earning working class was expanded. Nigeria also contributed resources by way of funds and raw materials. More tin and rubber were requested following the loss of southeast Asia, in addition to previous export commodities and newer ones such as cassava starch. Wartime scarcity brought economic prosperity which failed to last, as hardship followed the end of artificial demands.

The war ended with the failure of the allied forces to win without the support of the United States. Britain lost its position as a leading world power. The two new superpowers, the United States and the Soviet Union, had no colonies in Africa and both pressured the European colonial powers, for their own reasons, to decolonize. The Labour Party came to power in Britain with its leaders showing more sympathy for the colonies. An impetus was also given to the African freedom fighters by the Atlantic Charter which created the United Nations and supported the ideals of democracy and self-determination.

There were other conditions which contributed to the upsurge of nationalist activities. The concentration of economic power in the hands of European firms and Asian retailers frustrated Nigerian merchants and retailers. In the 1930s the UAC alone controlled 40 percent of the import-export trade. The UAC and five other firms formed the Association of West African Merchants (AWAM) which controlled over 60 percent of imports and 70 percent of exports. Wartime controls favored the European firms who became the buying agents for the government. Nigerian traders, who were excluded from profitable trade opportunities, identified with the nationalist cause. To the poor producers and farmers, the solution to low prices was also to be active in anti-colonial struggles.

There was also the pressure of the educated elite to be included in power and their request for the expansion of Western education. Many British officials continued to despise the educated elite while the government was unable to meet their desire for expanded education. A growing number of the educated elite joined political parties, organized and attended rallies, and carried political propaganda to as many places as possible.

The number of trade unions increased, formed by railway workers, teachers, post and telegraph workers, marine staff, civil servants, and others. There were other associations in the cities formed along ethnic lines (for example, Ibo State Union) or town lines (Oyo Progressive Union). More associations emerged in the 1940s, as hundreds of people entered wage employment. Nationalist leaders could mobilize these associations for support. More importantly, the workers had a platform from which to organize protest. In 1945 labor unions were strong enough to embark upon a general strike for fifty-two days. The strike was a challenge to the government, it enabled the trade unions and the nationalist movement to fuse, and it revealed the advantages of cooperation and the usefulness of threats to gain concessions. The north, which had been excluded from most of the previous nationalist agitations, was drawn into the strike, thus spreading nationalism and political consciousness to a region that the British had sheltered against new ideas. Many became emboldened to make demands for a transfer of power. In the early 1940s trade union leaders and students submitted memoranda to the government and wrote essays in the media calling for the takeover of power. In 1941 WASU called for the creation of "a united Nigeria with a Federal Constitution." Two years later, the same organization demanded ten years of representative government to precede five years of full responsible government led by Nigerians.

TRANSFER OF POWER, 1945–1960

The transfer of power to Nigerians was effected through peaceful constitutional changes after 1945. Within fifteen years the country attained self-rule made possible by a combination of constitutional reforms and the existence of Nigerian leadership and political parties working to ac-

quire power. Nigerian leaders organized political associations and mobilized different constituencies to gain concessions. The leaders appealed
to anti-colonial sentiments, and less to history, culture, and language.
They exaggerated what independence would bring to everybody, con-
trasting this with the limitations of colonial accomplishments. Younger,
radical nationalist leaders emerged. The organization of country-wide
political parties became important in the struggles to gain power while
the British increased the Nigerian membership in the Legislative Councils and approved a number of constitutional changes which culminated
in independence.

On August 26, 1944, the Nigerian National Council was formed, with
Herbert Macaulay as President and Nnamdi Azikiwe as Secretary General, to bring together diverse associations and people into one united
front. Membership was open to associations including political parties,
trade unions, ethnic unions, and professional and literary groups. To
allow the admittance of Cameroonian associations in Lagos, the name of
the party was changed to the National Council of Nigeria and the Cameroons (NCNC). For a decade, the NCNC served as the country's leading
national organization with branches in different towns. It called for self-
government.

The 1923 Constitution was revised in 1947 as the Richards Constitution, named after the governor. This constitution aimed to bring the
north and south together in a central legislative council, without destroying the power of the three regional assemblies or of the Native Authorities. The constitution affirmed a country with three regions, each with
its own assembly. The Executive Council was still European, the franchise was again limited to Lagos and Calabar, and the Regional Assemblies lacked legislative power. Both the assemblies and the legislative
council would include official and non-official members nominated by
the governor and local authorities. Nigerians wanted more than this in
the postwar era, and objected to the arbitrary manner in which the new
constitution was introduced. The NCNC took the lead in criticizing the
Richards Constitution. It organized tours all over the country to raise
funds to send a delegation to London to protest the constitution. The
tours raised political and national consciousness.

Trade unions and some radical groups were increasing the tempo of
militancy. The Zikist Movement, comprising militant members of the
NCNC, organized lectures and published materials to incite the public
against the government. Tied to Azikiwe and unable to popularize their
radical ideology, the Zikists failed to become a national organization.

The Zikists organized labor unrest, leading to the death of eighteen coal miners in Enugu in 1949, and additional protests thereafter. The Zikists took the lead in organizing violent demonstrations. Regarded as too dangerous by the government, and abandoned by Azikiwe, the Zikists were proscribed in 1951.

In 1948 the colonial government granted a number of concessions, the "turning point" towards decolonization. It reformed the Richards Constitution and announced measures to Nigerianize the civil service, democratize the Native Authorities, and expand higher education. Political reforms were introduced. Emerging leaders began to call for greater regional autonomy, creating associations to fight for this. The problems of ethnic politics that would consume Nigeria for the rest of the century had begun. Among the causes of ethnicity were the regional disparities created by colonialism, the competition in the urban environment for limited resources, and the instrumentalization of ethnicity by emerging politicians seeking the fastest means to mobilize support. Regional feelings eventually led to the emergence of regionally-based political parties. The Action Group (AG), based in the west, was led by Obafemi Awolowo, who used the Yoruba creation myth and the importance of the ancestral town of Ile-Ife to create a cultural organization, the Egbe Omo Oduduwa—"the descendants of Oduduwa"—that was transformed into a political party in 1951. The Northern People's Congress (NPC), established in 1949, revived the memory of the caliphate of the nineteenth century and used Islam to create a solid party for the north. A second major party emerged in the north, the left-wing Northern Elements Progressive Union (NEPU), led by Aminu Kano. The NCNC, which had started as a national party, became the party of the east, controlled by the Igbo. Things would never be the same again as the leaders abandoned pan-Nigerian issues and focused more and more on regional concerns. Within one generation, nationalists became tribalists, interested in independence for narrow gains. Regional Houses of Assembly and a central Federal Parliament were established.

As the country entered the 1950s, radicalism witnessed a lull. Regional politics opened tremendous opportunities for aspiring politicians to run for office or serve in other prestigious capacities. The civil service expanded and recruited many Nigerians. The first university was opened at Ibadan in 1948 as a university college, absorbing a number of young people who saw themselves as leaders of the future. Labor was no longer restless, in part because the economy had improved, and in part because the radicals in the Zikist movement had been abandoned in their moment of official persecution. Nigerian entrepreneurs were benefiting from Nigerianization and regionalism with better access to banks and government contracts and loans, in addition to acting as licensed buyers of a state-controlled export marketing scheme. New industries were being established and the domestic market was witnessing an upsurge. Exports of primary products expanded, allowing even the farmers to derive some small benefits. There was a massive increase in public expenditure in education, roads, energy, and industries. With very limited reflection on the implications of their actions, the politicians assured all Nigerians that development and improved standards of living were just around the corner. The 1950s became the golden era of hope and optimism in the history of modern Nigeria.

The Richards Constitution was revised under a new governor, Sir John Macpherson. Unlike Richards, Macpherson allowed the public to debate what they wanted. A new constitution came into effect in 1951, a compromise measure, including many irreconcilable elements. It retained the three regions but gave the north representation equal in number to the two other regions combined. The future was now to be determined by political parties competing within the bounds of an electoral system. The nationalists were now divided as each politician struggled for power. By the time of the General Elections in 1952, it had become clear that all parties had strong regional loyalty and none was able to command any national following. Only through regional-cum-ethnic alliances, rather than ideologies, did they try to forge a national image. Political agitation became common with a constitutional stalemate in the east and at the federal level. The enemy to fight was no longer the colonial government, which had indicated strong signs of dismantling itself, but fellow Nigerians. To minimize the conflicts, the British had to convene a conference in London in 1953.

The London Conference brought together competing representatives of political parties and regions who decided on the constitution for the country. Nigeria would be a federation with a strong centralized government and an Executive Council including four ministers from each region. The constitution set up regional governments headed by premiers and ministers, all Nigerians; and it granted the right to each region to request full internal self-government. Further, important changes followed in the next three years. Elections were held for the House of Representatives, and on March 31, 1953, Anthony Enahoro proposed a motion in the House of Representatives that Nigeria should become independent in 1956. This was opposed by the northern delegates who feared the domination of the southern elite. Regional politicians began to fight, to the extent that the north threatened secession, and British pressure helped to hold the country together. Another constitutional conference followed in 1954 with a constitution that gave more power to the regions. The last major conference was held in 1957 with the western and eastern regions opting for self-independence in 1957, and the north in 1959. The General Elections of 1959 saw Alhaji Abubakar Tafawa Balewa as the Prime Minister with the NPC in coalition with the NCNC.

Two issues delayed independence: the fear expressed by the minority groups that they would be stifled by regional politics controlled by the larger ethnic groups, and the fear by the north that it would be dominated by the south. Greater regional autonomy assuaged the fear of northerners. Minority groups clamored for constitutional safeguards to protect them, or for the creation of separate states to ensure autonomy. The three big parties were controlled by the dominant groups, not trusted by leaders of minority groups. A commission of inquiry to look into minority grievances failed to decide in their favor, as the dominant political parties rejected the creation of additional states. The commission recommended that safeguards should be added into the constitution to allay their fears. These included the centralization of the police, the legal guarantee of rights, decentralization of the functions of the provincial authorities, and the establishment of a development board to advise on the physical development of the Niger Delta area. Nigeria attained independence on October 1, 1960, and became a Republic in 1963. There were many issues outstanding, but these were swept under the carpet; most notable among these were ethnicity, minority complaints, violence, and growing corruption. In addition, the British successfully manipulated the decolonization process to protect their vital economic and other interests. The foundation stones of the post-colonial economic system were laid in this period, with continuing export production, and the withdrawal of foreign businesses from traditional fields (produce export, retail) into the more modern sectors of the economy. Here, the British partly cooperated with the emerging Nigerian comprador bourgeoisie. Gaining independence proved much easier than managing a modern nation-state, as Nigerians were to see in the first decade of self-rule.

NOTES

1. R. Cudjoe, "Some Reminiscences of a Senior Interpreter," *Nigerian Field*, 1953, p. 159.
2. *NNDP Manifesto*, Lagos, 1923.

7

The First Republic, 1960–1965

The first decade of Nigeria's independence witnessed the practice and demise of a parliamentary system of government from 1960 to 1965, the first and second military coups in 1966, a civil war fought and concluded under the leadership of Yakubu Gowon from 1967 to 1970, and attempts at economic development. These are the major issues explored in this chapter and the next.

GOVERNMENT AND POLITICS

The constitution approved in the last year of colonial rule, and modified in 1963, was fashioned along the lines of the British parliamentary system with a legislature, judiciary, and an executive. There was one popular election for members of the legislature without a separate one for the executive. The government received its mandate through the votes cast to elect members of the legislature (that is, the parliament). The parliament delegated its authority to some of its members, since the entire membership of the legislature could not constitute the executive. Four features characterized this system: the nominal position of the head of the executive and his separation from the effective head of government; the plurality of the effective executive which consisted of a cabinet of ministers headed by a prime minister; the parliamentary nature of the executive; and the responsibility of the ministers individually and collectively to the legislature.

There were three organs of government: the parliament was the principal legislative body; the executive was for the formulation and execution of government policies; and the judiciary's task was to ensure that the constitution and the statutes were obeyed. These three organs existed both at the federal and the regional levels. The parliament comprised a Senate and a House of Representatives. The president was the head of all the three organs (like the Queen of England). One of the duties of the president was to summon parliament, at least once a year. He also enjoyed the power to prorogue or dissolve parliament. In exercising the latter power, he acted upon the advice of the prime minister. The president could also dissolve the parliament if the House of Representatives passed a resolution of no confidence in the executive and the prime minister failed to resign within three days or dissolve the parliament after the resolution. He could also dissolve it when there was a vacancy in the office of the prime minister and nobody emerged to command the respect of the parliament.

The Senate had fifty-six members, representing Lagos and the three regions. Representation was on an equal basis and not on the basis of population numbers in order to take care of the interests of minority groups and forge national unity. Senators were chosen by a joint sitting of regional legislative houses from a list submitted by the governor. The federal territory was represented by four senators while the president, acting on the advice of the prime minister, selected the remaining four. The senators were not to be chosen on a political party basis. The House of Representatives had 312 members. These were elected on a single constituency basis, one member for a population of 100,000 people. Thus, the bigger the region, the more representatives it had. For instance, the North had more than half the entire membership. Out of the 312 members, the Lagos territory had 3, the West had 62, the East 73, and the North 174.

The president of the Senate or his deputy presided over the Senate. Where both were absent, the members could appoint any one of them to preside. The House of Representatives operated in the same way. The quorum for each house of parliament was one-sixth. The house should adjourn if a quorum was not formed at the beginning of business. Business was conducted in English, a provision which prevented a number of parliamentarians from contributing to debates. The decision of each house was reached by the required majority of the members who were present and who voted. The presiding officer exercised a casting vote.

Standing orders regulated the business of parliament. Under the Legislative House (Powers and Privileges) Act, members had immunity from criminal and civil proceedings in respect of resolutions, questions, motions, bills, petitions, or remarks made in the house or in a committee. Sections 4 to 13 of the statute empowered members to summon witnesses and request the production of documents in relation to matters before them. Section 24 made it an offense for anybody to publish scandalous or false reports that could bring members into disrepute.

Parliament made laws by means of bills passed through both houses and assented to by the president of the country. Either house could originate a bill, though only the House of Representatives had power on money bills. Both houses had to discuss and agree on a bill before it could be sent to the president for assent. The president could, however, withhold his assent. Members of the opposition could use the opportunity of debates in the house to voice critical opinions and kill bills which they thought were not in the best interest of the people. Since parliament did not meet often—it could even be just once in a year—it had many committees to do its work, such as the Committee of Selection which discharged the duties assigned to it by the house, and the Standing Orders Committee which debated bills after their second reading. The representation on these various committees depended on the strength of political parties in the house.

The federal executive comprised the president, the prime minister, and the ministers. The president was a ceremonial head of government and commander-in-chief of the armed forces. A president was elected by a joint meeting of both houses. The office of the president would be declared vacant either at the end of a five-year term, or when the incumbent died or resigned, or when he was removed in accordance with the provisions of the constitution.

Actual power was exercised by the prime minister and his cabinet of ministers. The president appointed the prime minister from a list of people who appeared capable of commanding the support of the majority in the House of Representatives. He also appointed other ministers on the advice of the prime minister. The ministers ceased to hold office when the office of the prime minister became vacant. This vacancy could occur when the House of Representatives was dissolved or when the prime minister ceased to be a member of it. The prime minister and his ministers were the key figures in the running of government. They were collectively responsible to parliament, except in matters dealing with the prerogative of mercy, the exercise of the powers conferred on the Attorney General, the dissolution of parliament, and the appointment and removal from office of ministers, members of the Council of Ministers and Parliamentary Secretaries to ministers, and the assignment of portfolios to ministers to perform the functions of the prime minister when he was ill or absent from the country.

The third organ of government was the judiciary. The constitution made provision for the establishment of a Supreme Court with no less than five members. The Chief Justice and Justices of the Supreme Court were appointed by the president on the advice of the prime minister. Four members of the Supreme Court were from the regions, and these were appointed by the president on the advice of the governors. The Chief Justice and the other Justices could be removed by the president, acting on the address from parliament that they should be removed for inability to perform because of misbehavior or infirmity of mind or body.

The four regions adopted a similar arrangement. Every region had two houses—the House of Assembly and the House of Chiefs. The House of Assembly, like the federal House of Representatives, was made up of elected members. The House of Chiefs comprised members not elected by the people. The executive powers of a region were vested in the governor. A governor was appointed and could be removed by the president on the advice of the regional premier. The governor was not, however, a delegate of the president. The premier and the Council of Ministers acted for the governor. A premier was chosen from the House of Assembly, although in the north he could also be chosen from the House of Chiefs. Other ministers were chosen by the governor on the advice of the premier. Two of these must be from the House of Chiefs. Like the federal ministers, regional ministers must also be members of the house of assembly. Each region had its High Court of Justice, made up of at least six judges and a Chief Justice. They were appointed by the governor, acting on the advice of the premier. Every region could establish Courts of Appeal, and the North also had a Shari'a Court of Appeal.

The parliamentary constitution can be criticized on several grounds. It contained little or no provision for the socio-economic transformation of the country. The constitution was more concerned with the distribution of power and less with the ends of power. In addition, it contained provisions that were not necessarily conducive to a federal system. To a large extent, the constitution affirmed regional differences and provided a strong institutional base for group sentiments. Political parties were able to exploit this base for the selfish ends of their members. Each of the regions had sufficient scope and power to struggle with the others. The constitution also encouraged an attitude of intolerance and separation between the regions. There were also problems within the regions, mainly because in each region a large ethnic group was allowed to dominate numerous smaller ones. This majority-minority regional structure created its own tensions as the "representatives" of the minorities struggled with those of the majority for power and resources. Throughout the First Republic, the representatives of minority groups in all the regions complained of discrimination, general misadministration, oppression, and neglect. In the north, for instance, agitation degenerated into two violent outbreaks in the Tiv area in 1960 and 1964.

The country borrowed a parliamentary model but left out the conventions and practices that make it function appropriately. None of the legislatures in the country sat for up to a total of forty-five days in a year. The Northern House of Assembly, for instance, never had a record of sitting for as many as thirty days in a year. The membership of the legislature was mostly part-time, with the result that the executive had its way most of the time. Only in two instances, in 1960 and 1965, did the government decide to withdraw a bill on a motion by the opposition. And even these (the Anglo-Nigerian Defense Pact in 1960 and the Newspapers [Amendment] Act of 1965) were both withdrawn because of hostile public opinion rather than because of opposition in the legislature. The three branches of government often acted as one, and sometimes conspired for selfish ends. In the few cases when one of the branches or any of its representatives tried to assert itself, the other two could gang up to frustrate it. For instance in 1963, when the Public Accounts Committee of the House of Representatives queried items of overspending in the audited accounts of the federal government, the executive quickly dissolved the committee, and it never met again. In the preceding year, the Auditor General of the federation, who was independent of the executive, was dismissed by the finance minister for raising a query about government overspending.

Elected members of the legislature came on party tickets while the executive was formed by the leading party, either alone or in coalition with another party or parties. There were several of these parties, but three achieved prominence: the NCNC (now the National Council of Nigerian Citizens), the AG and the NPC. Party manifestoes dealt with issues of rapid development and distribution of power. In the Cold War era, the parties also had to address the issues of communism, socialism, and capitalism. It was fashionable among a group of radicals to believe that socialism offered the rapid route to development.

From 1951 to 1966 the NCNC controlled the government of the Eastern Region and formed the major opposition party in the Western House of Assembly. From 1959 to 1966 it was in coalition with the NPC to form the federal government. The NCNC tried to draw its support from different interest and value groups, such as the Ibo State Union, the Bornu Youth Movement, and various cultural and labor unions. Until 1951 it was mainly these organizations, rather than individuals, that enjoyed membership. Azikiwe served as a major rallying force to individual members as well as the unions, and some of the internal crises within the party centered on loyalty to him. Although there was a "left wing" in the NCNC, Azikiwe only made use of its radical slogans to attain popularity. When he was accused of betraying the socialist cause by building a financial empire, he claimed that socialism is reconcilable with an accumulative urge.[1] During the 1958 Federal Elections, the party described itself as "a Fabian Socialist party which is stoutly opposed to communism as a way of life."[2] From 1960 to 1965 the party demonstrated clearly that its socialist slogans were mainly designed to secure votes.

The AG put forward a welfarist program. Its stronghold was the Western Region, although it enjoyed some support in Benue, Rivers, Calabar, and Ogoja Provinces. Throughout the First Republic, the party formed the opposition in the federal legislature. It drew on the support of the intelligentsia (lawyers, doctors, teachers), businessmen, and traditional chiefs. The party emphasized participation in the export-import trade, in order to enable its members to serve as the representatives of foreign firms and accumulate wealth. After the 1959 elections, the party became more vigorous in presenting a socialist ideology, partly as a way of appealing to more people. In 1962 the party formally proclaimed a new program and ideology, "democratic socialism," and this further intensified the ongoing rift within it, and its subsequent split. The AG never had the opportunity to put into practice its socialist ideas.

The NPC was formed in 1951 as an offshoot of a cultural organization, the Jam'yyar Mutanen Arewa (JMA—The Association of Peoples of the North), established in 1948 by some northern intelligentsia who wanted a platform to discuss politics. The NPC was a restricted party, open mainly to northerners. Most of its members in the 1950s were Native Authority staff or members of the Northern House of Assembly. Consequently, the party became welded into the native administration. Unlike the AG and the NCNC, the party made no pretense to socialism, and it conceived its program in such a way as to benefit the north and continue the colonial economic structure. Sir Ahmadu Bello, the *Sardauna* of Sokoto, was the party leader and premier until his death in the coup of 1966. His deputy, Tafawa Balewa, was the first and only prime minister in the First Republic. The NPC was the dominant coalition partner in the federal government from 1954 to 1966.

The other smaller parties included NEPU (Northern Elements Progressive Union), UMBC (United Middle Belt Congress), UNIP (United Nigerian Independence Party), BYM (Bornu Youth Movement), KPP (Kano People's Party) and MDP (Midwest Democratic Front). These parties provided opportunities for each of the three dominant parties to forge alliances which enabled them to extend their electoral reach beyond their regional base. For instance, the NPC reached the Midwest through an alliance with the MDP, while the AG extended to the North through its alliance with the UMBC. The small parties proved, however, to be of little electoral significance; they all polled less than 15 percent of total votes in the various elections. But the small parties benefited from the alliances: they had more access to votes through the assistance of the big parties, and their members enjoyed patronage mainly by way of appointments to boards and government parastatals.

One of the small parties, Northern Elements Progressive Union, deserves an additional comment because it was perhaps the most radical party. It also demonstrated that, ideally, political competition should be focused on programs and class interests rather than regionalism. It broke away from the NPC in 1950, criticizing the party for its autocracy, and at the same time declaring that "all political parties are but the expression of class interests." NEPU advocated the re-structuring of society in order to abolish privileges of birth and eliminate poverty. The party was led by Aminu Kano, a politician of great ability and integrity. Aminu Kano believed in the "rule of the common people, the poor, the illiterate," and his definition of democracy was unique:

> We interpret democracy in its more traditional, radical sense, and that is the rule of the common people, the poor, the illiterate, while our opponents interpret it in its modern Tory sense, and that is the rule of the enlightened and prosperous minority in the supposed interest of the common people.[3]

The party had to contend with the forces of the NPC. From 1952 to 1956 it had no representation in the Northern House of Assembly; in 1956, it had seven out of 131 seats; in the 1959 Federal Elections, it won eight out of 174 seats; and in 1961, it won only one.

The analysis of politics in the First Republic that is presented below revolves around party coalitions, inter-party conflicts, and intra-party crises. These conflicts and coalitions affected the interpretations of, and reactions to, issues of national significance such as the economy, foreign policy, the census, and elections. The politics of this era reveal the following features: power was exercised by a parasitic cabal and no genuine national party emerged; the electorate lacked the power to discipline its representatives (except to take to violence), which meant that a genuine democracy could not have been practiced; there was a failure to prevent public office holders from accumulating public resources, and this further encouraged the competition for posts and the elite-generated problems of religious, ethnic, sectional, and ethnic rivalries; and the power holders were unable to dismantle a neo-colonial structure that promoted the exploitation of the poor.

The first direct election covering the entire country was held in 1959. This was a significant election to decide the party which would rule an independent Nigeria. In the final result, the NPC won 134 seats, the AG 73, the NCNC 89, and independent candidates the remaining 16 seats. The Governor-General, Sir James Robertson, invited Tafawa Balewa to form a government. The NPC and the NCNC agreed to form a government, while the AG became the opposition. In spite of demands for southern politicians to unite against the north, the NCNC refused to form a coalition with the AG because of political and economic considerations. In a coalition with the AG, both would have an equal bargaining strength and pose an equal threat to each other. Pay-offs would also have to be shared on an equal basis. In a coalition with the NPC the NCNC reckoned that, though it would be a junior partner, it could exercise the power of blackmail by occasionally threatening to vote with the AG. Such a coalition would also make it possible for the NCNC to receive pay-offs out of proportion to its bargaining weight and also larger than it would have received in alliance with the AG. It was a good idea on paper, especially at a time when the regions were facing rising recurrent expenditure and declining revenues and were looking to the federal authority in Lagos for more development funds. The NCNC's expectations failed to materialize, however. By early 1961 the NPC had forged a working majority in the federal parliament because the sixteen independent candidates and some members of the minor parties allied to the AG had crossed over to it.

Politics was little concerned with good government or the reconciliation of competing demands. It was devoted primarily to primitive accumulation, the extraction of resources to satisfy the demands of politicians. Among these demands was the purchase of political support. To meet these demands, it became crucial to have control over the instrumentalities of government. This was one main reason why the NCNC thought it best to ally with the government in power. But it never had an extractive capability since the NPC had become stronger and succeeded in making the north the major beneficiary of federal spending. Since the NCNC did not meet its expectations in the coalition, it had to rethink its strategy, although collaboration with the AG offered even less promise. The best strategy was for the NCNC to extend its power base, especially to the West where it shared electoral support with the AG. If the NCNC were able to secure the control of the West, it would not only marginalize the AG, but would also undermine the NPC. This scheme did not succeed.

Both the AG and NCNC sought to alter the representational ratio between the north and south and also change the revenue allocation formula. The best way to achieve this was to contest the population figures of the country and the population ratio between the regions. A census controversy lasted from 1962 to 1964. The 1952–53 census made it possible for the North to have 174 out of the 312 seats in the House of Representatives. The southern politicians hoped that they would have greater access to power (and revenue) if a new census altered the balance in their favor. In July 1962 the results that reached Lagos were alarming: the population of the East had increased by 71 percent, that of the West by 70 percent, and that of the North by 30 percent. Checks were carried out in selected areas, at the end of which the figures for the North were adjusted from an initial increase of 30 percent to 80 percent. None of the parties was willing to accept the overall figures, and the prime minister had to cancel the census results with a promise that a fresh census would be held in 1963. The 1963 census was no improvement as indicated by the results: there was an overall increase of 74 percent for the North, 65 percent for the East, and 100 percent for the West. Once again, the strategy to dislodge the NPC had failed.

Meanwhile, the political situation in the Western Region was degenerating into chaos. In 1961 there was sporadic violence, especially between NCNC and AG supporters. A greater crisis and more serious violence occurred in 1962, occasioned by the rift within the AG which led to the split of the party. Disagreement had earlier been expressed in

1959 as to who should succeed Awolowo as premier, following his shift from the Western to the federal legislature. Chief S. L. Akintola succeeded him, consolidated his power, and took major decisions without reference to Awolowo. Personal differences were compounded by allegedly ideological conflicts as to whether the AG should embrace socialism, and how the party should relate to the NPC. Akintola was in favor of a coalition government with the NPC, while Awolowo was opposed to it. Indeed, Awolowo used his position as the opposition leader to attack the government on wide-ranging issues, notably the Anglo-Nigerian defense pact, the inefficiency of the federal government, and the need for more indigenous control of the economy.

The NPC was embarrassed and angered by some of Awolowo's comments, and sought the means to undermine him. The task was made easier by the conflict in the AG which degenerated into violence in the regional House of Assembly on May 25, 1962, when an attempt was made to remove Akintola as premier. The federal government intervened by dissolving the House and suspending the governor. It also proclaimed an emergency and appointed an Administrator.

Other developments created further ordeals for Awolowo and finally ended his political career in the First Republic. The federal government set up the Coker Commission to inquire into the investment policies and finances of six Western Regional government statutory corporations and their relations to political parties. The commission vindicated Akintola, found the AG guilty of shoddy financial dealings, and indicted Awolowo. In November 1962 Awolowo was arrested and charged with treason. In June 1963 he was sentenced to ten years' imprisonment.

The NCNC benefited from the crisis in the West. The party was able to introduce a motion in Lagos to demand the creation of a new state, the Midwest, out of Western Region. This motion was passed in the House, approved by the legislatures in the East and North, and ratified by the Administrator in the West. A referendum was held in the Midwest, and 83 percent of those present and voting gave their assent to the creation of a separate region. In 1963 the Midwest was created as the country's fourth region.

At the expiration of the six months' state of emergency in the West, Akintola was restored as premier, in spite of opposition from Chief Adegbenro, the candidate sponsored by the Awolowo faction. Akintola's group, now named the United People's Party (UPP), did not enjoy a majority in the regional assembly and decided to form a coalition with the NCNC. The NCNC was now a stronger party, with control in the

East and Midwest, and being in coalition in the West. The NPC was worried, especially as the NCNC's base could now create bipolarization between the South and the North, and this could affect its chance in the 1964 General Elections. The NPC acted swiftly by breaking the UPP/ NCNC coalition. Akintola was persuaded by the NPC to form a new party which became known as the Nigerian National Democratic Party (NNDP). He dissolved the UPP/NCNC coalition and ordered the NCNC members in his cabinet to join his new party or quit. Some NCNC members crossed to the NNDP, Akintola had a party with a majority in the Regional Assembly, and the NCNC lost the West.

The NPC converted Akintola's gain in the West to an advantage. Akintola's government ratified the disputed 1963 census figures of 66 million with the ratio between the South and North remaining unchanged. The Midwest was also coerced into doing the same—its new government was threatened with the withdrawal of federal aid on which it depended. The NCNC's opposition to the census could, therefore, not be sustained. By the end of 1963 the NCNC was looking forward to the 1964 elections to improve its bargaining strength, while the NPC was concerned with consolidating its power at the federal level.

The 1964 Federal Elections were contested by two main coalitions: the Nigerian National Alliance (NNA) comprising the NPC and a few minor parties, and the United Progressive Grand Alliance (UPGA) composed of the NCNC, AG, NEPU, and the United Middle Belt Congress. The NPC wanted to project the image of a national party, while the UPGA projected itself as both progressive and radical. Politicians with eyes fixed on federal posts and the federal treasury were not ready to lose the elections, and they resorted to all kinds of dirty tricks in order to succeed. Political violence escalated, as the country approached the election date in December. Parties recruited thugs to defend their members and harass opponents. Electoral officers were either bribed or threatened. The nomination papers of some candidates were rejected to ensure the victory of others. In the West the electoral process was so abused that 30 percent of NNDP candidates stood unopposed in a region where the party was unpopular. In the North 88 out of 174 NPC candidates were also unopposed, while the NCNC prevented elections in the East.

The Federal Electoral Commission ignored most of the irregularities. In a badly tainted election, the NNA achieved an overwhelming victory. Balewa called on the president to request his reappointment as prime minister and form a new government. Azikiwe refused, partly because of doubts about the result and his loyalty to his own party. A constitutional crisis was averted by pressure from other politicians, the Chief Justice, and the Head of the Armed Forces. Azikiwe invited Balewa to form the government. A deal was also struck, agreeing that the new government would be broad-based, including representatives from both coalitions. Elections would be held in the East in March, after which the NCNC members would be appointed into government, and new elections to the Assembly in the West should be held in October. This deal could not hide the deep cracks in the body politic. The president was interested in retaining his post in spite of his earlier threat to resign. The prime minister resorted to negotiations rather than to the constitution and the judiciary in order to have a second term. The judiciary weakened itself by intervening in politics in a partisan manner. Thus all the organs of government revealed problems. Subsequent events led to the final collapse of the republic.

In March 1965 elections were held in the East. The NCNC members were immediately rewarded with posts in the federal executive. Holders of prime cabinet posts now numbered eighty, or a quarter of the federal legislature. The government had now been converted into a holding company with every "big politician" becoming a shareholder. Those who were denied shares filled the pages of newspapers with complaints, and many Nigerians, who should have benefited from a judicious use of the nation's resources and from the newly won independence, began to grumble and to discuss the need for change.

The catalyst for change was provided by the elections into the Regional Assembly in the West in October 1965. The UPGA, humiliated by the Federal Elections, was optimistic about the October elections, hoping that it would win and use this as a source of change. The optimism was unjustified as elections had never been a factor of change. Massive rigging and electoral malpractices enabled the NNDP to win the elections. This victory brought immediate disaster. The government lost the support of the people. A weakened economy was complicated by massive tax evasion. The payment of salaries became both irregular and unpredictable. To avert bankruptcy, the government decided to draw from the "surplus" of cocoa farmers. Akintola's first major act as premier of a new government was to reduce the price of cocoa from £110 to £60 per ton, a major political blunder as it affected the majority of the population who expected that an UPGA victory would improve their lives. The farmers took to violence.

The violence was widespread, both in the rural areas and in the cities. Neither the NNDP nor the police had an answer to it. The NPC-dominated federal government believed that the NNDP had legitimacy and support in the West and the violence would soon be over. Rather than seek the means to overcome the crisis, Lagos concentrated its energy on the Commonwealth Conference it was hosting in January 1966. The army allowed the conference participants to depart before striking on the morning of January 15.

The picture that has emerged thus far is that of a society ridden with crises. There was hardly a year without a problem serious enough to undermine the political stability of the nascent republic. Many serious thinkers have pondered its rapid fall. It has been suggested that the fall was inevitable if we see it as part of the process of modernization by a newly independent country. It is argued that modernization is generally accompanied by political crises. Those who disagree with this view think that modernization is being equated with westernization, attacks on tradition, a denial of the success of indigenous societies in building successful states, and a failure to recognize that violence and crises also occur in developed Western countries.

Some analysts have noted the absence of "nationally shared values" necessary to overcome the limitations of regionalism and ethnicity. It is true that not many of the political actors had a commitment to a united Nigeria. Yet some other analysts have attributed the collapse to violence in the Western Region. This is like confusing the symptoms of a problem with the problem itself. Violence was a consequence and not a cause of instability. The conclusion has also been drawn that politicians regarded power as an end in itself, rather than the means to an end. They were not primarily interested in realizing the greater good of the electorate. Any method of achieving power was regarded as legitimate. It was not necessary to talk about the rules of the political game, since this would imply that there were certain ends in view which politicians intended such rules to serve. But since it is difficult to conceive of politics without a notion of rules, it means that there is no proper notion of politics either. And without a proper notion of politics, the predominant ethic is privatization, that is, the preoccupation of the politicians with personal considerations.

The most common explanation has been the ethnic factor. It is argued that "tribes" are too many and too autonomous to work together within a common national framework. The forces that pulled these "tribes" apart were greater than those that united them and this not only made management difficult at the center but also culminated in a civil war.

The constitution was deficient in arresting these centrifugal forces, since it recognized the power and status of these regions. Objections have been raised to the ethnic explanation, especially by analysts who believe that ethnicity was only used by the politicians, just as they used religion, to manipulate the electorate, trivialize important issues, and get away with moral and criminal offenses. Analysts who disagree tend to focus on the colonial factor as the obstacle to stability during the First Republic. The argument is that the British deliberately handed over a fragile country, difficult to operate because of the consequences of the colonial policy of divide and rule, the separatist tendencies which the colonial economic structure had fostered, and the educational system which gave rise to an elite that cherished Western culture at the expense of the indigenous culture.

An alternative explanation is to see the fall as an outcome of the inter-action of three interrelated factors, namely, the nature of politics, the char-acter of the state, that is, a weak state which inherited many problems created by colonialism, and the country's role in the international eco-nomic system which contributed to its underdevelopment. Politics took the form of a "winner takes all game," and politicians never accepted ex-clusion from government office. Politics involved primarily the ability to gain control of public resources, or the process of doing this, not for public ends, but for private ends. Losers had no rewards unless they allied with the winners. Self-aggrandizement, corruption, and accumulation were justified and rationalized, and this is where religion and ethnicity become useful tools. Violence, complaints about discrimination, and ethnic rival-ries rose to their peak in a period when the control of the instrumentalities of government at either the federal or regional levels threatened the access of a group of politicians to resources. Political stability is possible in this kind of system as long as politicians are satisfied with their privileges, but it is not possible when they are not.

The nature of politics had its root in the colonial period. In the colonial economy, opportunities for large-scale profit-making and wealth were located in trade and politics. A hierarchy of Nigerian traders serviced a host of foreign firms in trade in imports and exports. With the creation of state monopoly marketing boards, the government, too, began to ap-propriate a share of the value of agricultural exports. The Nigerian elite, comprising businessmen and professionals, fought for the control of po-litical power in order to have access to government funds, commercial opportunities, and jobs which they had been denied by the colonial gov-ernment and the expatriate firms. Those who gained political control consolidated their economic and political base by increasing the resources to appropriate and distribute. Politics also became the means of class formation, as rewards spread to new recruits. Politicians and businessmen forged a strong alliance with foreign firms. They were also able to distribute contracts, jobs, and licenses to their clients through the control of government and marketing boards. People and communities who wanted to share from the opportunities (such as schools, hospitals and factories) identified themselves with parties and politicians. These communities tried to protect their interests by excluding outsiders from other parties, regions, and areas from sharing in the resources which they felt should belong to them. And whenever the politicians who allegedly represented them lost power, the communities felt threatened. Changes in government were interpreted as changes in fortunes.

The decolonization process established regionalism as a major basis for political conflict. Political-cum-legal structures reinforced the economy. The constitutions of the 1940s and 1950s deliberately devolved political power to three regional governments controlled by three different political parties. These parties intimidated opponents in their regions. The contending regions and parties struggled for the control of the center, primarily to gain the best access to resources and foreign firms, and establish some control over rival regions and over political parties that had lost in the conflict. The NPC succeeded in dominating the center largely through its control of the North, the region with the most parliamentary seats. And having gained control, the NPC used all means, including coercion, to exclude its opponents from political office. The other parties and regions, similarly, adopted all conceivable strategies to dislodge the NPC.

The inherited colonial political-cum-legal structure failed to resolve the crisis that it helped to create. The country did not inherit the ability of the colonial state to employ force or coercion indiscriminately. It was still under the domination of foreign economic interests. Indeed, foreign firms and foreign countries (notably Britain) served as mediators and umpires to decide the best course of action and press for options that would benefit them. Political conflicts that would not put an end to trade were favorable to them since they would direct attention away from serious economic considerations (nationalization in particular). The conflicts would also enable them to bribe parties and politicians who needed finance to engage in combat and to exhibit their superiority (in terms of material acquisition) to their opponents. As a wise political insurance, foreign firms appointed politicians (and their business allies) as sole distributors, shareholders, and representatives. The Nigerian state became a regulator of the interests of the indigenous elite and foreign capital.

The state could not, however, succeed as an efficient regulator because the custodians engaged in intra-class conflicts. Other groups in the society, most especially the peasants who had been exploited in various ways (through tax, unfair prices for their products, unfulfilled promises by politicians), posed serious challenges to the state. These challenges were expressed in violence, refusal to pay taxes, and often protests. The genuineness of their challenges also served in part to galvanize a section of the army into action.

THE ECONOMY

Since the 1940s the country had ordered its capital expenditure in a number of development plans. A ten-year plan was drawn up for 1945–1955. In 1955 the federal and regional governments drew up a five-year plan, later extended for two years. In 1962 the first post-independence plan was formulated. The plans before 1962 were very much concerned with the interest of the colonial power. The 1962 plan also failed to remove foreign interest in the sense that the strategy was still the same—a capitalist option with emphasis on foreign investments, personnel, capital, and loans. Throughout the First Republic, the country could not resolve the contradictions in a neo-colonial economy that was foreign oriented and affected by changes in the international economic system.

The country inherited a backward economy. The state was the predominant agency of change with the primary role of supervising exports to Western countries. Agriculture emphasized the production of export crops. The industrial sector was weak, accounting only for 1.1 percent, 0.9 percent, and 0.8 percent of GDP in 1950, 1954, and 1960, respectively. Manufacturing was worse—its contribution to the GDP was 0.6 percent in 1950, 0.9 percent in 1954, and 4.7 percent in 1960. Its only components were food canning, brewery, soft drinks, matches, and cigarette industries. Most of these activities were also concentrated in Lagos and Ikeja. The balance of payments was in deficit, while international reserves declined from ₦562.2 million in 1955 to ₦343.3 million in 1960. Social and economic life was lopsided with an elite class that enjoyed varied economic opportunities and a rural peasantry functionally dependent on cities. The First Republic failed to solve this contradiction; rather it perpetuated the inegalitarian structure.

The first budget highlighted a ten-point economic plan: to maintain confidence in the value of the currency and to maintain a reasonable stability in wages and salaries; to continue to expand the basic infrastructure upon which all economic development depends; to give every support to increased agricultural production; to encourage the growth of industry and the further development of mineral resources; to promote the training of manpower especially in professional, technical, and managerial skills; to ensure that development works are undertaken in accordance with their priority and importance to Nigeria and that there is proper coordination between all the governments of the federation in this field; to make effective arrangements for the provision of the funds required to finance development, both by mobilizing domestic resources and attracting capital from overseas; to develop the social amenities increasingly required, in accordance with the ability of the economy to sustain them; to ensure that Nigeria plays its full part in the international institutions and organizations designed to promote development and freer and wider international trade; and to ensure that Nigeria plays its part, both as a donor and a recipient, in international technical assistance programs.

All the above were enshrined in the 1962–1968 plan, which envisaged a fixed investment of ₦2,366 million, comprising ₦780 million and ₦1,586 million of private and public sector investments. Financial allocations were concentrated in transport, electricity, primary production, trade, industry and education. An annual investment of 15 percent of the GDP and a savings rate of 15 percent of GDP were also anticipated. At the regional level, each emphasized what it considered important: the West sought industrial development; the North desired an increase in agricultural output; and the East a combination of agriculture and manufacturing. These were to be achieved through the revenues from the federal government and those generated within each region.[4]

The 1962–68 plan achieved little. Failure was ensured by the hope that 50 percent of the required finances would come by way of external assistance. By 1964 only 14 percent of the expected capital had been received. Neither was the political instability of the period conducive to serious implementation. Due to the coup and the civil war, the plan was abandoned. Other reasons, such as poor supportive administrative machinery and inadequate data to work with, also doomed the plan to failure.

The economy saw some changes. The GDP rose from ₦2,378.6 million in 1960–1961 to ₦3,405.4 million in 1966–1967, an annual growth rate of

5.3 percent which owed much to petroleum, the share of which increased from 1.2 percent in 1960 to 4.8 percent in 1966. The contributions of agriculture, fishing, and forestry to the GDP began to decline, due partly to petroleum production. The growth rate of agriculture declined from 4.5 percent in 1960 to 1.2 percent in 1964. Manufacturing showed some expansion with its share in GDP rising from 4.7 percent in 1960 to 6.1 percent in 1966. But manufacturing was mainly reprocessing and re-packaging imported components.

The balance of payments was in deficit, a trend that began in 1955 due to large-scale importation of consumer and capital goods. Massive importation was justified by the need for development. The current accounts deficit in 1960 was ₦138.6 million, falling to ₦111.0 million in 1963. Foreign reserves fell from ₦420.8 million in 1959 to ₦195.4 million in 1963. The government was disturbed by this and attempted in 1964 to reduce importation. An improvement in trade and capital accounts ameliorated the overall balance of payments by 1966. Meanwhile, internal and external factors in the economy had created an inflationary pressure with the cost of living index rising to about 5 percent per annum.

Fiscal and monetary policies were used instead of exchange controls (which became prominent during the civil war era and thereafter). Nigeria joined the International Monetary Fund (IMF) in 1961 and kept to the Bretton Woods Agreement that exchange restrictions and controls should be minimal. The First Republic witnessed expansionary fiscal policy, owing to large-scale increase in government expenditure and revenue. Recurrent revenue increased from ₦241 million in 1960 to ₦322 million in 1966, due to loans and taxes. Recurrent and capital expenditure, largely on administration, and social and economic services, rose from ₦162.5 million in 1960 to ₦278.5 million in 1966. This increase in investment necessitated importation of capital goods. Fiscal restraint measures had to be taken in 1964, and restrictions were placed on commodities such as textiles from Japan, while some goods attracted more duties in order to generate revenues. Fiscal measures after 1964 were aimed at curtailing the rate of expansion of aggregate demand, conserving external reserves, raising the level of domestic savings, curbing government expenditures, and raising customs tariffs. These measures brought about a fall in revenue, especially from custom duties, and a slow down in economic activities. Political instability accentuated the economic problems.

A Central Bank was created in 1958 to monitor monetary policies. The Bank filled the monetary gap created by the failure to secure sufficient foreign aid as envisaged in the First Plan. Consequently, money supply increased by almost 29 percent, thus contributing to inflation. From 1964 to 1966 a policy of monetary restraint was embarked upon to curb inflation and achieve an equilibrium in the balance of payments. Agriculture, the mainstay of the economy, began to suffer. The farmers were exploited to maintain the system. With the aid of Marketing Boards, the government skimmed off the "agricultural surplus" of the farmers. The boards determined the prices for the purchase of raw materials and sold them at an increased price, diverting the surplus to government treasuries.

The changes in the non-agricultural sector and the monetary and fiscal measures were either externally inspired or designed to benefit the private sector dominated by foreign firms. Reflecting on the state of the economy during the First Republic, Zana Bukar Dipcharima, the Minister for Commerce and Industry, rightly concluded that:

> The economy of our country, strictly speaking, is not in our hands. Over seventy-five per cent of our overseas trade is controlled by forces over which we have no control.[5]

NOTES

1. N. Azikiwe, "Presidential Address at the 1957 Annual Convention," mimeographed.

2. *Daily Times*, October 23, 1959.

3. Aminu Kano, "Presidential Address to the Party Convention," Zaria, January 1–2, 1961, mimeographed.

4. Revenue allocation is a contentious issue in Nigeria; thus far, no arrangement is considered satisfactory. The transfer of wealth derived from one area to another has been a lingering source of tension, in addition to the often-repeated argument that the north uses federal power to its own advantage.

5. Federal House of Representatives' Debates, November 16, 1961, Vol. IV, Col. 2943.

8

Military Rule and the Civil War, 1966–1970

Some analysts in the First Republic failed to foresee the possibility of a military takeover because they believed that the federal structure made it impossible and that the army was weak in training and numbers (10,000 men) and had a non-interventionist orientation. Such analysts forgot that the military was part of society, that it was politicized, and that it was not isolated from the problems created or inherited by the politicians in the First Republic. In addition, the mistake has always been made of omitting the top elite of the army from the ruling class. Even when not in power, the army provides the civilian regime with the force of coercion. In the First Republic, both the prime minister and the president consulted the military elite on major issues. Shortly before the 1964 Federal Elections, the army paraded the streets of Lagos to warn the electorate not to resort to violence, while the prime minister had to discuss precautionary measures with all the service chiefs. Similarly soldiers were used to quell disturbances in the West and among the Tiv in 1962 and 1964.

The Nigerian army was a colonial creation set up to protect the interests of the colonial state. Before the Second World War, recruits were drawn from among the poor, the politically marginalized, or minority elements. Improvements were later made by incorporating other social groups and the Western-educated middle-class. The early recruits either had grudges to settle or perquisites to gain from the colonial system. During the First Republic, the concerns of the army, especially those of its elite, found expression in promotion, which was important not only for the status it conferred but for the opportunity it provided in forging alliances with the civilian power elite. In 1960 the composition of the army was lopsided. Most of the officers were British (83 percent). The program of indigenization and the retirement of most British officers by 1962 did not produce a major change in balance, as most of the officers were now from the south. Indigenization and promotion became political issues, as politicians sponsored their favorites while the representatives of different ethnic groups lobbied for the appointment of their own people to strategic positions. A quota system was also introduced with implications for efficiency and merit, and putting northerners in military advantage.

There are major reasons why the military intervenes in politics: to defend a particular ideology or instigate a revolution; to protect the interests of the ruling class against opposition forces; to prevent an imminent collapse of society; to protect the interests of the army itself, especially if its officers want power and wealth; and to identify with a popular movement to bring about changes. From an analysis of the causes and aftermath of the two coups in 1966, the conclusion could be drawn that they were mostly influenced by a variety of factors. Given the political problems of the First Republic, the politicians failed to resolve the crises among their ranks, and between them and the people, and they failed to maintain a stable climate for foreign investments. Thus the ground was prepared for the military intervention of January 1966. Major Kaduna Nzeogwu, a self-styled revolutionary without a popular movement as a base, and his colleagues, were able to intervene, not because the army was more modern than other institutions in the country, or more educated or sophisticated, but because they controlled the means of violence.

The popular reaction to the coup was short-lived. The new leadership of Major General Aguiyi Ironsi did not announce any immediate policies to carry the public with it. The coup was believed to have been motivated by the desire of Igbo officers to attain regional domination. This was the popular perception in the north, but the justification for the coup was clear, in view of the problems of the First Republic, and the three leading participants believed that they were patriotic. In the inspiring words of Nzeogwu:

Our enemies are the political profiteers, the swindlers, the men in high and low places that seek bribes and demand ten percent, those that seek to keep the country divided permanently so that they can remain in office as ministers and VIPs of waste, the tribalists, the nepotists, those that make the country big for nothing before the international circle, those that have corrupted our society and put the Nigerian calendar backward. We promise that you will no longer be ashamed to say that you are a Nigerian.[1]

The stated motive of the planners did not reveal any attempt at Igbo domination. However, since they did not assume leadership, it is difficult to check their words against their actions. Their words, too, could have been clever rhetoric to buy their way to power. Certainly, the execution of the coup was a political disaster. Igbo officers were the architects of the coup, and none of the twenty-seven key politicians and military personnel that were killed was Igbo. Out of the four strategic areas where coup actions were to be carried out (Lagos, Benin, Enugu, and Kaduna), only in Kaduna was much success achieved. The failure enabled the General Officer Commanding, Major General Ironsi, to become the first military head of state.

As Ironsi and other officers after him were to realize, governance and politics were far more difficult and complicated than they had imagined. Social pressures and political problems plagued the Ironsi administration and he had no answer to the problems of ethnic rivalry. His regional governors failed to produce the radical measures which the people had expected and those of the West and East were even accused of nepotism. The politicians did not expect military rule to be prolonged and were still organizing themselves. There was no progress in the economy. In short, no coherent policy was formulated on how the new military era would differ from its predecessor, except in form of promises.

Regionalism and political wranglings did not abate. Ironsi played into the hands of the northern political and military elite. He failed to address the accusation that the coup was sectional and was confused as to how to treat the coup plotters, whether as traitors who had to be punished or as liberators who deserved pardon. He could not establish a broad-based government, preferring instead to work with a small group who incidentally were Igbo. This constituted a threat to the ambitious representatives of other ethnic groups. Added to all of this was the allegation that Ironsi was insensitive to the fear of northerners in the army, that they would suffer in matters of promotion. In spite of a one-year moratorium on promotion, he elevated twenty-one officers to the rank of lieutenant colonel, eighteen of whom were Igbo.

The final straw was the promulgation of the Unification Decree on May 24, 1966, which was to end Nigeria as a federation and inaugurate a unitary republic. There were four major changes: regions would be abolished and replaced with groups of provinces; military governors of groups of provinces would replace regional governors; military prefects would supervise provinces; and the administrative class of all the federal and regional civil services was to be unified. This decree ignored the real political environment. Ironsi either forgot or underplayed the strong loyalty already built around the regions since the 1940s, loyalty which politicians and soldiers had exploited to advance their careers and fortunes. Ironsi, too, never demonstrated that he could transcend his own ethnic loyalty. To those who believed that he was an Igbo agent, the decree only served as additional evidence. Rumors filled the air that the northerners in the army would be eliminated, while politicians began to warn of the consequences of Igbo domination of the country.

The first major reaction came in form of a demonstration by students of Ahmadu Bello University and the Institute of Administration, both in Zaria, on May 29, just five days after the decree. The students, with great potential as new recruits to the middle class, were threatened by the Unification Decree, which they thought would reduce their employment opportunities and force them to compete on a national basis. Regional autonomy had ensured that new graduates would secure jobs easily and move up the social ladder. The protest degenerated into physical attacks on the Igbo living in the north, especially in the urban centers where they had constituted rivals to others in commerce and transportation. The riots spread because of the widespread belief by northerners that the Igbo were exploiting their people.

The riots had far-reaching consequences. The atmosphere became tense as many Igbo fled back to the east. Rumors of Ironsi's scheme to dominate continued to spread, fueling more anger against the Igbo living in the north. When Ironsi embarked on a nationwide tour to explain the decree to the chiefs and kings, he was unable to complete his itinerary because of a counter-coup on July 29, 1966. The July coup put an end to the Ironsi administration and what northerners regarded as Igbo domination. Either because the leaders of the July coup lost control of their men, or because their organization was poor, the killing of Igbo soldiers was random, extending to people who were not even associated with the Ironsi administration.

Events were unpredictable for a few months. There was the need for a new leader. After a brief vacuum, Yakubu Gowon, then a lieutenant-colonel and the most senior officer from the north, became the new head of state. Gowon had to secure credibility, especially in the East where he was viewed as a northern agent. Lieutenant Colonel Odumegwu Ojukwu, the Igbo military governor of the Eastern Region, did not recognize Gowon's leadership, partly because he believed Gowon was anti-Igbo, and partly because he believed that there were other more senior and more competent leaders. The release of political prisoners, including Awolowo, placated a large section of the country.

THE CIVIL WAR

The counter-coup only replaced the fear of domination by the Igbo by fear of that of the Hausa-Fulani. Gowon promised to settle the problems of regionalism. In his first address, he proclaimed that "we should review the issue of our national standing."[2] But this review process ended with war, instead of peace. A meeting of the representatives of all the regions was convened on August 9, 1966. It recommended that all military personnel should return to their regions of origin, that Gowon should be in charge of the Lagos garrison, and that an Ad-hoc Constitutional Conference of delegates from all the regions should be summoned to review the constitutional future of the country.

The Ad-hoc Conference was held in September 1966. The army, politicians and the intelligentsia were divided, while regional representatives sought the best for their own areas. Every region presented a list of grievances. In the West, Awolowo had become the rallying force for the intelligentsia who wanted the Yoruba to exercise power in their domain and receive a good share of the national revenue. Awolowo became the "Leader of the Yorubas" with a mandate from "Leaders of Thought," an elite body recognized by the regional government. He presented a catalogue of problems: the Yoruba were victims of injustice—the Yoruba territory had been dismembered, Lagos, Ilorin and Kabba, and Akoko-Edo had been excised from the Yoruba homeland; the Yoruba were subordinate to other regions in governmental matters; they were the victims of the misuse and abuse of power in the First Republic and had suffered loss of life and property; they were envied by other groups in the federation for their human and natural resources; and other groups in the federation feared that the West and Lagos might come to dominate the federation in the future. In the Mid-West some wanted a merger with the East, while others wanted to remain an autonomous state. In the North opinions were divided into two: those who wanted one big region, and those who wanted the creation of states. Proponents of the former included emirs, staff of Native Authorities and others who had benefited from the one-region structure. The advocates of the latter argued that more states would bring more revenue. As to the accusation by other groups that they were afraid of northern domination, the delegates from the North had a collective response:

> We all have our fears of one another. Some fear that opportunities in their own areas are limited and they would therefore wish to expand and venture unhampered into other parts. Some fear the sheer weight of members of other parts which they feel could be used to the detriment of their own interest. Some fear the sheer weight of skills and aggressive drive of other groups . . . These fears may be real or imagined . . . Whether they are genuine or not, they have to be taken account of because they influence to a considerable degree the actions of groups towards one another.[3]

The Igbo took a more definite position in view of the counter coup, their fear of northern domination, and their refusal to recognize Gowon as the country's leader. The Igbo intelligentsia advocated the end of Nigeria as a territorial unit. In the East the propaganda on secession reached a crescendo.

In view of these divergent opinions, the Ad-hoc Conference could achieve very little. The delegates were mostly the politicians of the First Republic, men who distrusted one another and came together only because of their own economic and political interests. Gowon urged them to rule out a complete break-up of the country as well as a unitary form of government. However, the delegates had made up their minds on several issues. Their proposals were mainly along the lines of strengthening the regional base, either within a confederacy or a federation with a weak center.

The Ad-hoc Conference was yet to conclude its work when the September–October violence and killing of the Igbo in the north took place. The attack was more widespread than in May, involving members of the army. The number of Igbo who lost their lives has been put at between 7,000 and 50,000. The massacre ostensibly owed its beginning to a rumor that northerners resident in the East had been killed. A mass exodus of easterners from the North followed and those who were able to escape spread tales of horrors, stories which served to confirm the propaganda which the intelligentsia had worked hard to sustain. Igbo in the West, too, joined in the mass movement to the East. Ojukwu, the military governor, faced with the economic problems of thousands of refugees, ordered that non-Easterners should leave the East because he could no longer guarantee their safety. The refugee problems provided an additional justification for secession; the government argued that it could only take care of them if it had total control of the regional resources.

It was clear to Gowon and many others that the cleavages in the society had become too deep to be mended. Gowon attempted to use compromise to resolve the crisis, that is, if it was still possible to do so. Of all the compromise measures, the Aburi meeting held in Ghana on January 4 and 5, 1967, was the most famous. A study of the verbatim report of the proceedings reveal that the participants tried to paper over difficult issues, and there was little reason for optimism. They reached an agreement on the renunciation of the use of force to resolve conflicts, the reorganization of the army (which gave the governors more power over the security of their regions), the functioning of the Supreme Military Council (which again gave governors more power), the repeal of decrees which encouraged overcentralization, and the rehabilitation of displaced persons, mostly the victims of the riot in the North.

The Aburi agreement was beset by two immediate problems. The first was that of interpretation: Gowon thought that there would be a weak federation while Ojukwu assumed that the country would become a confederation, which would enable the East to run its affairs as it chose. The second was that of implementation; the steps subsequently taken by Gowon were interpreted by Ojukwu as breaking the Aburi agreement. On March 30, 1967, the government of Ojukwu enacted three important edicts: the Revenue Collection Edict, the Legal Education Edict, and the Court of Appeal Edict. The edict on revenue ordered that all revenues which originated from the East should no longer be paid to the federal government but to the Eastern Regional Treasury. The Court of Appeal Edict abrogated the rights of appeal to the Federal Supreme Court, while the edict on legal education broke the ties in education between the East and the rest of the federation. The two legal edicts broke the ties with the federation's legal system. Federal institutions and property in the East were also sequestrated. The East had virtually become an independent state though this had not been officially announced, partly because of the need to monitor the developments in the West (which the

East believed would also secede) and the reaction of Lagos. Other efforts at peace, including the granting of additional powers to the states, failed. Ojukwu took the final step on May 26, 1967, to secure the mandate of elders and leaders of thought "to declare at the earliest practicable date, Eastern Nigeria a free, sovereign and independent state by name and title of the Republic of Biafra."[4]

As if Lagos had anticipated this, its reaction was swift, coming only a day after Ojukwu had announced his mandate. Gowon proclaimed a state of emergency, assumed full powers over the army and government, banned political discussions, divided the country into twelve states (six in the North, three in the East, and one each in the West, Mid-West, and Lagos) to allay the fears of the domination of one ethnic group by another, and he announced measures to safeguard federal interests in the East. Ojukwu viewed Gowon's step as an act of provocation and interference in the territorial integrity of the East and he declared Eastern Nigeria a new sovereign state, separate from Nigeria. This signified the beginning of a civil war, since Lagos had made it clear that secession would be resisted by all conceivable means. In a radio broadcast on June 30, 1967, Ojukwu alerted all the citizens of Biafra to what would follow:

> Fellow countrymen, proud and courageous Biafrans, this is your moment. When we go to war, it will be a war against Nigeria for it is Nigeria that has vowed that we shall not exist. With God on our side, we shall vanquish.[5]

Both sides anticipated success. Lagos believed that Biafra could not defeat the combined forces of the other states in the federation. Biafra, on the other hand, based its optimism on two grounds. It anticipated massive foreign support, especially as profit-seeking oil companies had indicated their support for it. The companies knew that they would have more bargaining power in Biafra, which needed all the resources it could obtain to prosecute the war. Biafra, too, knew that these companies would act as pressure groups in their countries and in the international community. In addition, Biafra doubted the capability of Lagos; it regarded the federal leadership as weak, corrupt, and inefficient, all of which put it in a weaker position.

In the weeks immediately following both sides' declaration, the leadership of both parties consolidated their power. In Biafra civilian commissioners were appointed to broaden the political base, people of doubtful loyalty were flushed out of the decision-making process, and all citizens were mobilized for war and provided with brief military training. Biafra organized a massive propaganda with the phrase, "Be Vigilant," used to warn its people against so-called vandals. In Lagos, Gowon consolidated his power and broadened the political base by creating a Federal Executive Council comprising a civilian elite drawn from all states, excluding the East Central, the Igbo heartland. The civilian members were also commissioners, thus relieving soldiers of administrative duties. Awolowo became the Deputy Chairman, the highest status he achieved in his political career, and was able to use his influence to carry the Yoruba along in support of the federal cause.

The war was more prolonged than Lagos had anticipated. The first clash occurred on July 6, 1967, but what Gowon thought would be a quick "police action" dragged on for thirty months, claiming at least a million lives. The determination of the Igbo, the contributions of relief agencies to Biafra, and the shortage of managerial and organizational skills in the federal army were some of the reasons for the prolongation. Biafra, however, lost the war due in part to its inability to withstand a greater fighting force and inadequate food supplies. The federal side resorted to the strategy of starving the enemy.

The fighting followed conventional patterns: the two parties faced one another from strategic fixed positions, a barrage of artillery and mortar signaled an attack, and the infantry on both side approached each other until the weaker party retreated. The goal of fighting was to secure the control of roads and towns, and success in capturing one (by the federal side) or defending one (by Biafra) was given wide publicity. When a town was captured by the federal troops, the civilian population retreated with the Biafran army, a move which caused much suffering and starvation. Far more than the bullets, starvation led to the death of thousands, due in part to the displacement within Biafra, the difficulty of negotiating access to victims by relief agencies, and the federal war strategy of blockading Biafra, even at the cost of civilian suffering.

In the 1960s this was Africa's most internationalized war. Foreign nations, arms dealers, and mercenaries were interested in the war for reasons such as the need to procure a share of the country's wealth, or to ensure the break-up of Nigeria whose size was a threat to some. Biafra received diplomatic recognition from a few countries in Africa (Tanzania, Zambia, Gabon, and Ivory Coast) and from Haiti in the West Indies. It also received the sympathy and support of Portugal, Israel, France, and South Africa. For arms, Biafra relied on private traders as well as on France, South Africa, Israel, and Portugal while the federal government dealt mainly with governmental institutions in Britain, the USSR, Belgium, Holland, Czechoslovakia, and others. Relief organizations, notably Caritas International, the French Red Cross, the International Committee of the Red Cross, and Africa Concern, mainly from Western countries were also involved. This involvement was used by Biafra to secure an effective propaganda, food, money, drugs, and clothes.

Through propaganda, Biafra attracted a great deal of sympathy and relief. Locally, a Directorate of Propaganda mobilized the population for war. Internationally, it employed the Markpress Agency to present its case to the world. The strategy was to point to genocide and a possible attempt by the Islamic North to dominate the Christian East. Biafra won the propaganda battle although the federal side won the war. Biafra found it easy to put its views across and its message of genocide was convincing.

The war forced Nigeria to reexamine its foreign policy. During the First Republic, foreign policy was aligned to the West. International events were interpreted in a way that would not damage the close ties with the West. The civil war, coupled with the revenues from oil, compelled the country to reexamine its belief that the Western bloc was a friend while the Eastern bloc was an enemy. Britain's refusal to sell aircraft to Nigeria, France's recognition of Biafra, and the United States' refusal to sell military equipment to Nigeria all served to force policy makers to move to the East. And the Soviet Union was helpful. From August 1968 onwards, Moscow supplied MIG-15 fighter-trainers, Soviet technicians, MIG-17 fighters, small arms, and heavy artillery. Other links were also forged; for instance the Soviets won the contract for an iron and steel mill and new Soviet-Nigerian friendship associations were born. Other changes in foreign policy during the period included the attempt to strengthen relations with other African countries, especially those in the West African sub-region, and the widening of trade networks to include as many European countries as possible.

Attempts were made to end the war through the use of diplomacy. In all, four major peace meetings were organized by the Organization of African Unity and the Commonwealth Secretariat, at Kampala, Addis Ababa, Niamey, and Monrovia between 1967 and 1969. All were to no avail, since neither party was ready to compromise its objectives. Lagos in particular stressed that it wanted no peace proposal that would lead to the eventual break-up of Nigeria. To Lagos, peace talks must be "on the basis of one Nigeria."[6]

If millions of people suffered or died, a few others were enriched by the war as arms dealers and food merchants. Military officers in political roles and top civil servants consolidated their economic positions. The war also created an additional burden on the economy. The country had to cater to an army which increased in numbers, virtually overnight, from 10,000 to 270,000. The defense budget escalated from 0.2 percent of the GDP to 6 percent, from a mere ₦4.05 million in 1961 to ₦314.85 million in 1970. This increase was a big drain on the economy, especially as the army contributed little to the productive base. When the war was over, scarce resources were consumed by the army, and the officer corps became more and more parasitic and greedy.

Why did Nigerians go to war after six years of independence? Then and now, polemics and emotions have obscured analysis, and the government failed to create an archive. The issues revolved around ethnicity, the problems of the First Republic, division within the army, personality clashes, and the colonial legacy. Two explanations lack validity. The first puts all the blame on Ojukwu. He has been accused of being over-ambitious and presented as a man who entered the army to create an empire for himself. The war was "between one man and the rest of us," declared a fellow officer.[7] This is a gross exaggeration. Ojukwu was not the first to conceive the idea of secession. Before him, a number of leading politicians in all the regions had threatened to secede. Early in 1966, Isaac Boro and his followers declared an independent state of the Niger Delta and it took four weeks to suppress the rebellion. Ojukwu only went a step further by providing a strong and committed leadership to actualize what had hitherto remained only a threat. He was effective in capturing the mood of the Igbo. The colonial inheritance and the political crises of the time prepared the stage for him, and he was able to successfully exploit it. Other Igbo leaders shared his interpretation of the crisis. In 1966 and 1967 he enjoyed tremendous popularity, especially among thousands of refugees who were seeking new opportunities. Indeed, those in the East who opposed secession became an inconsequential minority. The second view is an extension of the first: that the Igbo were solely responsible for the war. The argument is that, without the Igbo-inspired coup of January 1966, the country would have been spared from the chain of events that led to the war. The sequence of events—the January coup, the July counter-coup, the massacre of the Igbo, and the secession—might have given credence to this view. However, other considerations must be borne in mind to reach a sound conclusion. The civil war was in fact the most extreme evidence of political instability after independence. The causes of the war cannot just be traced back only to January 1966.

The political class in all the regions contributed in one way or the other to the outbreak of the war, as every politician and military officer reckoned politics in terms of individual or sectional gains. In addition to issues already raised in the previous chapter, the knowledge that wealth would flow from oil affected the decisions of the political class. To those in the East, secession was a good idea, with the gains to be derived from oil wealth. But the oil which attracted the East was equally attractive to their rivals, especially when control over mining and manufacturing was becoming more lucrative than agriculture. Oil was produced in the East and Mid-West, and its potential for transforming the economy was already well known by 1967. Even as early as 1964, the NCNC had complained bitterly about the flow of money from the south to the north, and, in the crises of 1967, this issue had become paramount to the extent that the East believed that it created the substantial part of the country's wealth. During the war, both sides tried to control oil installations, and when this failed they tried to destroy them in order to disrupt exploration and cripple the economy of the enemy. The political class in the north which supported federation saw in all this a great economic advantage, including the gains from oil. For them to derive economic advantages from oil, they reckoned that they must control power at the center. The West, too, with its declining revenues from agriculture, was aware of the potential gains from oil, and had in fact supported the idea of a revenue allocation formula based not on derivation (which it had supported in the 1950s when agriculture was the lifeblood of the economy) but on population and need. As usual, multinational oil firms and foreign countries provided suggestions and "expert advice" on the basis of their own perception of how best their interests would be served.

GOVERNMENT UNDER THE MILITARY

The civil war did not prevent the development of a military system of government. While the military overthrew a civilian regime, it could not do without a civilian elite. Ironsi and Gowon chose active collaboration with the civil service for at least three reasons. First, in 1966 the military did not have the personnel with the requisite experience, education, and expertise to govern the country unaided. Second, the military thought that it shared some values with the civil service, those of merit and a unified command structure. Third, the military believed that the civil service had skill and integrity, both of which were lacking in the discredited politicians. Indeed, the bureaucratic personnel were better educated than the military, more adept at handling political matters, and better skilled in administration. Some civil servants eulogized this role, going a step further to suggest that the best way to attain the goal of national development was for them and the military to cooperate to formulate and implement policies. These civil servants tried to insulate themselves from blame with respect to government policies in the First Republic.

The alliance between the military and the bureaucracy was not without implications. To start with, top civil servants acquired more power, prestige, and influence. C. O. Lawson, the Secretary to the Federal Military Government, admitted in 1973 that civil servants were "heard a little more under the military regime"[8] than under the civilian. They attended cabinet meetings and took part in deliberations. They participated in an advisory capacity in key governing bodies, the ministries, the Supreme Military Council (SMC) and the Federal Executive Council (FEC). The same occurred at the regional level where civil servants became members of the Regional Executive Council (later the State Executive Council). In addition, permanent secretaries were appointed as Chairmen of Boards or Directors of public and quasi-public corporations. The danger in this was that the permanent secretary was accountable only to himself, since the corporation was under his ministry.

In a civilian regime, the administrative class is supposed to discuss and implement decisions which politicians have agreed upon. The minister is the head of the ministry and he takes into consideration the decisions of the party, the mood of the electorate, and the opinion of the legislators. Civil servants can persuade ministers, but if their suggestions are ignored, they have no right not to implement government decisions. In other words, the service is subordinate and subservient to legitimate political institutions. For a government to be effective, the civil service has to be competent and efficient.

Under the military, however, a minister was not solely responsible for all policy executions and implementation. The military-civil service alliance meant that political control was not exercised solely through a minister's supervision of his ministry. Throughout 1966 civil servants performed the role of ministers. By 1967 when the first set of ministers was appointed at the federal and state levels, top civil servants were already used to an unprecedented amount of influence, prestige, and

power. There were other obstacles in the path of the ministers. First, they
had little security of tenure because of the manner of their appointment.
A military fiat that appointed them could also dismiss them. Dismissal
was easier since they did not represent any party or interest group which
they could appeal to. Unlike politicians, they did not need to work for
a career or a cause. Secondly, since permanent secretaries were members
of cabinet, ministers could not keep them out of discussions and decisions. There were even cases when civil servants, instead of the military
and the ministers, provided political guidance. Permanent secretaries regarded themselves as colleagues of ministers.

The arrogance of power and the lack of control over civil servants led
to general inefficiency. In addition, civil servants became insensitive to
public opinion, concerns, and complaints. The service also became corrupt. The bureaucrats who had enjoyed power also wanted to protect
this by encouraging the military to perpetuate itself in power. They gave
misleading advice and insulated military leaders from the public. The
alliance promoted more centralization of political power than ever before. Obtaining the support and goodwill of key civil servants in the
federal and state capitals became very important to communities seeking
projects and spawned a legion of contract seekers, further encouraging
a tendency to abuse office.

The structure of government that emerged under the military recognized the alliance between the bureaucracy and the military. In January
1966 Ironsi abolished eighty-eight political associations and removed all
ministers and legislators from office. He became the sole legislative and
executive authority. A decree amended the constitution to take care of
these changes. Military governors in the regions also assumed executive
and legislative roles. To aid him in governing, Ironsi created two bodies,
the Supreme Military Council (SMC) comprising himself, the four governors, the Chief of Army Staff, and the Inspector General of Police, and
the Federal Executive Council (FEC) composed of federal permanent secretaries. Regional Executive Councils were made up of regional permanent secretaries. The FEC met more regularly than the SMC and Ironsi
was in regular touch with the permanent secretaries. More decisions
were taken by the FEC than by the SMC, which was on paper the senior
of the two. The SMC met infrequently and its key members were more
concerned with regional matters.

Gowon retained Ironsi's structure, though he included civilian ministers to strengthen his legitimacy and shore up his government. The FEC

now comprised both military and civilians. Bureaucrats continued to enjoy influence, especially in the first nine months of the administration when there were no civilian ministers. Bureaucrats had a strong hand in monitoring the Ad-hoc Constitutional Conference, the meetings to end the strife between Lagos and Enugu, and the creation of twelve states. Gowon's regime witnessed the emergence of "super permanent secretaries," who constituted a strong power group. Cases were even reported of secretaries ignoring their ministers, dealing directly with Gowon.

THE EMERGENCE OF A STRONG CENTER

The war promoted the development of a greater centralization of power which, in subsequent years, led to authoritarianism and the undermining of the federal system. In 1968 Gowon blamed political instability on regionalism:

Under the Constitution, the regions were so large and powerful as to consider themselves self-sufficient and almost entirely independent. The federal government which ought to give lead to the whole country was relegated to the background. The people were not made to realize that the federal government was the real power.[9]

His administration retained the federal structure and deliberately strengthened the power of the center over the regions. The creation of twelve states was significant in changing the nature of the relations between the center and the states. As a political strategy, it was meant to protect the rights of minorities, especially those in the East in order to prevent them from identifying with Biafra, and also to re-distribute power between the federal government and the states in such a way as to eradicate the impact of the large regions. The aim was that none of the new states would enjoy sufficient size and wealth to enable them to control the center. Also the hope was expressed that there would be no areas of conflicts between the center and the states, though the underlying theory that the center would not be so powerful as to dominate the state at will was negated in practice. By splitting the East into three, the oil-producing region was split into three. By breaking the federation into twelve, the power of each to threaten the center was reduced to virtually none. In later years, the states became so financially weak that they had to rely on the federal government even to pay their civil servants. The weakening of the states enabled the center to impose its own policies as well as take full control of foreign policy.

Throughout the war years and thereafter the states were subordinated to the center. The war years witnessed an era of federal supremacy in politics and economy. The centralized command of the military encouraged the rise of a strong center. Under Gowon, the governors must conform to the decisions of the SMC. After Gowon's departure, the governors became field officers who must obey their commanders. Fiscal relations were also used to weaken the states. Before 1967 the regions were, to a large extent, fiscally self-sufficient, though they still needed the center for support. For instance, from 1953 to 1960 the revenue of the federal government increased by 74.4 percent; that of the regions combined increased by 181.5 percent. During the First Republic, federal revenue increased by 32.5 percent while that of the regions combined rose by 72.0 percent. This trend was reversed during the war, as federal revenues increased substantially because of increasing revenues from petroleum, the expansion of the sources of federal tax, and the federal government's prevention of the states from raising more internal revenues. The growth rate of revenues in the states fell, and many found it difficult to meet their rising expenditure without the allocation from the center.

The military also used the war and its centralizing policy to arrive at a revenue allocation formula that favored the federal government. The war and the organizational structure of the military precluded the usual acrimony between the regions over the right formula. The federal government assumed responsibility for financing higher education, acquired a majority share in mining rents, and made tax legislation in the country uniform. In 1970 a decree further curtailed the power of the states and gave the center a greater share of revenues accruing from export duties, mining rents and royalties, excise duties, and the distributable pool account.

Major amendments were made to the constitution to invest the center with more power. Both Decrees No. 1 of 1966 and No. 28 of 1970 (Supremacy and Enforcement of Powers) declared as null and void the decisions of all courts which purported to show the invalidity of any decree or the power of the federal government to enact any decree. In other words, the center could add to, delete, or modify the constitution as it deemed fit. This power was used to limit the influence of the judiciary and to interfere in the affairs of the states. The military made decrees and edicts superior to the constitution. Many of the provisions of the decrees and edicts were meant to delete from the constitution those things that the military thought were incompatible with its rule. The Ironsi and Gowon regimes showed that a rigid constitution was not suited to their regimes and the political issues that they had to address. Consequently, they made it clear that they were not bound by any complicated procedure in order to amend the constitution. In a civilian regime the constitution is the supreme law: its provisions have binding force on all persons and authorities while any law that is inconsistent with the constitution is void. The military reversed this by provisions which made it clear that the constitution would not prevail over a decree, and that nothing in the constitution should render the provisions of a decree void to any extent whatsoever. In other words, the constitution was no longer the supreme law.

The rule of law—an idea that human beings should be governed by law rather than the whims and caprices of rulers—was similarly subjected to modification. A military regime is based on force. The initial act of coming to power is a violation of the constitution. But the military itself operates under the law, especially those laws that specify the structure of government and the functions of the various organs. To say this, however, is not to confuse a government under the law with a government under the rule of law. While the military operated under the law, it did not run a government under the rule of law since the necessary requirements were lacking: the military was not accountable to any institution other than itself, there were no elections, and no legal guarantees of fundamental liberties. The undemocratic nature of military rule creates problems for the pursuit of fundamental human rights.

The war compounded the problem. It allowed the federal military government to operate in a manner that was even less conducive to the pursuit of human rights. The government had the power to detain anybody considered a threat to public order. The Public Security Decree No. 31 of 1967 suspended chapter three of the constitution on fundamental rights and the writ of *habeas corpus*. Related decrees allowed the government to take over any land or material needed to prosecute the war, prohibited the formation of labor unions, and restricted the right of access to the courts.

The system which emerged during the war was consolidated in subsequent years. The constitutional powers of the states were gradually reduced. In the immediate post-war years, the center forbade the states from possessing any police force of their own. Thus, the need to prevent secession turned the federal government into a dominating force. The war did not help to resolve the controversy over which political and constitutional models to adopt. Indeed, some of those who fought as federalists during the war were later to advocate confederalism. Neither did the war put an end to the problems of ethnicity. In subsequent years, especially in the 1990s, Nigeria moved closer to disintegration, meaning that the blood sacrificed in the civil war was in vain.

THE ECONOMY

The military inherited a weak economy in 1966. Three issues were clear: the nation's foreign exchange reserves were inadequate; it was necessary to increase both domestic savings and foreign exchange in order to finance capital imports; and it was difficult to insulate the economy from inflationary pressure. The civil war created additional complications. However, oil assumed a crucial significance and enabled the country to finance the war and formulate new development plans. The search for petroleum had begun in 1937, although it was not until 1958 that Shell-D'Arcy, a consortium of Royal Dutch Shell and the British Petroleum Company, made the first exploitation and exports. By 1967 about 627 wells had been drilled, with almost 67 percent of these concentrated in the Niger Delta. The production of crude oil increased from 1958 to 1966 (Table 8.1). The war disrupted exploration, but full activities were resumed in 1970. The contribution of petroleum to overall export earnings increased from 1958 to 1970, to the extent that it became the single most important export (Table 8.2) and the major component of government revenue, accounting for 16 percent in the late 1960s and 26 percent in 1970 (Table 8.3).

From 1967 to 1970 what was important was how to manage the economy to win the war, rather than how to encourage development. The government spent ₦600 million at least, while Biafra spent not less than ₦300 million. The country had to take drastic measures such as a reduction in budgets, a surcharge on duties and a levy on pioneer companies. War conditions created obstacles to the development of agriculture and industries. Capital expenditure fell and the growth rate in the manufacturing sector decreased from 15.1 percent in 1966 to 6.7 percent in the war years. Investments declined at an annual rate of 3 percent while national output in 1967 and 1968 were worse than in 1962. Agriculture declined by at least 1 percent per annum. The inflation rate was high. The 1962–68 development plan had to be modified in order to finance the war. War-time monetary and fiscal policies were directed

Table 8.1
Crude Oil Production and Exports, 1958–1970 (Thousands barrels per day)

Year	Production	Exports
1958	5.14	4.99
1959	11.22	10.84
1960	17.40	17.06
1961	46.03	45.22
1962	67.46	67.45
1963	76.47	75.89
1964	120.21	118.67
1965	272.20	265.71
1966	417.61	381.28
1967	319.32	299.38
1968	141.82	139.70
1969	540.29	540.25
1970	1084.48	1050.56

Source: Petroleum Inspectorate, *Annual Reports* (Lagos: NNPC, various years).

Table 8.2
Crude Oil Exports as Percentage of Total Exports, 1958–1970

Year	Crude Oil Barrels (OOO)	Exports Value (₦ million)	Growth rate %	Proportion of crude oil in total export
1958	1,820	1.8	—	0.7
1959	3,957	5.2	188.9	1.6
1960	6,244	8.4	61.5	2.5
1961	16,505	22.6	161.4	6.7
1962	24,680	34.4	45.2	10.5
1963	27,701	40.4	21.0	10.9
1964	43,432	64.0	58.9	15.2
1965	96,985	136.2	112.2	25.9
1966	139,550	184.0	35.1	33.1
1967	109,275	142.0	−22.8	30.5
1968	52,130	77.6	−45.4	18.9
1969	197,246	301.2	237.6	45.1
1970	383,455	509.6	94.5	58.1

Source: Federal Office of Statistics, *National Accounts of Nigeria, 1960–1961, 1975–1976*, Lagos.

Table 8.3
Contribution of Oil to Federal Revenue, 1958–1970

Year	Oil Revenue ₦ million	Total Revenue	Oil revenue as % of total revenue
1958	0.2	154.6	0.10
1959	3.3	177.6	1.80
1960	2.5	223.7	1.08
1961	17.1	229.0	7.45
1962	16.9	231.6	7.31
1963	11.0	249.2	4.43
1964	16.1	299.1	5.38
1965	29.2	321.9	9.06
1966	37.7	339.2	11.1
1967	41.2	300.0	13.7
1968	23.3	299.9	7.8
1969	72.5	435.9	16.6
1970	196.4	633.2	26.3

Source: Federal Office of Statistics, *National Accounts of Nigeria, 1960–61, 1975–1976*, Lagos.

Table 8.4a
Gross Domestic Product (₦ million)

Country	1960	1963	1970
Nigeria	3,380	4,125	7,872
Canada	39,918	43,055	82,810
U.S.A.	506,696	594,501	981,199
U.K.	71,401	84,933	121,859

Source: United Nations, *Year Book of National Accounts* New York: United Nations, 1979).

Table 8.4b
Per Capita GDP (Naira)

	1960	1963	1970
Nigeria	192	215	202
Canada	2,229	2,270	3,884
U.S.A.	2,804	3,142	4,789
U.K.	1,358	1,586	2,199

Source: United Nations, *Year Book of National Accounts*, 1979.

towards solving the problems of declining revenues, increasing expenditure (especially on defense), falling reserves and balance-of-payments problems. To raise revenues, a number of capital projects were abandoned, income tax was increased, and a 1 percent compulsory savings was introduced in the expenditure of all ministries, except Defense and Internal Affairs. In spite of these and other measures, the civil war years were characterized by budgetary deficits, reduction in revenue, and an increase in non-capital expenditure.

In Biafra, a siege economy was created, in addition to a number of experimental institutions. The Biafran government imposed administrative controls on virtually all sectors of the economy. Ten administrative directorates were charged with the function of centralizing food production, food supply, transport, clothing, fuel supply, price control and rationing, manpower utilization, and employment. The general performance of the economy was undermined by the ad-hoc approach to policy implementation, the concentration of population in areas under Biafran control, the high proportion of productive assets which had to be consumed in war, and blockades by federal forces. The initiatives which characterized the economy in 1967 were not sustained towards the end, as the Biafran politico-military elite tried to survive at the expense of the larger population.

Finally, the war period witnessed the attempt by the military elite and their civilian counterparts to divert a portion of proceeds from oil into private pockets. Though this sharing process was perfected in the 1970s—the boom years—the foundation was laid in the late 1960s. It was made easier by military rule. The military was not accountable to the people and its system of governing encouraged corruption since most discussions on finance were not subject to debate or public scrutiny. The military elite, together with its civilian counterparts, became a rentier class working in alliance with foreign business interests to make substantial wealth out of oil. Thanks to several public revelations in the 1970s, the forms which this collaboration took are now well known. They included, among others, rewards from the award of contracts, kickbacks from suppliers of goods to the government, and participation in "joint enterprises."

From the above analysis of the economy from 1960 to 1970, it is clear that the country was still underdeveloped by 1970. Indeed, by this date, the economy of Eastern Nigeria had been ruined and the country was far away from closing the development gap in per capita incomes (Tables 8.4a and 8.4b). And though the GDP and the per capita GDP show indices of economic advancement, they obscure other features such as socio-economic security, the state of the development of natural resources, the condition of the health of the people, and the stability of the economic system. By 1970 Nigeria revealed most of the features of underdevelopment: an economy dependent on a few export commodities; low agricultural productivity; dependence on the industrialized (notably the Western) nations for foreign exchange, technology, and manpower; unemployment and underemployment; poor medical facilities; a high rate of illiteracy; poor infrastructure; rural-urban inequities; and intra-urban inequalities. Nigerians were however optimistic that transformation would come when the war was over. Indeed, the 1970s marked the peak of Nigeria's glory during the twentieth century, thanks to oil revenues.

NOTES

1. Radio Broadcast, Kaduna, January 15, 1966. See full speech in J. Ojiako, *Thirteen Years of Military Rule, 1966–1979* (Lagos: Daily Times Publication, 1979).

2. See full text in *The Struggle for One Nigeria* (Lagos: Federal Ministry of Information, n.d.), pp. 37–39.

3. Northern Delegation to the Ad-hoc Constitutional Conference, Lagos, September 1966.

4. C. O. Ojukwu, *Biafra: Selected Speeches with Journals of Events* (New York: Harper and Row, 1969), pp. 146–47.

5. Lt. Col. Ojukwu, Broadcast to the People of Biafra, June 30, 1967.

6. *New Nigerian*, September 13, 1969, p. 1.

7. Statement made by Major General Hassan Katsina, quoted in O. Obasanjo, *My Command* (Ibadan: Heinemann), 1981.

8. C. O. Lawson, "The Role of Civil Servants in a Military Regime," *Daily Times*, December 11, 1973, p. 24.

9. Yakubu Gowon, Broadcast to the Nation, May 26, 1968.

9

Oil and Politics under the Military, 1970–1975

Nigeria entered a politically stable and prosperous phase in the 1970s with substantial revenues from crude oil. Three successive military regimes, those of Yakubu Gowon, Murtala Mohammed, and Olusegun Obasanjo managed this prosperity. This chapter examines the oil industry, focusing on the achievements and failure of the 1970s, in addition to the major events in the last years of Gowon's administration. The administration of Gowon turned the military into a political force and used oil revenues to minimize the trauma of war. The patterns for the continuing forms of impact of oil developed in the 1970s.

THE OIL INDUSTRY AND THE ECONOMY IN THE 1970s

Nigeria has oil in great abundance. Low in sulfur and light in consistency, the oil is also of the highest quality, attracting the best prices in the world market. The major production center is in the Niger Delta, with substantial offshore reserves in the Gulf of Guinea. As with the trade in slaves and palm oil, geographical proximity to the European and American markets also gives Nigeria a competitive edge, compared with the Middle East. Multinational corporations seek a stake in the country's oil, the United States purchases a large percentage of its oil imports from Nigeria, and other countries such as France promote economic relations with Nigeria. In 1971 Nigeria joined the Organization of Petroleum Exporting Countries (OPEC), an association of oil exporters and developing countries. Since the 1960s, OPEC has played a role in influencing prices and supply, although it weakens itself with its inability to effectively punish members that fail to implement collective decisions. OPEC's fortunes are unstable. It reached its peak in the early 1970s when it controlled over 50 percent of world production. This enabled it to create an oligopoly, allowing Nigeria to experience a boom in 1973. Its influence waned in the 1980s, as its production slumped to 30 percent in the mid-1980s. In the 1990s its contribution has risen to 40 percent, but it retains only limited international clout. While Nigeria is an important member of OPEC, it also undermines the organization by exceeding its production quota and ignoring instructions to sell at an optimal price. Nigeria produces up to 8 percent of OPEC's output.

Oil has been both a blessing and a curse to Nigeria. It is the most coveted of all natural resources, it generates money, affects world politics, creates leverage for diplomacy, and, if revenues are well managed, it can transform a poor country into a rich one within a short time. Oil gave Nigeria all these opportunities, an autonomy it never had before and the ability to rapidly change its society, dominate the West African region, become a continental power, and pursue a radical foreign policy.

Revenues from oil transformed Nigeria in the 1970s into the thirtieth wealthiest nation in the world, a regional power, an emerging industrializing country, and an assertive country with a prosperous middle class and a rising number of millionaires. The country experienced a rapid economic growth, more than ever before, reaching a rate of 8 percent per annum. Public fiscal expenditures, imports, exports, investments, and money supply all expanded in the 1970s. Substantial oil money was accumulated between 1970 and 1973, and a boom followed in 1973 and 1974 due to OPEC's pressure which quadrupled oil prices. The prices of Nigeria's light crude rose from $3.8 per barrel in October 1973 to $14.7 per barrel in January 1974. Oil revenues as a whole rose from ₦1 billion in 1973 to ₦4 billion in 1974. In 1975 prices declined because of the slump in world demand, and by 1976 the boom had ended. However, production never ceased as oil had become the primary revenue source, constituting half of the total revenue in 1971, rising to 81 percent in 1974, and even more in later years. It was the principal export: in 1970, oil exports constituted 58 percent of total exports, rising to 94 percent in

1976. Government fiscal operations increased rapidly, tenfold during the span of a decade. Budget surpluses were recorded from 1970 to 1975, in addition to huge balance of payments surpluses. Thereafter, budget deficits became the norm, brought about by inaccurate projections of oil income, the need to finance the new states, and also to meet the requirements of two development plans. At the same time, balance of payments recorded deficits. External assets increased in the early 1970s, from ₦180 million in 1970 to ₦3.7 billion in 1975. In 1974 Nigeria had sufficient external reserves to finance two years of imports. This gain was soon wiped out, as foreign reserves began to decline from 1977 due to excessive import of luxury items and technology for development, and a decline in the demand for oil. In 1978 the government had to borrow $1 billion from the Euro-dollar market and the World Bank, starting a process that was eventually to turn the country into a major debtor nation. By 1979 as the oil euphoria was about to end, the government was already talking of abandoning a number of projects and scaling down the size of many more.

The currency became strong and attained a high level of international respect in the 1970s. Huge fiscal expenditures and foreign reserves led to a large increase in the domestic money supply at a staggering rate of almost 40 percent a year with an abnormal rise of 74 percent in 1975 due to massive wage increases. The economy recovered from the civil war at an impressive speed and immediately exhibited a remarkable growth rate. National output increased at 8 percent per annum, and real investment grew at 35 percent between 1970 and 1975. The government embarked upon an indigenization program to transfer the control of businesses to Nigerians, but the benefits reached only a few, thus widening the gap between the rich and poor. Two development plans revealed the country's wealth and confidence as bold attempts were made to expand all aspects of social and educational institutions, and establish new capital projects including three steel mills, two refineries, petrochemical plants, fertilizer projects, paper and pulp companies, and cement factories. The first of the plans under Gowon, the Second National Development Plan (1970–1974), aimed at reconstructing the facilities damaged during the war in addition to promoting social and economic development. Among the achievements of the plan were the restoration of some farms, airports, industries, and roads damaged during the war, and an expansion in schools, from primary to university level. The federal government was able to finance the new states, embark upon low-cost housing projects, start seven new universities, and initiate in 1973 the National Youth Service, which compelled university graduates to work in states other than their own.

Sectoral growth was not uniform. The oil industry, manufacturing, building, and construction witnessed a phenomenal growth of over 10 percent while agriculture declined by 1 percent yearly. High tariff protection to ensure import substitution allowed the growth of the manufacturing sector. By 1970 foreigners controlled manufacturing, owning 63 percent of paid-up capital, while the government owned about 27 percent and the public 10 percent. The indigenizaton program was expected to increase the participation of Nigerians in various businesses. Small businesses were to be operated only by Nigerians while larger ones would have 40 percent equity participation by Nigerians through shares. When the decree was revised in 1977, equity participation was increased to 100 percent in many sectors while in the large industrial and commercial enterprises it was increased to 60 percent. However, equity sharing did not mean that Nigerians gained control, while indigenous ownership did not necessarily translate to better management. Indeed, manufacturing retained some of its old features. Important tools were still imported while Nigerian entrepreneurs avoided investments in the iron, steel, and engineering industries which required heavy capital input. Industries were confined to a few cities and they concentrated on consumer goods. Throughout the 1970s they were protected by high tariffs. Benefiting from a strong Naira, merchants and industrialists resorted to the use of imported materials, either at the expense of existing local materials or without regard for developing local substitutes. In addition, they did not export manufactured products, thus failing to contribute significantly to diversification.

Infrastructure was slow to catch up with the huge spending, thus creating high social costs and disruption to economic activities. In the development plans, energy and transport sectors took enormous shares. The road network, admittedly, improved greatly. While energy and telephone services received a boost, however, they were never sufficient or efficient as demand continued to mount, again due to the increase in the middle class population and a phenomenal growth in residential and commercial buildings.

The highlights of the continuing forms of the effects of oil unfolded in the 1970s. To start with, a comprador relationship grew up between the oil-extracting multinationals and the Nigerian state. Notable multinationals such as Mobil and Shell were granted licenses to drill oil. Granting the licenses and collecting revenues has become the primary role of the state. Thus, although the state controls oil, it depends on external technology, expertise, and firms for its extraction. For the tiny elite that awards the contracts, it is lucrative to collect kickbacks from the multinationals. Millions of Naira of state money can disappear, and highly-placed leaders can take huge cuts from oil companies. Although lacking direct state power, a local elite also has to work for the multinationals in different but lucrative careers.

Oil wealth came at a time of political stability and greater centralization of power in the federal government. The major arena of capital accumulation shifted to the center. Although the regions also benefited, access to the multinationals and enormous revenues settled in the center. This in itself became a source of instability. Coups and counter-coups, bitter competition for federal power, and access to the corridors of power were all important in ensuring control of oil revenues. Those with power sought to retain it. Gowon changed his mind about relinquishing power until he was forced out. All but one of his successors did the same, initially promising to leave, but later changing their minds after realizing the benefits and corruption that came with oil. The multinationals and other foreign interests began to support only the regimes and leaders that allowed them to exploit the country, or at least only those who were willing to grant the most generous concessions.

Nigeria's relations with the multinationals are generally friendly, to the annoyance of left-wing labor unions and intellectuals. During the colonial era, British firms enjoyed a monopoly which Shell turned into an advantage up to the present. Shell D'Arcy, an Anglo-Dutch consortium, pioneered exploration in Nigeria. Oil was discovered in 1956 and Shell moved quickly to establish exploration rights in virtually all the known productive fields. Competing oil companies did not gain any inroad until much later when they were granted off-shore concessions. The Shell Petroleum Development Corporation (SPDC), the Nigerian subsidiary of the Royal Dutch/Shell multinational, is both productive and lucrative. It has produced more oil than other companies; in the 1970s, 1.3 million barrels per day out of the total production of 2.3 million; in later years it has maintained production of almost 50 percent of the OPEC quota of 1.8 million barrels per day. At the very least, it makes a profit of $1 per barrel.

Indigenization was extended to the oil industry. Unlike the nationalization advocated by the left, indigenization was merely designed to allow Nigerians greater access to the management levels of the oil companies and a greater share of profits. The country would use part of the oil revenues to minimize dependence by acquiring a 100 percent share in all new concessions, and 35 percent in existing oil concessions. The 35 percent was later changed to 60 percent. In addition, in 1971 the government established a holding company, the Nigerian National Oil Company (NNOC), to manage and supervise oil extraction and provide guidelines to multinationals and local subsidiaries. Five years later, the NNOC and the Ministry of Mines and Power merged to become the Nigerian National Petroleum Corporation (NNPC), with wide-ranging powers and active involvement in oil production and sale. In later years the Ministry and the NNPC became two agencies, a cumbersome arrangement that led to a number of conflicts. The NNPC was also responsible for domestic refineries, petrochemical industries, and pipeline networks.

There were, however, signs of trouble in the 1970s associated with the dominance of multinational companies, the dependence on oil revenues, and the management of these revenues. To start with the multinationals, the state did not establish a strong mechanism to monitor them, to ensure that they did not cheat and collude with leading political figures to divert public funds into private hands. The industry has always operated as an autonomous unit with limited connections to other spheres; its technology is imported with little or no connection to local industries. Only limited efforts are made to transfer technology, while the high cost of imported technology has a negative impact on the country's balance of payments. The employment effect remains small as the industry is not labor intensive. Its operations are restricted to a corner of the country, and it has its own support and security system and limited interaction with local people. Oil companies have adopted a strategy of satisfying the men in power, not the masses. Their contributions to welfare programs were very low in the 1970s. They are not interested in gas which is flared into air. Oil leaks are more prevalent than elsewhere, seriously damaging the environment. The government ignored the early signs of environmental degradation; by the 1980s oil leaks had become a routine occurrence, far worse than in other oil-producing countries.

Revenues from oil have created a "mono-crop economy." Oil is central to the economy, the revenues from it have ensured dependence on imports while mismanagement has turned Nigeria into a debtor nation. Until 1965 agricultural products sustained the country. Thereafter, oil became the primary export with the result that such viable products as cocoa and peanuts were gradually neglected. Incentives for diversification were reduced and the country became a mono-crop economy relying on oil exportation. The market is volatile, oil prices shifting with little or no notice. The two development plans grossly exaggerated oil revenues and the government had to resort to severe adjustments to deal with an "oil bust" and price reduction. The economic growth driven by the boom was miscalculated in terms of the extent to which the country was stable, and it failed to account for unpredictable swings. Even today, long-term government planning is financially unstable, even without taking into consideration the additional factor of gross mismanagement.

The country became a rentier state, that is a state whose revenues rely exclusively on royalties. Grave consequences have followed. Unlike an economy dependent on production and taxation, royalties come from the outside, not from within, and from a sector unconnected to the rest of the economy. In spending the royalties, the rentier state can ignore its people, thinking that it owes them less responsibility since it is not the people's money or tax. Neither does it have to justify revenue allocations to projects and states. When the people are angry and take to protest, production losses and labor withdrawal do not necessarily cripple the economy as long as the state collects its "rents" from abroad. The rentier state becomes stronger and more autonomous with the ability to procure weapons with which to weaken or destroy opposition forces. The ability to increase or decrease oil production also gives the rentier state the control to determine its income and plan its expenditure accordingly. Public finance can be dominated by short-term concerns, rather than the long-term needs of the nation. Short-term needs can provoke the rentier state into maximizing wealth creation by increasing production, or borrowing with the anticipation of paying later with royalties. When there is a windfall, as in 1973 or 1980, the state scrambles for ways to spend the money, again ignoring long-term considerations.

The 1970s were an era of massive spending, as reflected in conspicuous consumption and countless projects of the government and the middle class. The government in fact boasted in 1973 that it had so much money that it could not finish spending it and sowed in the minds of its middle class the idea that opportunities were both abundant and unending. Thinking that development could be purchased overnight, the government embarked upon a grandiose series of projects and its policies encouraged price-distortions. The bureaucracy at both the federal and regional levels expanded far beyond the real needs of the government. From half a million public servants in 1973, the figure increased to one and a half million in 1981 without corresponding increases in productivity. In an attempt to spread the benefits of oil money and purchase public support for the administration, wages were increased by over 100 percent in 1975. This was known as the "Udoji Award." Large sums of money were paid as arrears of pay, and generous benefits, notably low-interest-rate car allowances, were added. Inflation reached double digits, compounded by the government's deficit financing and the demand for imported goods. The consumer price index increased enormously from 150 in 1970 to 423 in 1977. Food prices increased in some cases by 500 percent. A task force on inflation had to be established, strikes for more wages were prohibited, and control measures were taken to enforce reasonable rent and food prices, but to no avail.

The government aggressively encroached on the private sector, taking over or creating new enterprises and parastatals. With so much money pumped into them and little to show in return, most became avenues for the privileged elite to enrich themselves. Enterprising individuals wisely calculated that it was better to struggle to join a government enterprise rather than create their own.

Allocation to defense continued to rise. The Gowon regime was unable to demobilize soldiers with the army reaching 250,000 men in 1977. For peacetime, this was too large. Without a modernizing role to play, without contributing to the economy, and with an insatiable appetite for scarce resources, the army became a parasite. Defense expenditure increased from ₦314.5 million in 1970 to ₦1116.70 million in 1975, 7.6 percent of the GDP, much higher than that of many other countries. This does not take into account the wages and benefits of military men in political offices. Using the privilege of being in power, the military sacrificed the demands of the people and the long-term interest of the country to squander money on itself, pursuing a professional agenda that is uncorrelated to the country's wealth or the extent of any external threat.

The contribution of agriculture to national output fell below 30 percent. Agriculture stagnated, a major problem considering the fact that it employed the majority of the labor force. The production of export crops had virtually collapsed by 1977. The emphasis on oil, unsuccessful government policies, increasing rural-urban-migrations, the use of outdated technology, and the Sahelian drought of 1972–1973 were some of the reasons for the agricultural decline. Urban areas consumed the bulk of the oil revenues, leading to a serious marginalizaion of the countryside. The consequence was a sharp decline in food production which compounded inflation. The food production index declined to below that of the pre-civil war years, food demand outstripped supply, and the nation failed to feed itself. The country took to food imports which increased at the rate of 25 percent per year. Urban dwellers relied on imported sugar, wheat, milk, meat, fish, and rice. The price level of domestically-available food soared, while food imports impacted negatively on the balance of payments. Rural dwellers, who did not see much of the gains from oil, now had to suffer from the failure of agriculture as they had to use their limited amount of money to buy imported necessities at inflated costs.

Increasing domestic food production became a top priority, although by the end of the 1970s, little had been achieved. Among the measures taken were the supply of technology and fertilizers to farmers at reduced prices, the reform of the marketing boards, and the introduction of guaranteed prices to farmers whenever they sold their crops. There were two nationwide food campaigns, the first in 1972 with the National Accelerated Food Production Program and the other in 1976 with Operation Feed the Nation. The latter mobilized thousands of university graduates to work in villages. Neither campaign brought down inflation and food prices or reduced food imports. Enormous sums of money were spent to establish River Basin Development Authorities in different locations with the aim of setting-up extensive food plantations in fertile areas and assisting neighboring farmers with irrigation and flood control. In 1978 a Land Use Decree was enacted to make large tracts of rural land available for large-scale farming. The decree vested land in the government. This provided opportunities for those who had made some money in government to invest in farming. However, since they had other investments and cash reserves, failures on the farm did not cause their economic downfall. They were quick to retreat to politics in order to recoup their losses.

Reforms were also embarked upon to boost export crop production, again with limited success. New commodity boards were expected to work in the interest of farmers, rather than act as an agency of revenue collection for the government. The pricing policy that had favored the government—produce sales tax and export duty—was abolished, so that the farmers could gain more money and thus produce more.

POLITICS IN THE POST-WAR YEARS

The Gowon regime laid the foundations of an active foreign policy during the 1970s. The country's disappointment with the West during the war plus its economic prosperity paved the way for bold revisions in foreign policy. In the 1960s while ostensibly a member of the non-aligned movement—to avoid supporting any of the Cold War rivals—Nigeria was actually pro-West and regarded very highly by the Commonwealth under the leadership of Britain. In the early 1970s Nigeria was able to make six major changes. To start with, it re-ordered its foreign policy priorities. In the 1960s its concerns were with the Commonwealth, Africa, Europe, and the rest of the world in that order. In the 1970s Africa came first, followed by Britain and the Soviet Union, while the Commonwealth lost its influence. Second, Europe, rather than just Britain, became a trading partner, an arrangement from which France was to benefit. Third, Nigeria redefined its pro-West attitude by recognizing the People's Republic of China, engaging in only lukewarm relations with the United States, and developing closer ties with the Soviet Union. The West did not see any cause for alarm as Nigeria did not pursue a policy of nationalization or of radical anti-multinational regulation. Indeed, Gowon was popular in Western countries as an example of a mild-mannered and rational head of state, unlike the crude, dictatorial, and excessively corrupt leaders in some other countries. Fourth, the country undertook a major review of its African policy and worked aggressively to establish the Economic Community of West African States (ECOWAS). An association of sixteen countries, ECOWAS became a reality in 1975 with the aim of uniting all the member countries into a common market which would promote the free flow of capital, property, and people within the region. The expectations were that the various economies would become better integrated, and ownership and control of capital would be indigenized. Fifth, Nigeria normalized relations with African countries that had supported Biafra and strengthened relations with its immediate neighbors. Sixth, it saw itself as a champion of the black race struggling to achieve a new world economic order. To this end, it called for a number of new initiatives to negotiate with the European Economic Community. Projecting itself as a rich country, Nigeria believed that it could not only lead Africa into the modern era but also assist many poor countries, financially and technically.

If success was recorded in external relations, it was not so at the domestic level where failure to curb abuses of power brought about the downfall of the regime. Gowon tied his exit from politics to a so-called nine-point reform program which was supposed to transform the country's politics and economy. Against the background of the successful prosecution of the war, his own popularity, and the oil money, he announced with exaggerated optimism that his regime would reorganize the army and the civil service, rid society of corruption, invest in development, approve a new constitution, create additional states, conduct a new census, establish new national political parties, return the country to a democratic government, and embark upon a postwar program of reconciliation, rehabilitation, and reconstruction. The expectation was that everything would be accomplished by 1974, although this was later extended to 1976.

Winning the war proved much easier than accomplishing any of these other tasks. The civil service was reorganized, as outlined by a fact-finding commission, but it could not easily become result-oriented as had been anticipated. Gowon lost control of accountability and fiscal discipline and was unable to manage the increasing oil wealth with prudence or efficiency. Corruption was on the rise with his key ministers and governors implicated and publicly ridiculed. A new census in 1973 generated limited public trust and had to be declared void because of allegations of rigging, especially in the north where the population was said to have increased by 72 percent. Because of the connection with revenue-sharing and allocation of electoral seats, each state tried to add to its population figures. By 1974 the media and members of the public were already complaining bitterly about the government, blaming it for corruption, creating abundance for a few and great want for the majority, and neglect of the rural poor. The administration failed to address the general perception that it was corrupt or even to engage in a serious fight against patronage. Available funds were large enough for power holders and senior civil servants to display patronage, accumulate great wealth, and distribute resources to their clients. Patrimonialism was getting out of control, as more and more people saw ties with government officials as opportunities to enrich themselves. In one glaring example, a group of intelligentsia formed an ill-defined organization, known derisively as the Kaduna Mafia, in order to acquire power and wealth by ties with government officials.

Unable to meet his reform program, surrounded by ambitious civil servants and cronies, and enjoying power himself, Gowon announced in October 1974 that he was delaying the transition to civilian government, saying that a "precipitate withdrawal . . . will certainly throw the nation back into confusion."[1] He refused to lift the ban on politics and accused a number of people of "sectional politicking, intemperate utterances and writings, all designed to whip up ill-feelings within the country to the benefit of a few . . . it is clear that those who aspire to lead the nation on the return to civilian rule have not learnt any lesson from past experiences."[2] He asked for more time to create a stable political system in order to ensure the survival of the country. He made new promises: the appointment of a panel to draft a constitution which would be approved by the people, the creation of more states, and the inclusion of more civilians in the administration. He hinted at a major reform of his government, such that those who had served for long as ministers and governors would be replaced, while there would be a vigorous fight against corruption.

This was his last major political speech. The public was stunned by it, and he lost credibility and respect as well as the opportunity of becoming the country's first post-independence political hero. Reneging on his promise to restore democracy was a gross miscalculation which dissatisfied all the major segments of the population and different factions of the political class. Senior officers in the army who had been excluded from power and contracts were dissatisfied with him. Radical intellectuals and students condemned him. Earlier, in 1973, he had antagonized and humiliated university teachers who embarked upon strikes to demand better wages. Now alienated from his regime, they became prominent critics. Loud complaints came from unexpected quarters: Islamic leaders such as Alhaji Abubakar Gumi accused Gowon of moral decadence and an anti-Islamic attitude. Fellow officers, even from his own region, disassociated themselves from him. His most bitter critics were the politicians, who felt betrayed and began a campaign alleging that he wanted to perpetuate himself in power. Expecting a commitment to a 1976 transition date, politicians had been active in underground activities. The military had promised disengagement, thus encouraging leading politicians to develop ambitions for power. To legitimize his government and win the war, Gowon had made use of prominent politicians. When the war was over, the politicians were sidelined as technocrats, and civil servants became more active in managing the economy and implementing economic policies.

If Gowon had had strong support from the public, perhaps this could have been a source of strength or manipulation. On the contrary, many ordinary people were also tired of his government, partly because of his failure to reduce inequalities and spread the benefits of oil revenue. Nothing illustrated the malaise of the time better than the cement "armada" of 1975. An order was placed for 20 million metric tons of cement to build army barracks, private housing, and the nation's cultural venue for the pan-African Festival of Arts and Culture (FESTAC). Ships had waited for as long as one year to unload their cement, while the country paid a demurrage fee. While waiting, the cement had turned into crystals, which had to be thrown away. But those who attacked Gowon's government for corruption were harassed. Inflation was unchecked, and there was the impression that Gowon was too weak to control his cabinet members and state governors. On July 29, 1975, he was overthrown in a bloodless coup which brought Lieutenant-General Murtala Mohammed to power.

NOTES

1. Independence day broadcast to the nation, October 1, 1974, full text in *Daily Times*, October 2, 1974.
2. *Ibid*.

10

Reforms and Military Disengagement, 1975–1979

The coup that brought Lieutenant-General Murtala Mohammed to power was well received. His regime was so short and eventful that he is the most eulogized of the country's leaders. Following an unsuccessful coup on February 13, 1976, in which Mohammed was killed, power went to Lieutenant-General Olusegun Obasanjo who continued with the programs of his predecessor. These were years of reforms as corrections were made to some of the lapses of the Gowon years while the public and the media enjoyed freedom and security. A successful transition to a Second Republic was also accomplished. This was the first government to articulate and implement a philosophy of administration based on nationalism, probity, responsibility, and discipline. It tried to cure the ills of society, if only for a moment.

In his first speech to the nation on July 30, Mohammed announced a bold agenda. His would be a "corrective regime" to save the nation from Gowon's insensitive government which had been "characterized by lack of consultation, indecision, indiscipline, and even neglect."[1] Senior officers of the rank of general were retired, all ministers in the federal and state cabinets were dismissed, and three panels were appointed to consider the suitability of Lagos as a federal capital, the need for additional states, and the nature of asset sharing in the old Northern and Eastern regions. Mohammed's government would ignore the 1973 census, post-pone the hosting of the Second World Black Festival of Arts and Culture (FESTAC), establish a structure that would allow discussion among key members of the government, and reduce the size of the army. He ended on a tough note that became part of public discourse: "This government will not tolerate indiscipline [and] will not condone abuse of office."

If Nigerians had been used to unfulfilled promises, Mohammed showed that he was different. He moved fast to implement everything he promised, purifying the political process, considering public opinion on some issues at least, and stressing official probity. A day after his speech new governors were sworn in with a warning that they must show exemplary leadership, run open governments, and make the inter-est of the public their priority. Again in a remarkable speech, Moham-med said that the previous governors were removed

> because of allegations of graft and misuse of public funds and widespread dissatisfaction with their personal conduct. There were complaints of ostentatious living, flagrant abuse of office and dep-rivation of people's rights and property. Other allegations were per-version of time-honored government procedures, nepotism and favoritism, desecration of traditional institutions and humiliation of highly respected traditional rulers. All this gave the impression that the states were being run as private estates.[2]

He repeated the theme of a "clean government" many times, and the public came to trust him as a honest leader. All retired governors were ordered to declare their assets, some powerful individuals lost their assets after investigations, many contracts were either reviewed or can-celed, and boards of parastatals and public service commissions were dissolved and reconstituted. Public officers who owned assets beyond their legitimate earnings would forfeit them. A Corrupt Practices Inves-tigation Bureau and a Special Tribunal were established to handle cases of corruption. A Public Complaints Commission was set up to investi-gate cases of complaints by the public against government officers.

The anti-corruption crusade was successful only for a few months. While the leadership was sincere, entrenched interests were opposed to the confiscation of stolen wealth, and the officers who assassinated Mo-hammed thought that he was leading the country on a communist path. For a political class not used to productive enterprises, learning the tricks to survive corrupt practices became the game of the moment.

At this juncture, it is appropriate to pose the question: in spite of the sincerity of the regime and the cooperation of the public, why was corruption so difficult to eradicate, or why is it endemic to the system? All its various guises—bribery, theft, extortion, nepotism, and patronage—are prevalent in Nigeria. The most serious is the use of political power to advance self interest and limited interests, a violation of the social contract between the people and their government. Most cases of corruption have their roots in power, in how it is distributed and deployed. When power is concentrated in a few hands, as in Nigeria, it tends to be misused and to break out of the restraints that the people can provide to protect themselves. In cases where power is organized along patriarchal lines, the patriarch has an obligation to show loyalty to "family members" at the expense of others. When power has been authoritarian, as in the colonial and military eras, it has been used for limited ends, and accountability has been minimal. A government could lose both its loyalty and responsibility to the people and resort to a system of patronage to govern. In a patronage system, only a few are satisfied at the expense of others; power is for the governors, not the governed.

The major cases of corruption in Nigeria are linked to patrimonialism, involving bribery, nepotism, extortion, and clientelism by civil servants, politicians, and military leaders. Members of the public have cooperated, serving as clients to a set of patrons. The business elite, too, has been happy, able to enjoy the fruits of an expanded economy, secure contracts, reduce competition with foreigners, and get away with shoddy deals. In a patrimonial system, a person with power can abuse it, ignore the guidelines that check the use of authority, and distribute public resources as if they are personal. Regarding himself as a patron of members of his ethnic group, town, community, or church, the power holder shows loyalty and prestige by distributing largesse and opportunities in ways that ignore objectivity and rationality. He can also demand payment in return for favors, such as kickbacks from contracts. Revenues from oil created greater opportunities of making personal gains from public expenditures. What Mohammed's regime did was to punish a few people, thus gaining acclaim as an anti-corruption crusader, but he failed to change the patrimonial system.

CIVIL SERVICE REFORM

The civil service was implicated in the political and economic mismanagement of the early 1970s. The belief was that it was corrupt, too powerful, and had conspired with Gowon to cause the country's "drift and indecision." In Mohammed's view, it had to be overhauled if the country was to make progress. A great purge followed, the like of which had never been seen before. Within eight weeks, over 11,000 civil servants were retired or dismissed with ignominy. The slow civil service procedure was ignored, minor complaints led to termination, the innocent and the guilty suffered the same fate, morale suffered, manpower shortages followed in some agencies, security of tenure was destroyed, the era of "super permanent secretaries" came to an end, and many became too cautious to offer opinions that would antagonize their political bosses or administrative seniors.

Yet the public supported the government and regarded the purge as evidence of a sincere and committed leadership. It was expected that a leaner, more polite, less corrupt, and more efficient bureaucracy would emerge, and the purge was a small price to pay. As vacancies were created for promotions at all levels, it was also popular among those who remained behind and were able to move up. The purge achieved within a limited time what would have taken years to accomplish by civil service procedure. The permanent secretaries were also stopped from contributing to deliberations in the Federal Executive Council in order to reduce the power that they had acquired under Gowon. Many of those who lost their jobs or who resigned because of insecurity moved to the private sector and were in fact able to secure lucrative government contracts. In the decades that followed, the successful among them became fervent supporters of privatization of public businesses, so that they could acquire them.

The purge also affected the armed forces and police with the retirement of many senior officers; the judiciary (the Chief Justice was retired); the universities (four vice-chancellors were removed); and all government parastatals. Retirement or dismissal was always attributed to malpractice, inefficiency, poor health, declining productivity, or old age. It was a routine occurrence in 1975, creating panic in many quarters and applause from anti-elite members of the public. The reform destroyed the preeminent role of the civil servants in politics. However, the government was careful not to transfer the power to the politicians, but to professionals and academics who were appointed as ministers and expert members of various specialized commissions. When it came to deciding on the constitution, veteran politicians were involved.

REFORMS OF GOVERNMENT STRUCTURE

A number of reforms were made to improve the federal system of government. These covered the creation of states, the streamlining of the pay structure of the state and federal civil service, changes to local government administration, and modifications to the revenue allocation formula. With regard to the civil service, the problem of rivalry for power between the professionals and the administrators for senior positions was solved by opening leadership to all cadres. Instead of a multiplicity of salary scales, an integrated structure was implemented all over the country, simplifying the budget and eliminating tension between federal and state bureaucracies.

A panel was established in August 1975 to consider the necessity of establishing new states. Five months later, seven new states were created, bringing the number to nineteen. Carved out of the existing states and given creative names and new governors, the new states provided opportunities for the creation of thousands of jobs and rapid promotion. The elite was happy, for it benefited considerably. Ethnic leaders, too, were satisfied, for the move created more openings for political appointments. A new federal capital, Abuja, was also established in the center of the country to be managed independently of any state government. As the states were not economically viable, they all depended on federal revenues. More states were created in the 1980s and 1990s, raising the issue of why the country continues to adopt this option of managing inter-governmental relations. As states proliferate, they become nothing more than large local governments, their revenues go more and more into salaries with little left to create industries or improve infrastructure, and the power of the center is further enhanced. In spite of these problems, agitation for more states has continued in the 1970s and beyond. The reasons are related to the need for development and the desire of members of the political class for access to power and money. As instruments of the center, the states collect money which is controlled by ethnic notables. For the ethnic notables and other elites to obtain more money, one strategy is to call for more states, to atomize what already exists. When an ethnic group splits itself into more states, the calculation is that a greater share of the "national cake" will accrue since the federal government uses a principle of equality as one of the formulae by which to share revenues. In addition, since the constitution stipulates that "federal character" should be reflected in the distribution of power, indigenes of each state will be able to secure positions as ministers, senior administrators, and diplomats, to mention only a few, and also demand that ethnic-cum-state considerations be applied to the award of contracts and the location of federal projects. Demands for new states are also fueled by the fact that every new state creation produces new (sub) ethnic minorities who in turn demand their own.

A major reform turned local government into a third tier of government, following the federal and the state. The aim was to take government closer to the people and extend democracy to the grassroots by having democratically elected leaders. The need to reform local government began in the 1960s. In the north, the Native Authorities were strong and controlled by traditional rulers, but there was a need to modernize them and promote popular participation. In the south, where no strong local governments existed, new ones had to be created. Reforms were introduced in the 1970s. In 1976 the military enacted the States Local Government Edicts which provided that the members of the local councils must be elected, the elected members would appoint a chairman, while decisions must be by majority vote. The hope was that these local institutions would become "the training ground for democracy."[3] Each council would also enjoy a financial allocation from the federal government. However, local government never fully evolved in the 1970s as an autonomous third tier of government, while a poor caliber of politicians controlled many of the local councils. In later years the local governments provided opportunities for aspiring politicians to start their careers. The more experienced, and already rich, secure politicians sponsored their followers in local government elections as an extension of their own power to the grassroots.

The regime also tried to tackle the politics of revenue allocations between the state and the federal levels, a contentious issue. It tried to seek the means to depoliticize the formula, although without success. The politicians and intelligentsia from the south had argued that the bulk of the revenues derived from their region flowed to the north, that northerners held on to power in order to dominate the revenue arrangement, and that secession might be necessary to solve the problem. All constitutional reforms have involved discussions on revenue sharing, with debates as to whether to emphasize the principles of derivation (where the money is made), even development, or national integration. Revenue sharing affects the ability to conduct an accurate census, as each area inflates its population figure in order to obtain more money. The country has yet to come up with an arrangement that will satisfy all the ethnic groups on the issues of the percentage of revenues to be retained by each tier of government and the criteria by which to share statutory and non-statutory revenues among the states. Revenue sharing formulae have been changed many times, and the reports of two specialized commissions have been rejected. As oil is derived from a minority area, there have been complaints that minority groups are being cheated by the larger ethnic groups. The federal military government has changed the system many times, simply because the state governors, usually junior in ranks to those at the center, cannot complain in public. In addition, the concentration of power at the center has given the federal government far more privileges, gradually making some federal agencies far more powerful and far richer than any state government. The Mohammed/Obasanjo regimes kept close to the guidelines issued by their predecessor in 1975:

(i) The 45 percent mining rents and royalties paid to the states of origin were reduced to 20 percent while the balance was credited to the distributable pool account;

(ii) The federal government retained 65 percent of import duties on all goods except motor spirit, diesel oil, tobacco, wine, potable spirit, and beer. The rest of these duties as well as the duties on motor spirit and tobacco were paid in full into the distributable pool account;

(iii) Fifty percent of the excise duties was paid into the distributable pool account while the rest was retained by the federal government;

(iv) The distributable pool account was distributed 50 percent on the basis of population and 50 per cent on equality of states;

(v) Personal income tax was standardized throughout the federation. In effect the state governments' power to change income tax rates was taken away from them.[4]

Two years later, a technical commission was appointed to recommend new proposals. The commission recommended a new sharing formula based on five principles: equality of access to development opportunities, national minimum standards for national integration, absorptive capacity, independent revenue and minimum tax effort, and fiscal efficiency. Each of these was carefully weighted so that each state would know what to expect well in advance. The military accepted the recommendations.

Since they came at a time when a new constitution was being fashioned, the military requested the Constituent Assembly to consider them, in the hope that they would become law. The politicians from the north were able to ensure the rejection of the recommendations, describing the plan as too technical.

The military regarded trade unions as chaotic and unnecessarily hostile to the government. In 1975 the Nigerian Labor Congress was formed, an amalgamation of four powerful trade unions. The military was threatened by what it saw as a strong radical movement. In December 1975 the government arrested hundreds of trade unionists and initiated a probe. Later, eleven union leaders were denied participation in future political activities, all existing unions were dissolved, workers in so-called essential services (oil and banking sectors) were banned from joining strikes, and new unions were restructured in a way that subordinated them to the government.

ECONOMY

Oil revenues declined because of an international glut and the fall of the dollar in 1978–1979. The government acquired a billion dollars in external debts but was still able to leave adequate reserves for the next administration. Defense continued to consume large sums of money, mainly as salaries, although the regime succeeded in reducing the size of the army by 50,000 men. Soaring food prices and widespread inflation plagued the administration. With respect to food shortage, a land use decree attempted to change the land tenure system by making it possible to acquire land for large-scale agriculture in the countryside and reducing land speculation in the cities. The land use decree was hard to implement as people continued to sell land even though it was officially rationalized. Research institutes were reorganized and strengthened, although with no major results during this period. With respect to inflation, the government pursued a frugal policy. Imports of expensive cloth and champagne were prohibited while the government abandoned the use of Mercedes cars. To conserve foreign exchange, food imports were reduced, further adding to domestic shortage and inflation, and trade restrictions affected other imports. Recurrent expenditure for higher education was cut, the enthusiasm for Universal Primary Education waned, and power supplies became erratic. Other highlights were the government's acquisition of 60 percent of the equity in two national newspapers, the *Daily Times* and *New Nigerian*, and the building of a second port in Lagos, thus ending the long line of ships waiting to berth. As the economic changes began to have deteriorating effects on living standards, the military was attacked in the media. A crisis occurred in April 1978 when secondary and university students took to widespread demonstrations and protests. They were energized by the need to respond to increases in tuition fees and living costs. The administration reacted angrily by closing down schools, proscribing the National Union of Nigerian Students, and dismissing some lecturers. By and large, the public was forgiving as the government was always the first to admit that there were problems, while the preparations for the Second Republic made the politicians less enthusiastic in attacking the military.

In keeping to the commitments of its predecessor, the government spent large sums of money on international projects that portrayed Nigeria as rich. It hosted FESTAC, a scout jamboree, and an international trade fair. In spite of these grandiose projects, the government showed an awareness, as reflected in the Third National Development Plan (1975–1980), that the country was poor. It promised to mobilize all citizens for full participation in the economy, buy technology from all parts of the world, assume greater control of oil production, processing and distribution, and pursue an indigenization program more vigorously. With respect to the latter, the government enacted a decree that forced a number of foreign businesses either to sell them to Nigerians or participate with Nigerians as joint ventures.

FOREIGN POLICY

This was the most radical moment in foreign policy, with Nigeria assuming a leadership role in anti-colonial and anti-apartheid struggles and in a regional economic union. With courage and vision, Nigeria was able to challenge the positions of the West in Angola and South Africa. It also demanded a new world economic order to reduce the control of the industrialized world over poor countries while it continued to strengthen its relations with other African countries. Nigeria regarded itself as a continental power—its stature at the United Nations was enhanced, world leaders and dignitaries visited the country, and it served as a mediator in all the African conflicts of the period.

In Angola, three movements struggled for power—the Popular Movement for the Liberation of Angola (MPLA), the National Front for the Liberation of Angola (FLNA), and the National Union for the Total Independence of Angola (UNITA). Originally, Nigeria opted for a government of national unity. However, when South Africa and the United States of America supported the FLNA-UNITA alliance in order to install a puppet government and exploit Angola's minerals, Nigeria saw the need to oppose this. Such an alliance would also undermine Angola's neighbors, Zambia and Botswana. In 1975 Nigeria announced that it would support the independence of Angola and the use of Cuban and Soviet forces by the MPLA, and would contribute resources to get rid of the invading force from South Africa. U.S. President Ford sought to discredit Nigeria by asking other countries not to follow its lead, warning that they must not support the MPLA as it would mean the spread of communism. The Nigerian government reacted in a way designed to humiliate Ford, canceling a scheduled visit by Henry Kissinger, the American Secretary of State, and taking over the U.S. Information building and radio monitoring units in Lagos and Kaduna. Nigeria asked the Organization of African Unity to recognize the MPLA as Angola's only government. It was bold in calling the United States a dangerous imperialist power, eager to collude with Europe to recreate the nineteenth-century partition of Africa "into spheres of influence where the predominant consideration will be the interests of the big powers without any consideration of the inalienable rights of the Africans."[5] Jimmy Carter and Olusegun Obasanjo were later to normalize the relations between their two countries, adding an arrangement to expand trade.

In 1976 Anglo-Nigerian relations also soured following allegations that Gowon was involved in the unsuccessful coup. An exile in Britain, Gowon refused to return home to defend himself while the British government also refused to extradite him. A decision to diversify Nigeria's reserves held in sterling hurt the British currency badly. Relations were, however, normalized in 1977. Nigeria did not move to the Eastern bloc as an alternative or in retaliation. The Soviet Union was disappointed that post-civil war Nigeria did not choose a socialist ideology or closer ties with them. Previous agreements on assistance to build an iron and steel mill were not kept, while Nigeria did not have a need for financial loans from the Soviet Union. Unlike the United States of America, the Soviet Union was self-sufficient in crude oil. Although Moscow wanted to open its schools to Nigerian youth, many did not find the opportunity attractive. Although relations were cool, they did not lead to any major conflict. Bilateral treaties were signed and a number of students went to the Soviet Union on scholarships. As if to indicate that Nigeria had nothing against the Socialist bloc, closer relations were promoted with Poland and Romania.

Nigerian-African relations acquired greater visibility and the country enjoyed respect abroad. Its stand on Angola received praise, its hosting of FESTAC brought international prestige, and it cooperated in ratifying the treaty that established ECOWAS. The government refused the call by radical citizens to annex the small neighboring country of Equatorial Guinea for maltreating Nigerian migrant workers. Instead, they were repatriated and resettled in paid employment or on farms. Liberation movements in Zimbabwe and South Africa received financial assistance, while Nigeria voiced its opposition to the increasing military and diplomatic interventions in Africa by the great powers. On many occasions, the country threatened to punish companies who had dealings with South Africa, and even to use its military resources to march on South Africa.

Nigeria acted as a continental power. Oil money enabled it to maintain ninety diplomatic missions, pay all its dues and special levies to international and regional organizations, assist other African countries in need, and support liberation movements. However, contrary to popular thinking, and in spite of brushes with the United States, it was unable to use oil money to confront Western powers for three reasons. To start with, without a diversified economy, oil as a weapon is severely constrained in view of the reliance on it for revenues, the importation of technology, and market volatility. A second reason is that the government was unable to control the multinational oil companies that had the power to subvert production and to divert crude oil even to such enemy countries as South Africa. Finally, Nigeria was not the only oil producer, and its Western importers could go elsewhere if relations degenerated into prolonged conflict.

TRANSITION TO THE SECOND REPUBLIC

In October 1975 a four-year five-stage transition program was announced: the appointment of a Constitution Drafting Committee, the creation of new states, elections into a Constituent Assembly, ratification of a draft constitution, and State and Federal Elections to be held in October 1979. The program was to restructure the federal government, allow new states to develop a satisfactory bureaucracy, and demilitarize. A forty-nine-member Constitution Drafting Committee was appointed on October 4, 1975, and submitted its report a year later. Its draft report called for an executive presidential system, with an elected president and vice-president with well-defined powers. The president would be expected to work with a cabinet drawn from different parts of the country. Nigeria would remain federal. With the ills of the First Republic in mind, the draft called for an arrangement that would decentralize power, promote consensus politics, eliminate bitter political rivalries and the winner-takes-all approach, and the formation of national political parties. A Constituent Assembly discussed the draft and submitted a constitution in August 1978 for ratification by the military. Meanwhile, a Federal Electoral Commission (FEDECO) was appointed to compile a list of voters, delimit electoral constituencies, register parties, and organize elections.

The sincerity of the army in its desire to disengage was reaffirmed in July 1978 when military governors and soldiers in the federal cabinet were reposted to the barracks and the constitution promulgated. The military established broad guidelines, warned that it would not allow politics similar to those of the First Republic, especially the resort to violence, and prevented those who had been found guilty of corrupt practices from participating in the political process. Members of the army were allowed to vote for any candidate or party of their choice, but must not join or form political parties. Officers interested in politics were asked to resign their commissions, while the new administrators in charge of states were also commanders of military units and resident in barracks. Traditional chiefs and religious leaders were requested to be non-partisan, while media executives were asked to maintain objectivity.

The ban on politics was lifted on September 21, 1978. In less than seven days, a number of political parties had emerged, showing that underground activities had been enthusiastically pursued. Indeed, politicians had formed long-standing "social associations" to discuss the strategies with which to acquire power. The first party to go public was the Unity Party of Nigeria (UPN), led by Obafemi Awolowo. It was by far the most orderly and efficient of the parties, with four cardinal principles: free education at all levels, free health facilities, full employment, and integrated rural development. Awolowo became the party's presidential candidate and Philip Umeadi from the East the vice presidential candidate. All attempts by the UPN to recruit major political candidates from the north failed. The second party to announce itself was the Nigerian People's Party, a coalition of three associations. At its first convention in November, there was a split, leading to two new parties: the Great Nigeria People's Party (GNPP) was led by a former minister, Waziri Ibrahim, also its presidential candidate and chief financier; the other retained the older name, with Nnamdi Azikiwe as leader. Both the NPP and GNPP promised to promote the unity and integration of the country as a secular state, promote equal opportunity, and work towards free education and full employment. The National Party of Nigeria (NPN) was the third. Although highly disorganized, it soon became the largest party, drawing most of the prominent politicians from the First Republic and the Gowon era. Next was the People's Redemption Party (PRP), the only party of the left, led by Aminu Kano.

New men in politics also attempted to establish political parties, forming in all over fifty small parties which ultimately failed to obtain official recognition from FEDECO. The UPN, GNPP, NPP, NPN and PRP fulfilled the requirements for registration, which stipulated that their membership must be open to all Nigerians, their headquarters must be located in the federal capital, their names, emblems, and mottoes must reflect national, rather than ethnic or parochial, orientation, and party branches must exist in two-thirds of the states. The emphasis was on the creation of a party that would be national, to avoid the parochialism and regionalism of the First Republic. Only national parties could canvass for votes, while ethnic, religious, and cultural groups were prohibited from contributing funds to the parties. Still, much of the new party system had similarities to the First Republic. As for the orientation of the registered parties, the UPN was the reincarnation of the Action Group, dominated by professionals and academics, led by Awolowo, and with a manifesto that regarded the provision of welfare and social programs as the primary objective of the government. The PRP was the most ideological, with a promise to create a "national economy" that would distribute resources equitably and benefit the common person. It attracted a number of academics and labor union activists. The GNPP did not promise a fundamental restructuring of society and was able to establish a stronghold in the north, especially among the petty bourgeois. The NPP tried to revive the NCNC under the leadership of Azikiwe. The NPN was the party of the political heavyweights from the north, like the old Nigerian National Alliance that controlled the federal government during the First Republic. Three veteran politicians emerged as key actors in the NPN: Shehu Shagari, a northerner, as the presidential candidate, Alex Ekwueme, an Igbo, as the vice presidential candidate, and A. M. A. Akinloye, a Yoruba, as party chairman. The party allocated offices to zones representing different parts of the country; for example, the north was to produce the president, the east the vice president, the west the party chairman, and the minority areas the leader of the senate. From its inception, the NPN was more preoccupied with the distribution of offices than the goals of government, although it announced that its aims would include the promotion of social justice and social welfare, equality of opportunity for all citizens, personal liberty and fundamental rights, supremacy of the will of the people democratically expressed, and unity of the country.

Contrary to the military's expectations, a set of politicians with new political philosophies did not emerge. The parties were dominated by established politicians of the First Republic. Personal credentials, rather than political ideologies, were important in organizing campaigns and recruiting new party members. Appeals to ethnic and religious cleavages were made as before, while the parties did not regard democracy as a means to liberate the poor. Since students, academics, and civil servants were prohibited from participating in politics unless they first resigned their appointments, the field was left open to the self-employed and the career politicians. The formation and running of party offices in various locations was made possible by men with money, who also saw power as an avenue to recoup their expenses. As the labor unions were excluded from participation, a source of ideological pressure, especially of the socialist tradition, was also removed. Both the process and the constitution ensured the entrenchment of the propertied political class. In spite of these shortcomings, by disengaging itself from power as promised, the Obasanjo regime restored the image of the military.

NOTES

1. Brigadier Murtala Mohammed, Broadcast to the Nation, July 30, 1975.

2. Brigadier Mohammed, Swearing-in ceremony for new governors, July 31, 1975.

3. Brigadier Shehu Yar 'Adua, Chief of Staff, Supreme Headquarters, Speech to the Commissioners of Local Government, November 21, 1978 (full text in *Daily Times*, November 23, 1978, p. 26).

4. Oyeleye Oyediran and Olatunji Olagunji, "The Military and the Politics of Revenue Allocation," in Oyeleye Oyediran, ed., *Nigerian Government and Politics under Military Rule, 1966–79* (London: Macmillan, 1979), p. 201.

5. Murtala Mohammed, Speech to the OAU Summit, *Daily Times*, February 21, 1976, p. 1.

11

The Second Republic, 1979–1983

Nigeria adopted an American-style presidential constitution, hoping that it would correct the lapses of the Westminster system of the First Republic. Ever since, the essentials of this presidential constitution have been retained with minor modifications in the 1980s and 1990s in preparation for a Third Republic. A strong president with real power was believed to be better suited to African conditions. Unlike the earlier system, the president and his deputy had to be elected by the people. To ensure that the majority of states and ethnic groups accepted the president, he must win a majority of votes spread across the entire country, not less than one-quarter of the votes in two-thirds of all the states in the country. The president was the chief executive and the commander-in-chief of the army. He would stay in office for a maximum of two terms, four years each, and enjoyed the power to appoint all ministers, the attorney general, members of many federal executive bodies, and the heads of the army and police. Restraints upon these wide powers were vested in the legislature.

The legislative body was a bicameral National Assembly, comprising a Senate and House of Representatives. With a life-span of four years, the Assembly had power over government spending, the investigation of the executive when abuses were reported, the removal of the president, and a bill which had to be assented to by the president to become a law. The third organ of the government was an independent judiciary, with its head appointed by the president, subject to confirmation by the Senate. The rights of the states vis-à-vis the center were spelt out to avoid the threat posed by regionalism during the First Republic, while their government was similar to that at the federal level. The functions of local governments were also clearly spelt out in such a way that state governments could not trample upon them.

Anticipating that politicians would abuse power, and in order to minimize a tendency to greed, the constitution stipulated a code of conduct that prohibited members of the executive and legislature from operating foreign accounts, usually an avenue to hide stolen money, earning two wage incomes from the public accounts, and running a private business, trade, or profession. Far more innovative was the inclusion of a section on "Fundamental Objectives and Directive Principles of State Policy," which identified the responsibility of the government in all domestic and foreign spheres, although these were "non-justiciable," meaning that the government could not be sued for non-performance. The constitution regarded the government as the major source of development with a mixed economy philosophy, thereby investing it with authority over resource allocation, with control of land and the power to subordinate individual rights to the collective.

In sum, the constitution solved some of the problems of the First Republic by creating a strong executive, minimizing the dangers of regionalism, and providing for the establishment of national parties. It was clear about how power was to be distributed among the various organs of government and about the relationship between the states and the federal government. What would ultimately doom the constitution was not its inadequacies, but the nature of competitive politics, the primary goal of turning politics into business, the limited power granted to the civil society to check their leaders, and the subversion of the democratic process by the political class.

Over a six-week period in 1979 five elections were conducted for the Federal House of Representatives, the Senate, the state assemblies, the governorships, and the presidency. The army and the police maintained order, a number of lapses in the conduct of elections were reported, and the turn-out was rather low. Of the 47.7 million registered voters, only 16.8 million voted in the presidential election. The NPN maintained a lead, with 37 percent of the seats in the House of Representatives, 36 percent in the State Assemblies and 38 percent in the Senate. The UPN followed with 25 percent of the seats in the House of Representatives, 25 percent in the state assemblies, and 30 percent in the Senate. The NPP won 17 percent of the seats in the three legislative bodies and the other two parties the remaining 10 percent. In the governorship race, the NPN won in seven states, the UPN in five, the NPP in three, the GNPP in two and the PRP in two. The presidential candidate, Alhaji Shehu Shagari, did not enjoy a convincing mandate, failing to satisfy the rule that he must win at least 25 percent of the votes cast in two-thirds of the states. He fulfilled this in only twelve states, but a last-minute interpretation by the judiciary supported by the military, which regarded two-thirds of nineteen states as 12.7 percent instead of 13 or 12⅔ percent, enabled him to be declared a winner. This was an acrimonious ending to a carefully managed transition program, but the public accepted the president and other elected officers, hoping that democracy would bring positive changes.

Although the parties had tried to be national through the appointments of their officers and leaders, and nationwide campaigns, the results revealed that ethnic rivalries and regional parochialism remained. Ethnic-bloc voting brought many politicians to power, as the parties were linked to their predecessors in the First Republic. Thus the UPN did well among the Yoruba and the NPP among the Igbo. The NPN claimed a national spread, but it was controlled by northern politicians who regarded it as the reincarnated NPC and successfully curbed the ambitions of southern politicians, notably Chief M. K. O. Abiola, the Yoruba multi-millionaire. However, the rules for winning the presidency ensured that a single ethnic bloc was not sufficient. Thus, Shagari was able to obtain significant votes in all the "minority states."

DOMESTIC ISSUES

The performance of the Second Republic was a dismal failure, although large amounts of funds were expended on agriculture, shelter, and education. The revision of the revenue allocation formula in 1982 gave more money to the states and allowed them to collect income tax and sales tax. Educational facilities were expanded partly to meet the requirement of Universal Primary Education (UPE). Started in 1976 this program led to the massive expansion of teacher-training schools to produce thousands of school teachers. In states controlled by the UPN, mainly in the west, hundreds of new primary and secondary schools were established. Elitism was shattered as the UPN governments gave

opportunities to the majority of the population. Higher education received a boost; a polytechnic was established in every state and seven
new universities were created in addition to an open university for distance learning. As is common in cases of rapid expansion, there would
be problems of shortage of finance, personnel, and materials, but parochial nationalism stressed the importance of establishing the schools
rather than their limitations. And without relating educational progress
to economic development, there was little or no thinking about the job
prospects of thousands of new graduates, a problem that the Second
Republic and later governments could not solve.

Similarly, there were efforts to expand social services, notably the expansion of five teaching hospitals, the completion of five new ones, the
upgrading of three more hospitals to teaching hospital status, and the
establishment of a national eye center. Rural health was marked by a
new infrastructure of 362 health care clinics. At a time when medical
personnel were migrating out of the country, and of food shortages and
scarcity of drugs, the impact of the expansion was more visible in the
buildings than in the improvements of the health of the populace.

A new crisis was posed to the nation by the pervasive role of religion
in politics. Beginning during the Shagari administration, religious violence became one of the most serious crises of the 1980s and beyond. A
large-scale riot broke out in 1980 in Kano and spread to a number of
major cities in the years up to 1985. Known as the Maitatsine riots, these
claimed thousands of lives in addition to extensive damage to property.
The federal government blamed foreign countries for instigating all this,
allegedly to derail its positive programs. When it set up a tribunal to
investigate the violence, there was no credible evidence to support the
accusation of external instigation. Rather, religious violence was a response to internal economic and political decay. Pressure had been building since the 1970s, in large part over the role of religion in politics.
Northern delegates to the Constituent Assembly had fought over the
inclusion of the Shari'a in the judicial system. During the election campaigns, the NPN manipulated religion as one of its strategies. Vigorous
attempts were made to obtain the support of religious leaders and emirs
and to use religious verses as political songs.

From the records of religious organizations, it was abundantly clear
that they rejected the corruption of political (and even religious) leaders.
They characterized the society as decadent and excessively materialistic.
Electoral malpractices and rivalries among the political parties convinced
reformist religious leaders that the secular state was not ideal for the

country. Some began to reject the constitution, calling instead for a theocratic state with moral leaders. Colonel Ghaddafi of Libya and the Ayatollah Khomeini of Iran provided alternative models of leadership, both widely believed to be strong, popular, honest, moral, and committed to their people.

The leading figure in the 1980 religious crisis was Muhammad Marwa, better known as the Maitatsine. Combining Islam with sorcery, he attracted to himself a large crowd of dedicated followers willing to die for their beliefs. Marwa offered a compelling alternative to the secular government and its modernization agenda. In his belief, a leader must be spiritual, and symbols of materialism, the West, and technology must be rejected. Among his followers were youths who had migrated to Kano from the surrounding villages, the urban poor, and a handful of foreigners from Niger, Chad, and Cameroon. The government encroached on religious matters by issuing regulations designed to control preachers. Marwa's example was to be replicated by others, although they were different in orientation and motivation. Worsening economic conditions pushed more and more people into radical Islamic organizations.

The relationship between Islamic and Christian organizations also entered a period of great tension. In October 1982 Muslim rioters set on fire eight prominent churches in Kano, marking the beginning of what would become a complicated national problem. A government tribunal attributed the violence to the growing influence of Christians in an Islamic city and the influence of radical literature from Iran, and recommended that caution must be exercised in locating churches among the Muslims. But this was an opportunity for the Christians to make wide-ranging complaints of discrimination in jobs, land allocation, and access to radio broadcasting, and the takeover of their schools. The incident marked the beginning of a long and bitter confrontation between Christians and Muslims that eventually led to fear of religious wars that would divide the country.

A major and long-standing source of Christian anger was the belief that Muslims were trying to turn the new capital of Abuja into an Islamic city. Very quickly mosques and an Id el Fitr praying ground appeared, a National Mosque was built close to the presidential mansion, and the designs for the city gate and some other places were Islamic. Using the Hausa language and wearing the Hausa garb and cap associated with the president became common as a way to attract notice, while some southern Christian politicians shamelessly converted to Islam for political advantage. In the contest for re-election in 1983, northern politicians demonstrated their commitment to hang on to power and to promote the cause of Islam.

The expectation was that the new government would inherit a sluggish economy, cope with a mounting balance of payment problems, and be forced to address the problems of inflation and declining agriculture. However, the republic was welcomed with good news: due to the crisis in the Persian Gulf, oil revenues increased in 1980 with the federal treasury acquiring a windfall of $22.4 billion. When prices stabilized, the income for 1983 was $10 billion. But then, a global recession and decline in oil revenues became the justification for taking external loans with commitments reaching close to $15 billion. Internal debts were even more reckless, with the states joining the federal government to acquire a staggering total of ₦10.2 billion.

With the ease of collecting oil revenues, the government failed to carry out in any tangible way any of its promises to diversify the economy, and, rather than solve inherited problems, it multiplied them. The government was largely concerned with creating opportunities for party members to secure contracts and import licenses. Food imports, especially of rice, and the building of Abuja, the new capital city, were avenues of making quick big money. The ambition was not to create an efficient state capitalism, as in Latin America or Asia, but to keep expanding expenditure to consume all revenues and even borrow more. Investments did not have to satisfy rigorous criteria of productivity or sustainability but only the rather crude concern of allowing the ethnic notables to display power and accumulate illegal wealth. More and more resources were devoted to consumption rather than investment opportunities. To address mounting budgetary deficits, the government had to meet short-term necessities. Budget deficits mounted, rising from ₦3,295.6 million in 1980 to ₦4,882.6 million in 1981, and ₦5,371.1 million in 1982. As these were financed by domestic and external loans, severe strains were imposed on the economy.

Other problems included smuggling, unemployment, inflation, and massive looting of the treasury. The manufacturing sector declined in addition to manifesting the negative characteristics of the previous era: dependence on imports, concentration of key industries in Lagos and a few other cities, and the production of a limited range of goods. Due to the scarcity of imported raw materials, many manufacturing enterprises were either put out of business or forced to produce at a minimum, leading to large-scale retrenchment of workers. Low productivity was reported in almost all economic sectors. Although the federal government made agriculture its number one concern, productivity did not increase due to the continuing problems of technological inadequacy, rural-urban migration, and diversion of government funds to private pockets. Smuggling was a problem as the country received inferior or fake goods, including drugs. Petroleum resources and scarce foods were also smuggled out of the country to the neighboring countries of the Republic of Benin and Togo where they attracted higher prices.

To buy public support and create avenues for personal enrichment, the government embarked upon massive food imports reaching a staggering ₦8.3 billion between 1979 and 1983. In addition, the importation of fertilizers reached its highest ever level, mobilization for internal production was weakened, and it became convenient to link food imports to foreign loans and dependence. Unlike the situation in the First Republic, the peasantry had lost its ability to exert pressure on the political leaders through such tested means as failure to pay tax and withdrawal of crops. In the Second Republic, wealth came from oil, not from agriculture, and those in charge of public expenditure ignored the rural majority, having no fear that they could retaliate, even through their votes.

As the economy plunged, the government blamed it on global recession, ignoring the plea to reform itself and reduce the scale of mismanagement. It failed to check its financial recklessness and resorted to borrowing. The loans were not invested in successful production of goods and services, while the government's economic policy, especially on agriculture, promoted capital flight and drained its foreign reserves. A Central Bank report for the year which ended on December 31, 1983, the last day of the Second Republic, presented a very gloomy picture:

> The Nigerian economy was in severe stagflation in 1983: there was a deep and general recession amidst a sharp increase in the general price level. The Gross Domestic Product fell by 4.4 percent, which is more than the 3.4 percent decline recorded in 1982. . . . The external sector was not spared from the general malaise. The recorded value of external trade (imports and exports) fell from ₦21.3 billion in 1982 to ₦17.3 billion in 1983; the external payments situation deteriorated further, leading to the largest accumulation of payment arrears ever recorded. The external payments situation was so bad that some of the trade debts had to be refinanced while negotiations were commenced with the International Monetary Fund (IMF) for a balance of payments support loan and the World Bank for a structural adjustment loan. . . . On the whole, the index

of agricultural production declined substantially by about 9.4 percent, compared to a rise of 2.7 percent in 1982, 3.4 percent in 1982, and 2.5 percent in 1980. Industrial output also plummeted, the index of industrial production declined by 11.8 percent. . . . As a consequence, there were serious unemployment, retrenchment of labour (including management staff), low productivity, acute shortages of consumer goods, intensification of inflationary pressures, and increased smuggling activities.[1]

EXTERNAL RELATIONS

The constitution specified the country's foreign policy objectives: to promote African unity; to achieve the total political, economic, social, and cultural liberation of Africa; to promote all other forms of international cooperation conducive to the consolidation of universal peace and mutual respect and friendship among all peoples and states; and to combat racial discrimination in all its manifestations. This was the policy vision of the late 1970s, based on the assumption that Nigeria had the resources to be a world power and the leader of the black race. By and large, the Shagari administration tried to consolidate the previous government's achievements in terms of ECOWAS and opposition to apartheid. While the regime promoted a philosophy of non-alignment, it identified more with Western interests, while relations with Eastern Europe were slow and cautious. The country supported movements to end European rule in Zimbabwe and Namibia and apartheid in South Africa by rhetoric, and monetary and material gifts. Nigeria consistently supported the demands of the Palestinians for an autonomous state and refused to restore diplomatic relations with Israel, in spite of the insistence of strong business relations.

Although the power of the presidency was weakened at home, Shagari identified with the radical demands of the 1980s for a New International Economic Order. As if Nigeria was the leader of the Third World nations, Shagari remarked in 1980 that: "we must refuse to subsidise the economies of the rich by continuing to sell cheaply our raw materials and labour to them (the industrialised nations) in return for their exorbitantly priced manufactured goods."[2] Nigeria called for a set of new rules to redistribute world income, promote trade in favor of developing countries, and help with their industrialization. The country hosted the O.A.U. summit which came up with an important document, the Lagos Plan of Action, with concrete plans on how to turn Africa around by the end of the twentieth century. The country was also active in OPEC, although it undermined the organization in 1983 when it reduced the price of its crude oil.

Relations with Western countries were normal, if not close to subservient, driven by Nigeria's desire for external investments and loans, by the need to be in the good books of the International Monetary Fund and the World Bank, which served to guarantee some loans, and by a misplaced optimism that the World Bank would assist in transforming the country's agriculture, again with special loans. The administration regarded the United States of America as its best ally, a relation cemented with the exchange of visitors, mutual discussion on African affairs, new joint ventures in agriculture, and vigorous attempts to woo investors from the United States of America. Relations with Britain were cordial, while France and Germany became the major suppliers of military hardware.

There were major problems. Although Nigeria wanted to be a regional power and promote ECOWAS, in January 1983 the government expelled all its so-called illegal alien residents, numbering over a million. This dented the country's image in the region, making it appear uncaring and callous to smaller countries with battered economies. Cameroon and Chad showed little respect for Nigeria, the former over border incidents and the latter over its civil war, which brought refugees to Nigeria. In general, the country's response was slow in external affairs, always behind that of articulate public opinion, and it was undermined by the alternative agenda of rival political parties. For instance, the UPN pressed for diplomatic relations with Israel and withdrawal from OPEC. Radical elements criticized Nigeria's role in the Chad civil war and in denying Ghadaffi the chairmanship of the OAU in 1982 as being in support of Western imperialism. In general, Nigeria opted for a cautious, less ambitious role in international diplomacy.

THE FALL OF THE SECOND REPUBLIC

The Second Republic was consumed by its own inadequacies, by the failure of the political actors even to work for their own survival. Politics achieved a bad name. A number of characteristics undermined both the constitution and the republic itself. All the major components of a democratic system were abused: the rule of law and the independent judiciary were set aside, especially in the conduct of elections; there was no fair competition; checks and balances between the organs of government were not allowed to work; many people were denied the opportunity to choose their leaders; and politics did not fulfill public goals. Agencies of government exhibited lawlessness, as if the country was under a dictatorship: the police violated human rights at random; thugs harassed and wounded political opponents; and senior police officers and some judges were coopted to assist in electoral malpractices. The politicians completely ignored the spirit and intention of the constitution to maintain a balance between competitive politics and consensus.

The primary goal of political parties was to acquire power so that their members would obtain privileges and fulfill their selfish desires. The behavior of politicians was so egregious that democracy received a negative connotation. The presidential constitution became cumbersome, expensive, and difficult to operate. The president could create his own cabinet, and this was done to such an extent that most party faithfuls demanded one office or another. Political excesses and abuse demeaned the constitution and accountability was set aside.

To the politicians what was important was how much money could be made from state coffers within a limited period, an attitude in line with the philosophy of prebendalism. This philosophy promoted and justified stealing, decadent leadership, and political immorality. Nowhere is prebendalism more visible than in the economy. To import, licenses were required. Political cronies, rather than genuine entrepreneurs, obtained these licenses, which they in turn sold to importers who added the license cost to the goods. Fake goods could be imported to meet approved government contracts for supplies. Hoarding of essential commodities such as rice and milk became common to create artificial scarcities that would then push up the price. The building of a new capital, schools, and hospitals rewarded party men who inflated contracts and provided shoddy work, if indeed they did any job at all. Those who awarded the contracts collected a cut. To finance political parties, a percentage of bribes from contracts and other deals went to party coffers, thus turning political parties into kleptocratic organizations.

The politician was a patron distributing largesse to a large army of dependents and followers. He used money to buy support, recruit loyalists, reward favorites, and punish opponents. He was expected to attract government projects to his area and show favor to people from his own town in contracts, employment, and admission to universities. For all the politicians to be rewarded, the government had to control virtually all the profitable sectors. Access to state power meant access to status and wealth; failure to win an election or to win and not be assigned to a profitable agency was synonymous to a colossal business failure. Also, to have supported a candidate who failed to win could lead to retaliation, as the farmers who were denied access to fertilizers for not voting for the NPN realized.

The NPN promoted itself as a patronage party, recruiting support by distributing rewards, jobs, and opportunities to its members. Policies became secondary to issues of distribution, and the party was unable to discipline its leading members. But as the network grew and resources contracted, the NPN began to lose support and witness internal struggles for power. Those already in positions of authority refused to relinquish them, even at a risk to their lives and security, while new members struggled to acquire power, even if this would bring down the entire political system.

The outcome was an intense social malaise. As the number of jobless increased, they became a menace in urban centers. They were recruited very easily as party thugs by politicians, or else they joined anti-government protests. Rural-urban migration brought youths into the cities. In the north, many joined the Maitatsine, as religious protest became a social movement to protest the degeneracy of secular institutions and attack corrupt politicians and military leaders. Smuggling, armed robbery, and drug trafficking grew as alternative occupations, especially in southern cities. Patriotism and national consciousness were eroded—to many people Nigeria was not worth defending, it should be exploited for self-promotion, and hard or honest work was unnecessary or ineffective. When the government embarked upon a so-called policy of "austerity measures" and called for an ethical revolution to improve declining morality, the public saw it as nothing but a joke, coming from the people grossly unqualified to provide moral and political leadership, and flaunting ill-gotten wealth.

Public institutions experienced rapid decay. In many states, the salaries of government workers, especially of teachers, went unpaid for over a year, causing not just a deterioration of morale but a justification for avoiding work altogether. Public buildings were not maintained and some prominent ones suffered from fire disasters. These the public attributed to arson by officials and politicians who wanted to destroy records of theft and contract deals. Medical personnel, university teachers, and others went on prolonged strikes to demand better pay and conditions of service. Hospitals became "consulting clinics, without drugs, water, and equipment."[3]

Issues of law, order, and security were important, as cases of violence,

armed robbery, abuse of human rights, police harassment, and legal un-
fairness were rife. The representatives of the government were first and
foremost lawbreakers. To those who acquired power through electoral
malpractice, they violated the constitution. For being unable to manage
the country very well, the government created an insecure and unstable
environment. As many expressed doubts as to the longevity or survival
of the republic, those with power saw corruption as the most urgent task.
Not knowing when the military would strike, the first assignment in
office was to steal as much money as possible. Behaving as predators,
they set negative moral standards for society. To protect themselves from
public wrath and violence, it was necessary to spend more and more on
the police as if citizens were criminals. Justice was rarely available to the
poor, the public lost confidence in the police and the judicial system, and
the rich used their money "to put themselves above the law."[4] Rather
than reform the conduct of public affairs, the government spent more
and more money on weapons for the police in order to protect the lives
and properties of public functionaries. For instance in 1980, the federal
government spent an additional ₦83 million to buy equipment for the
police, citing the incidence of armed robbery. Three years later, money
was also allocated to buy armored cars, but this failed to reduce the scale
of violence or robbery. So insecure did the political class become that
some among them began to wear bulletproof vests. Personal security
systems and fortified walls were also common features of the landscape.

As the first term of the civilian administration drew to a close, many
believed that the system could be reformed through the ballot box. This
was not to be. The electoral process was marred by violence, arson, mur-
der, looting, and massive corruption. In all the parties, the Primary Elections to select governors and other candidates led to bitter rivalries and
violence. Alliances among parties reflected the need to win and share
power, rather than to discuss policies and programs. When the UPN led
a major attempt to create the Progressive Parties Alliance, comprising
the UPN, NPP, and factions of the PRP and GNPP, they failed to agree
on a presidential candidate or a list of candidates to present for elections,
as virtually everybody was interested in power. The PRP, the party of
the left, was torn by wrangling, as some members wanted to join the
ruling NPN. FEDECO lost its credibility to organize a fair election, as it
brazenly conducted its business to favor the NPN. Through an unprecedented extent of electoral fraud, the NPN was returned to power in the
presidency, claiming that they had gained success in areas previously
controlled by other parties. The NPN chieftains were greedy, fraudu-

lently winning the governorship race in such areas as Oyo and Ondo states, the strongholds of the UPN. In the case of Ondo, the scale of violence was such that FEDECO had to arrange a so-called recounting just to save face. When Shagari began his second term in October 1983, the public, the media, and the opposition forces were united in concluding that he would not last. The election that brought him to power was neither free nor fair. Poverty, lawlessness, and widespread insecurity engulfed the country. On New Year's Eve, 1983, the military struck again, bringing to power Major General Muhammad Buhari, who promised to salvage the country.

NOTES

1. Central Bank of Nigeria, *Annual Report* (Lagos: CBN, 1989), p. 1.

2. President Shehu Shagari, Address to Nigerian Institute of International Affairs, mimeographed.

3. Coup announcement, Brigadier Abacha, December 31, 1983, *Sunday Concord*, January 1, 1984.

4. Comment by Alhaji Isa Keita, Chairman of the Code of Conduct Bureau, *New Nigerian*, November 22, 1983.

12

The Military, Economy, and Politics, 1983–1993

Following the fall of the Second Republic, the country again returned to a prolonged period of military rule, widely regarded as the worst phase in its modern history. Unlike the "sober" generals of the earlier decades, the new ones were far more authoritarian: they carelessly discarded the principle of accountability, failed woefully to tackle the problems of corruption, and very readily resorted to the use of force to silence any opposition to their power. In this chapter, we will focus on the two regimes of Muhammad Buhari (1983–1985) and Ibrahim Babangida (1985–1992). Although different in style, they were both concerned with issues of economic reforms and stable politics. Both vacated office unwillingly, the first in a coup and the second in disgrace.

THE CONTEXT

The 1980s saw Nigeria in deep economic decline. The standard of living declined even further than before, external debts increased, and 1970s programs of development that had emphasized the provision of basic human needs were abandoned in favor of export-led strategies. It was also a period of conflict as poor people protested government policies.

Further, religious conflicts were on the rise in Nigeria, fueled by economic decay and political mismanagement.

Global politics were altered after the end of the Cold War in the late 1980s. In previous decades, Nigeria had conducted its foreign policy by negotiating with the super-powers, although it identified more with the West. The East, however, provided a growing number of Nigerian radicals and left-oriented scholars with the opportunity to keep calling for a socialist alternative. In the 1980s and beyond, the East lost its influence, the Soviet Union was no more, and Russia had no positive lessons to offer Africa. Where Marxist-oriented regimes emerged—Ethiopia, Guinea, and Mozambique—they failed, further causing disrepute to the socialist model. Liberal and right-wing ideologies gained dominance, with the Bretton Woods institutions (the World Bank and the International Monetary Fund) dictating the options to be pursued. In the 1990s, the concept of "good governance" was added to economic management for African countries seeking foreign assistance. It was hoped that governments would reform themselves by becoming more responsive to public needs, promoting democracy, and avoiding military rule. In line with domestic and international demands Nigeria promised a transition to civil rule which it failed to fulfill. Autocracy and development can go together, as General Abacha confidently asserted in 1995.[1]

There was a democratic wave in Africa marked by protest movements in different countries, the radicalization of civil society, and a few cases of successful elections and democratic changes. Nigerians also demanded civilian rule and the expansion of democratic space. Hundreds lost their lives in the process, but the military tenaciously clung to power.

THE BUHARI YEARS, 1983–1985

The Buhari regime was more concerned with the immediate political circumstances that brought it to power and less with the context that shaped the decade. Like Mohammed in the 1970s, the Buhari administration regarded itself as a corrective regime, promising to avoid "immorality and impropriety in our society."[2] The administration would, in its own words,

maintain national unity and stability, give the nation a better and more purposeful sense of direction, embark on prudent management of the available resources and diversification of the economy, achieve self-sufficiency in the production of the major staple food commodities and essential raw materials within a targeted period, encourage labour intensive projects with a view to creating more job opportunities, re-phrase development projects involving large foreign exchange commitments, clean the society of the canker-worm of pervasive corruption, maintain law and order and ensure the security of life and property, uphold the principle of public accountability and encourage the development of improved work ethics among Nigerian workers, and check the activities of hoard-ers, smugglers and all other social and economic saboteurs.[3]

Assuming that the politicians of the Second Republic were corrupt and that the people lacked discipline, the regime adopted draconian tactics which failed to win friends abroad. The Western media saw the coup as a subversion of democracy. Anglo-Nigerian relations were damaged over the case of a fugitive politician, Umaru Dikko, a key figure in the Second Republic accused of masterminding electoral fraud and theft. Eager to bring him to justice, the plan to forcefully abduct him was aborted by the British police. A diplomatic rift between Nigeria and Great Britain ensued.

On the domestic front, the administration was oriented towards de-cisiveness and promptness. In contrast with the slow process of decision-making that characterized the civilian administration, the Buhari regime moved fast on many issues, such as changing the colors of the currency (following mounting evidence of counterfeiting and currency traffick-ing), and abolishing the new local governments created by the civilians. In probing and punishing the civilian leaders of the Second Republic, there was a popular perception that many members of the NPN were spared, creating the impression of government bias against the other parties and even against southerners in general. Two decrees made the government widely unpopular. One eroded the power of the judiciary by subordinating it to military decrees: the decisions of military tribunals could not be challenged in a court of law. The other curtailed press free-dom. No institution remained available to serve as a check on the mili-tary.

Issues of accountability and "house-cleaning" were at the top of the government's agenda. The eradication of corruption would go hand in hand with "the development of improved work ethics." A decree em-powered the government to confiscate the illegal assets of political par-ties and political leaders. Public officers suspected of corruption in all the tiers of government were to be investigated and severely punished with long prison terms. A number of prominent politicians fell victim to this and were duly dispatched to prison. A code of conduct was published for all public officers, with instructions that they should close some of their bank accounts and declare their assets.

As if the members of the public were guilty of the failure of the Second Republic, a crusade was launched to reform them in the War Against Indiscipline (WAI), the most prominent of all the "ethical campaigns" since the 1970s. The objectives were "to instill in the minds of our people and gear them up to a sense of nationhood, patriotism and, above all, discipline."[4] Now the only program for which Buhari is remembered is the "war" which forced people to stay in line for their turn, to report to work at the right time, and to clean their neighborhoods. Ridiculous as it may seem, WAI was for some time an inspiring subject to many people who indeed believed that Nigeria's problems arose from confusion and chaos. The impact was short-lived, destroyed by bad leadership and the craze for quick money. Enforcing public discipline could not produce patriotism or instill a feeling of national pride; the regime wrongly equated people's silence with willing cooperation in the "war."

The regime was not innovative in its economic policy, simply repackaging that of its predecessors. It failed to reduce the high cost of food, create new jobs, or escape reliance on oil. Shortages of raw materials crippled local industries. The government believed that so-called saboteurs such as smugglers, counterfeiters, and exporters of foodstuffs were to blame for the economic woes, and therefore enacted severe measures, including capital punishment, for offenders. Strict control was imposed on foreign currency exchange in and out of the country in a way that denied scope to legitimate entrepreneurs. Wastage and large deficits were eliminated from the budgets, contracts were re-evaluated to scale down costs, public expenditure was curtailed, and the government payroll was reduced. Dependence on imports was reduced with respect to consumer items.

Although mismanagement was reduced, the economic recession remained. Foreign reserves were low and repayment of interests on external debts consumed resources. The failure of agriculture created opportunities for local merchants to grow wealthy from food and fertilizer imports. Industries—excluding the oil sector—relied on imports and contributed little overall. Debt service mounted and attempts to engage in countertrade deals with European countries and Brazil failed. Armed robbery was endemic, becoming a barometer of the state of internal insecurity and the hopelessness of many.

The iron-fist methods of the administration provoked public antagonism. As the administration remained close to many previous leading civil servants and traditional rulers who had collaborated with the NPN, the public had doubts about the quality of leadership being offered; as the probes antagonized many politicians, the regime acquired powerful enemies who schemed for its destruction; as the administration was dominated by northerners, southern politicians cried of injustice; and as its measures failed to alleviate suffering and create jobs, it lost the support of the civil society. Without providing any indication as to its duration, or offering a program of transition, the Buhari administration failed to create a useful diversion for the politicians or use the possibility of a future new government to appease the public. The regime also failed to pacify the anger of a cabal of senior military officers who wanted to push an alternative policy agenda in order to benefit from power themselves. Capitalizing on all this, Major General Babangida staged a palace coup on August 27, 1985. Nigeria moved from the frying pan to the fire.

THE BABANGIDA YEARS: STRUCTURAL ADJUSTMENT PROGRAM

An astute but misguided officer, Babangida fell "from grace to grass," as Nigerians would say. If Buhari was straightforward and sincere, Babangida was an evil genius—affable and cunning, he was a master of double-speak, deceit, and ambiguity. The regime was dominated by two issues: an economic policy of structural adjustment, and the politics of transition to a civilian government.

As before, the Nigerian economy was still dependent on oil. Growth rates could no longer be sustained, the GNP declined, and external debts increased. It was difficult to embark upon new projects. Recurrent overhead costs (to run the infrastructure, thirty universities, and a large public service) were high. Adequate maintenance of existing utilities and buildings was ignored while such negative economic practices as external debt acquisition, budget financing, and reduced expenditure became the norm, all at a time of high unemployment and unprecedented corruption. Access to oil revenues also complicated politics, being one of the reasons why a corrupt military regime failed to relinquish power. More reserves were discovered; in 1992 proven reserves were as high as 17.9 billion barrels, rising again to 20 billion four years later, enough to be exploited until the mid-twenty-first century. Both established and new companies invested huge sums of money in looking for additional reserves.

The option that the Babangida regime adopted to deal with the economic crisis was the Structural Adjustment Program (SAP), launched in June 1988. This started as a tricky policy of declining to accept the IMF demands—thereby appealing to the anti-imperialist patriotic feelings expressed by Nigerians—and, at the same time putting the IMF policies into practice, but without the advantages of the loan. A policy of economic liberalism compelled the state to redefine its role in managing the economy. The government was required to privatize many of its companies, which were regarded as impediments to economic growth. From being a leading participant, it should become more of a "supervisor," providing the guidelines to enable a market economy to thrive. The five major objectives of SAP were: (i) to restructure and diversify the productive base of the economy in order to reduce dependence on the oil sector and on imports; (ii) to achieve fiscal balance of payments viability, that is to say, reduction and, possibly total elimination of budget deficits; (iii) to lessen the dominance of unproductive investments in the public sector and improve the sector's efficiency, as well as intensify the growth potential of the private sector; (iv) to lay the grounds for sustainable noninflationary or minimally inflationary growth; and (v) to reduce the strangulating regime of administrative controls in the economic sector. As outlined by the government, the strategies of implementation included: (i) the establishment of a realistic external value for the Naira through the operation of a Foreign Exchange Market (FEM); (ii) the adoption of measures to stimulate domestic agricultural and industrial production, including non-oil exports; (iii) the rationalization of tariffs to grant protection to local industries and, thereby, facilitate industrial growth and diversification; (iv) investment in the direction of improved trade and payments liberalization; and (v) relaxation of administrative controls combined with a greater reliance on market forces for purposes of resource allocation.

Since independence, SAP has been the most far-reaching attempt to reform the economy, blending World Bank and IMF ideas with those of the government. It was to lead to a disaster of unimaginable proportions for the economy, enormous suffering to the people, widespread protests, and state violence. While relations with external creditors improved, SAP weakened the country's foreign policy, added to its external debts, and ensured capital flight. Each year the government touted the gains of SAP and promised the public that the end of their pain was in sight. Listing the advantages of SAP, the government would mention the local sourcing of industrial inputs (for example, breweries used local corn instead of imported wheat), the curtailment of rural-urban migration as people remained in the countryside to grow crops for industries, the emergence of many new enterprises, and the interest in the cultivation of cocoa and rubber for exports, reducing reliance on oil. In addition, the privatization of government enterprises and better use of foreign exchange were also mentioned.

These policies failed entirely to correct the county's massive economic ills. Two years after implementation the government began to waver, and by 1991, only its most ardent supporters still found merit in the program. Eventually, the economic reform collapsed, although the government refused to admit it. SAP caused the devaluation of the Naira. For a currency that had been strong for years, devaluation was a great economic shock. It generated a great decline in the standard of living as the cost of food, housing, transportation, and other necessities increased to an unbearable level. Devaluation increased the cost of all imported items, with the result that cars, spare parts, machines, and other items became unaffordable to the middle class. When the government increased the cost of petroleum products, the rate of inflation multiplied ten-fold, creating untold hardship. The decline in living standards devastated both the poor and the middle class. Local industries suffered from limited access to foreign currency while debt added to the country's dependence. Professionals left the country in thousands, migrating to the West and elsewhere, with the result that shortages of personnel in all leading occupations became acute. Anti-SAP protests degenerated into riots, leading to long closures of institutions of higher learning.

To meet the demands of external creditors and the domestic pressure for better living standards, the government resorted to a variety of strategies which included political manipulation, elite patronage, and coercion. In the process, Babangida and his regime lost credibility and respect.

Domestic and external debts mounted. Two years into SAP, external debts increased from $15 billion to $23.45 billion. A high proportion of revenue went into debt servicing, and the government had to set aside not less than $2.3 billion annually for debt repayment. By 1988 servicing the public debt had reached $7 billion per year, equivalent to half the estimated government revenue. Public expenditure in education, health, and housing was severely cut to accommodate debt servicing. A policy of privatization enabled those connected with power to buy previously state-run enterprises, thereby diverting more money to the wealthy and accentuating the problems of inequality.

While the government promised a fiscal policy that would eliminate wasteful consumption, most of its activities negated this. Babangida bought support with public money, bribing army officers and key civilians. Rather than maintain existing facilities and assets, the government preferred to establish new agencies to reward major allies and create an impression of progress. For instance, the WAI under Buhari became MAMSER (Movement for Mass Mobilization for Self Reliance and Economic Recovery) to create supposed "awareness" among the people and to encourage them to defend their rights. For the first time, an office of first lady was established with a budget to promote women's issues. Known as the Better Life Program for Rural Women, it was controlled by wives of the president and governors and dominated by urban women, providing an opportunity for fashion parades rather than gender empowerment. This was an era of flamboyant and ostentatious living, discrediting the government's program of austerity measures.

Like its predecessors, the Babangida administration also emphasized food production. A Directorate of Food, Roads, and Rural Infrastructure (DFRRI) was established in June 1986 to serve as a focus for food production and rural development in three core ways: (i) to mobilize the rural people for national development; (ii) to use available resources to develop rural areas; and (iii) to improve the quality of life and standard of living of rural dwellers. Budgets were allocated for rural roads, food production, the creation of community banks, simple technologies, and the use of local materials to build more houses. Unfortunately resources flowed more to the cities than to villages and control was exercised by urban-based technocrats.

By 1993 when the regime ended, the results of SAP were a currency that had been badly devalued and weakened, the closure of many factories, a high rate of unemployment, a widening of the gap between rich and poor, inflation, a fall in living standards, a decline in all educational and social institutions, and increased corruption.

The Babangida years saw a rise in drug trafficking. Nigeria does not produce narcotics, but it is infamous as a transit trading post for Southeast Asian heroin heading for Europe and the United States. Trafficking organizations emerged, some with connections to leading government officials, although the cartels cannot be compared in efficiency or volume to those of Asia or Colombia. A 1989 INTERPOL report put Nigeria third in the world in drug seizures from its nationals abroad. Its international image has been tarnished, as its citizens, usually innocent travelers, are subject to humiliating searches in international airports. The National Drug Law Enforcement Agency has been tainted by charges of collusion with major drug barons and of selling confiscated drugs.

PROLONGED TENSION: RELIGIOUS RIOTS AND PROTEST

Thousands of people lost their lives, buildings and properties were destroyed, and the country was pushed to the brink of a religious war between Muslims and Christians. The diversity of the country was both a source of problems and an opportunity for manipulation by the political leaders. The failure of SAP further fueled discontent and the search for alternative means to social and political survival. Millions of people were driven to religion, as both Islam and Christianity accelerated their conversion process, drawing from angry, poor, frustrated people. A new trend of fundamentalism emerged, as radical organizations preached against military rule and secularization. Among the Christians, fundamentalism took the form of evangelism that could be reactionary and conservative in form. Among the Muslims, the influence of the West, materialism, and secular governments was severely attacked. Discontent with the military led to the resurgence of the idea of the Mahdi, the coming Messiah who would save the country and reform Islam. The Shi'ites were also growing in number, led by Sheikh Ibrahim El-Zakzaky, a courageous preacher who demanded the creation of an Islamic Republic of Nigeria. The Shi'ites also engaged in clashes in diverse places such as Katsina, Maiduguri, Kano, Bauchi, Zaria, and Kaduna. Generally against the government, the demands were for a theocratic state governed by just and God-fearing leaders.

There were also mainstream religious organizations with leaders who had access to the media and to government. Among the Muslims, the Supreme Council for Islamic Affairs and the Jama'atu Nasril Islam (JNI) defended the interests of Islam and made demands of a political nature, such as replacing Sunday with Friday as a holiday and removing the symbols of the Judeo-Christian tradition in schools and courts. Among the Christians, the Christian Association of Nigeria (CAN) was the most prominent defender of Christians, calling for the government to distance itself from Islam. These organizations began to resemble political parties; not only did they make important demands, they also mobilized their members, sometimes for protest. Military rule succeeded in turning religion into a platform from which to organize politics. While the politicians were afraid of being excluded from power or being put in detention, religious leaders were relatively free of harassment.

In 1985 the Babangida administration registered Nigeria as a member of the Organization of Islamic Conference (OIC). The OIC unites Islamic countries in political and economic issues. Member nations must commit funds to the OIC and can also take loans from it. Previous Nigerian leaders had rejected such a move but Babangida clandestinely pushed the country into the organization. A period of prolonged tension followed as Christians interpreted the move to turn the country into an Islamic state. In later years, Christians and Muslims engaged in major clashes in a number of cities, Bauchi, Kano, Kaduna, and Zangon-Kataf, all with severe damages to places of worship and the deaths of many people.

TRANSITION TO THE THIRD REPUBLIC

The attempts at military disengagement under Babangida were costly, fraudulent, unpredictable, and ultimately a failure. While the general was trusted in the beginning, it soon became clear that he had no intention of relinquishing power, as he constantly changed the rules of the game and rigidly controlled the process to meet his own personal desires. Originally promising to leave in 1990, he changed the date to 1992 and again to 1993. The personal ambition of the general, his lieutenants who benefited from military rule, the desire to keep controlling oil revenues and allocation of licenses to lift oil all ensured that the transition would not be peaceful. Critics of the transition program became enemies of the government, while there was a press clampdown in 1993 when events gave indications of a possible civil war.

The transition program by the government assumed that the military was wise and charitable enough to yield power to reformed politicians. In a clever populist strategy, Babangida began in 1986 by calling for a national debate on the political future of the country. To monitor these debates and present a consensus on the political model to the government, a Political Bureau was established. Every ethnic group and major interest group made its views known while the media was saturated with discussions on the constitution, political parties, and issues of political behavior. The report of the Bureau analyzed the ills of the Second Republic and recommended changes, many of which were ignored by the government.

Rather than allow the politicians to control the transition process, the military decided to dominate it and set all the rules. "Old-breed" politicians were banned from participation, and the government regulated the parties and established an electoral commission. A motley collection of new institutions was established to create the ethical and philosophical foundations of the transition. MAMSER would reform ethics and energize the populace, the Center for Democratic Studies would be a training ground for politicians, and the National Council for Inter-governmental Relations would resolve disputes among the various tiers of government. Many conferences were also sponsored and the leaders of all the various agencies were co-opted into the scheme by Babangida in his quest to perpetuate himself in power. Although they were expected to facilitate the transition, the agencies defended military rule, arguing against any hasty handing-over, and even projecting Babangida as the best leader for the country.

The incorporation of a corps d'élite into different government agencies coincided with a period of economic difficulty when college professors and other highly educated people found it difficult to maintain their lifestyles, drive expensive cars, and send their children to elite schools. Government patronage became the key to good living. Babangida was clever at manipulating the economic situation to his advantage as he also co-opted army officers, contractors, businessmen, and a number of politicians, using a strategy of generosity to buy their loyalty. At the same time, he used the military against the civilian leaders, either criticizing them for their ambition or exaggerating their mistakes to justify the prolongation of his rule.

When party formation was allowed, with stringent rules, the government was not satisfied with the thirteen freely formed parties. In a historic decision, the government itself created two political parties, one "a little to the right," the Social Democratic Party (SDP), and the other "a little to the left," the National Republican Party. The government invented manifestoes for them and paid for office buildings and party executives. The two parties refused to antagonize the military, keeping quiet on the failures of SAP and dictatorship. The military exercised the right to ban any politician from participation, compelling a number of articulate politicians either to go under or keep quiet. The executives of parties could be dissolved, court orders ignored, and the electoral commission manipulated.

Unlike his predecessor and his successor, Babangida received the support of Western countries until his last few months in office. After promising the public not to take foreign loans, he changed his mind, implemented IMF conditionalities, and pursued a foreign policy that emphasized the promotion of liberal democracy and laissez-faire economics. Babangida became the darling of foreign leaders and multinationals as the best example of the type of leader that they wanted for Africa— corrupt, but not crude in his authoritarian devices. The support of foreign leaders and multinationals undercut the efforts of pro-democracy organizations to build an international coalition against him. Indeed, the government launched a crusade against those they called radicals; naturally, they preferred conservative elements that would support the programs backed by international financial institutions.

In spite of all the obstacles, there was no shortage of political candidates who had ambition and the money to spend. Although still regarded as "new-breeds," those who had made their wealth in the 1970s were able to consolidate themselves in the 1980s. There were also the retired generals, with plenty of money made from connections to power. The retired generals established a number of businesses but without the acumen to run them and they realized that a role in government brought easier economic rewards. The ambitious ones joined the political parties where they used their money and connections to create a measure of control. They were joined by a large number of rich civilians obsessed with power. Some of the civilians were propped up by the army with generous contracts. Contrary to popular expectation, the new entrants did not espouse any new vision, neither did they eschew extravagant lifestyles and public displays of affluence. However, the old politicians were not easily beaten: they called the shots, pulled the strings, and bankrolled the parties. Major political associations were shaped according to the vision of the "old-breed" who, in addition, sponsored new men into offices and local government elections. Ruthless and Machiavellian, they used ethnicity and religion to manipulate the process.

Babangida was able to use government resources and coercion to undermine the political ambitions of many politicians and to emerge himself as the only credible leader. He overlooked the corruption of his governors and ministers, rewarded a large number of people with positions and money, courted the friendship of traditional leaders, and manipulated government newspapers such as the Daily Times and New Nigerian. He gave his blessings to an undemocratic organization, the Association for Better Nigeria (ABN), which embarked on a well-financed campaign of Babangida-Must-Stay-in-Power. He played off one party against the other, Muslims against Christians, and the north against the south. He exercised the right to ban and unban the participation of everybody in politics. This power enabled him to determine who could participate and when such participation was desirable. As no one knew when he would be banned and "unbanned," most erred on the side of caution. As a revised constitution stipulated, elections were held in local governments, state and national assemblies, and even to governorships, although the military retained control.

Presidential election on June 12, 1993, was the last and most difficult stage of the transition. Babangida had set up many safeguards to ensure that no one was actually victorious. Two candidates were given clearance to run, Chief M. K. O. Abiola from the south and Alhaji Bashir Tofa from the north. Babangida's thinking was that the election would not produce a winner because of the north-south divide and the fact that both candidates were Muslims. Abiola organized the better campaign and was able to overcome antagonism from the north and from Christians. A week before the election, there was no major obstacle to stop the process. But five days before the election, the ABN went to court to seek an injunction to stop it. Although the ABN was not a registered organization, it was public knowledge that it was being funded by Babangida and although the decree that established the National Electoral Commission allowed it to escape such frivolous suits, a pro-government judge ruled two days before the election that the "NEC is hereby restrained from conducting the presidential election."[5] In an illustration of the confusion of the time, a Lagos High Court judge ruled the next day that the election should proceed.

As it turned out, Abiola won 58 percent of the votes in the most peaceful, freest, and fairest election in the country's history. The mandate was also widespread with large amounts of votes even in non-Yoruba areas and a majority in his opponent's home town of Kano. The public was already fed up with the military and Abiola offered hope of improving economic conditions. Babangida's next scheme was to discredit the election, using the ABN, corrupt judges, and the electoral commission to prevent the inauguration of a new president. Before the electoral commission could announce Abiola's victory, Babangida annulled the election on June 23, thus throwing the country into a state of confusion that lasted five years. Pro-democracy movements were energized with violent protests in different parts of the country, most notably in the southwest. Hundreds of people began to migrate from host communities to their homelands.

The annulment of the election brought the country to the peak of a political crisis similar to that of the mid-1960s. Domestic political forces lost the ability to resolve the crisis. Abiola's ordeal became both a personal and a national tragedy. To the Yoruba and other southern groups, it appeared as a clear case of the ambition of a northern hegemony to control power and oil revenues in perpetuity. Indeed, a number of generals and notable northern politicians urged Babangida not to transfer power to Abiola. Thus, the factor of ethnic domination came into the open in bold relief. Representatives of the northern oligarchy presented Abiola as dangerous—rumors circulated that he would retire some officers, reverse Babangida's policies, and embark on a populist program. There is no evidence that Abiola would have done any of these. He was himself a beneficiary of the military government, making huge amounts of money in federal contracts. As to whether Abiola would have disgraced Babangida, this was unlikely as he had the greatest respect for him until they quarreled after the annulment. If one were to search for the difference that Abiola would have brought to the government, it is most unlikely to have been a challenge to the northern interest, but rather in better economic management. Abiola was brilliant in his investment strategies, a skill that would have been useful in political management, although there is no evidence to suggest that he would have initiated far-reaching revolutionary reforms.

Issues of personal ambition were important. Babangida never had a desire to leave power. As later events also showed, his key lieutenant, General Abacha, was also eager to succeed him. A man of limited intellectual ability, Abacha was nevertheless a master of intrigue who manipulated his way to power. In the eyes of Babangida and his lieutenants, therefore, Abiola's victory could bring not just a shift of power to the south, but also the loss of control over oil revenue distribution.

In the aftermath of the annulment and in spite of the escalating crisis, Babangida was still scheming to stay in power. He promised to reconstitute the Electoral Commission and hold another election with new conditions that presidential candidates must fulfill. To set off conflicts in the political parties, he unbanned all the "old-breeds," so that many more could enter into the arena of presidential politics. To discredit Abiola, he accused him of a conflict of interest since he was a contractor to the federal government which owed him money. Although the plot worked with ambitious politicians, it did not do so with the public, which took to violence, thus necessitating yet another strategy. After unsuccessfully trying to persuade Abiola, his friend of two decades, to publicly renounce his claim, Babangida resorted to the politics of divide and rule, using one party against the other and one ethnic group against the other. In the opinion of Babangida and his supporters, Abiola, as a Yoruba, was only interested in power to further the interest of his people. Political parties and the military were divided, falling prey to the politics of ethnic strife and to the inability of civilian politicians to unite in defense of democracy and the June 12 election. Babangida threatened to abolish the two parties and other democratic institutions unless they agreed to a new election or the setting-up of an interim government. Unable to maintain control over society, fearing a coup, and aware of escalating political tension, Babangida vacated office on August 26, 1993, after unceremoniously installing a friendly Interim National Government led by Chief Ernest Shonekan. General Babangida was not successful in improving the country's economy or politics and the troubles that he created were to consume Nigeria for a long time after his departure.

NOTES

1. General Sani Abacha, "This is how we do it in Nigeria," *The Economist*, July 22, 1995, p. 40.
2. Major General Muhammad Buhari, Maiden Address, January 1, 1984 (full text in *Daily Times*, January 2, 1984).
3. General Muhammad Buhari, *Daily Times*, January 7, 1984.
4. *The Guardian*, March 21, 1984.
5. *African Concord*, June 12, 1993, p. 12.

13

Predatory Rule, 1993–1998

The Interim National Government was a sham. It lacked legitimacy, credibility, and respect. The politicians who had invested heavily in the transition felt betrayed. Shonekan's grip on power was so weak that most segments of the population ridiculed him as a usurper, traitor, and lackey. Challenged in the courts by regular public demonstrations, the ING was embattled from beginning to end. An increase in the cost of gasoline led to anarchy in many cities. The beneficiary of the chaos was General Abacha, who overthrew the ING, abolished all the elected national and state assemblies, dismissed all the state executives, dissolved all the local government councils, and banned all political parties.

While Abacha used the need to preserve the country as his excuse, there is no doubt that he had nursed a presidential ambition for many years. He had nothing new to offer: he had been in government for decades, he was Babangida's right hand man, he had participated in the failed transition, and he was never known for making intelligent contributions to economic policies. A number of politicians, including Abiola, believed that Abacha would transfer power to them, while a few pro-democracy activists accepted his invitation to serve in government, thus weakening the opposition to his regime in the first critical year. Notable politicians were also drafted, thus revealing once again the opportunism that characterizes Nigerian politics. Abacha was to become the country's worst dictator yet and the most brazenly corrupt and cruel. Under his regime, Nigeria's foreign policy was in a shambles, the country became a pariah state, and living standards reached their lowest level during the twentieth century.

AN ERA OF DESPOTISM

The rise of Abacha to power changed the political terrain and brought the country to the verge of total collapse. While his predecessors had managed a comprador, patrimonial state in which the political class distributed largesse to its clients, Abacha moved much further to create a predatory government with a set of rules that privileged the despotism of one person, himself. As before, politics relied on a network of loyalty to the military rulers and of patron-client ties. Under Abacha, a state of permanent political instability discouraged foreign investments except in the oil sector and long-term investments in general. Smuggling of oil products to neighboring countries, currency trafficking, and speculative ventures were the most productive economic activities. As before, political leaders appropriated government money for private ends. However, the situation worsened under Abacha. The fear of instability and possible collapse of the government, coupled with the erratic changing of governors and ministers to compensate those close to the administration, created an atmosphere of "rush to steal," not steadily or even with caution, as no one was sure of when power would be lost, but rapidly and callously. Because of inflation and the weakness of the Naira, stealing small sums of money would have limited usefulness for someone aiming to build a mansion, ride the best car, entertain lavishly, or use charity to display prestige. Abacha was interested in billions, his loyalists in millions, all milking the nation in spite of declining revenues.

Far more than Babangida, Abacha concentrated power in himself, thus altering the long-established pattern of clientelist relations with many patrons ministering to different constituencies in a diffuse political arrangement. He had little regard for rule or protocol, failed to keep appointments, signed many important documents late at night, and appeared in public in dark glasses. He did not respect his ministers or convene regular cabinet meetings. He offered no vision, ideology, or program, and most of his speeches were about the coercive ability of the government rather than what the government would do for its people. He resorted to a reward system in which his core loyalists would get power and money, especially in the oil sector. However, in dealing with the majority of the population, he based his legitimacy on fear and successfully turned the government into a repressive machine. A Presidential Strike Force humiliated and destroyed opponents and critics. Intelligence operatives enjoyed unlimited opportunities to encroach upon human rights and monitor all the so-called enemies of Abacha. Rather than assuage the fears of labor unions, students, professional associations, and pro-democracy organizations, the Abacha government chose to repress them and subvert their activities. He did not wait for abortive coups before purging the army; instead he invented coups against himself and used them to fire or incarcerate officers and punish civilians perceived to constitute threats to his regime. A draconian decree, No. 22 of 1994, allowed Abacha's agents to detain anyone without reason and to deny them access to family members, lawyers, and the judicial process. The courts had no jurisdiction to entertain any case of wrongful detention, while the government did not need to release or charge the detainee.

The consequences of this despotism were grave. The army, police, and civil service were degraded to agencies in support of authoritarianism and repression. The role of the police was not to protect anyone but to kill and injure Nigerians who protested against the regime, while their spare time was used to collect bribes from motorists and petty offenders. In the army, officers were cowed into silence, and to further weaken them, foreign personnel were brought in for security and intelligence. The civil service had little to contribute to policy issues, and those civil servants with access to the public victimized them by demanding bribes for the smallest services. When political parties existed, none could criticize the regime, and the judiciary was equally subordinated. The articulate media was driven underground.

Ethnic problems were compounded. Abiola was kept in jail throughout Abacha's regime, a case of gross injustice to him personally and to the cause of democracy in Nigeria. To many southerners, it was also an example of northern domination. In maintaining his personal rule, Abacha had to exclude those he perceived as enemies, thereby resorting to some loyal northerners and his Lebanese friends for support. The members of the ethnic groups excluded from power complained of marginalization and called for secession.

The military was discredited both as an institution and as an agency of governance. Although the public knew that civilian politicians were corrupt, they were prepared to pursue the democratic option as the military offered no more hope or promise. Military leaders became so corrupt that there was no longer any need for contrast with civilians, except in the scale of theft and abuse of power.

The country lost prestige. It alienated the Commonwealth, the European Economic Community, and many Western countries. Although Abacha contributed to the restoration of civilian rule in Sierra Leone following a coup in 1997, this added little to his legitimacy since at the same time he was suppressing democratic forces at home.

The regime attracted enemies, both nationally and internationally. Issues of human rights and democracy merged to produce many anti-military, civil liberty, and pro-democracy organizations which were united by opposition to Abacha although divided by strategies and approaches. Many were urban-based, dominated by the elite, and lacking firm connections to the grassroots. While they were weakened by their failure to unite and the ambition of some of their organizers for prestige and attention, they constituted a powerful challenge to a repressive regime. It is in the light of a regime of dictatorship that its economic and political programs have to be analyzed.

ECONOMY AND SOCIETY

Dependence on oil reached a peak, accounting for over 90 percent of export earnings. The avenue for accumulation revolved primarily around oil, as other sectors had become devastated. Shell continued to maintain its dominance in production, and, with its profits in Nigeria, became one of the most profitable companies in the world in the mid-1990s. Although the country was politically unstable, oil companies kept investing in it because they realized huge profits. In 1995–1996 Shell spent over $1 billion to upgrade its equipment and infrastructure. Other companies such as ELF, AGIP, Chevron, Mobil, and Texaco also invested in their operating costs. Some also collaborated with the government in a project to conserve gas, instead of flaring it off. Known as the Liquid Natural Gas Project, it is an added source of revenue and energy, especially for domestic use in a country where the majority rely on firewood.

The decline in the economy and the failure of the military to overcome it further radicalized the civil society against both the state and the multinationals. In the minds of many, both the military and multinationals like Shell were one and the same, conspiring to destroy them. In the oil-rich areas, the breadbasket of the country, development has been slow and the standard of living low. Many of the locals recruited into the oil industry were in menial positions with a couple of hundred in security-related jobs. With their means of livelihood—farming and fishing—devastated by oil production, and their environment degraded by oil spillage and pollution, local communities became rebellious. In 1993 alone oil companies suffered damage to their equipment and production worth more than $200 million. Companies such as Shell bought weapons for the Nigerian police, again implicating them in a conspiracy with the state to undermine local communities. Forced by protests and fear of occasional stoppage to production, oil companies began to contribute to welfare in the surrounding areas and devote some money to development. Shell for instance instituted a scholarship and educational program costing over $21 million a year.

The event that most clearly publicized the atrocities both of the oil companies and of the Abacha regime was the execution of Ken Saro-Wiwa, a writer, and eight others on November 10, 1995. All representatives of the Ogoni, a community in the Delta where oil is produced, they had for years asked for just treatment of their people in the distribution of oil revenues and in preventing further environmental degradation brought about by pollution. Comprising half a million people, the Ogoni argued that their land (650 square kilometers) produced more than half the nation's oil, but with little to show for it. In October 1990 they established the Movement for the Survival of the Ogoni People (MOSOP) to fight for justice, autonomy, and protection from environmental crisis. A Bill of Rights, increasing activism, and the mobilization of the majority of the Ogoni for demonstrations in January 1993 provoked state-sponsored riots in the community and with false charges against MOSOP's leaders. In May 1994, when four Ogoni chiefs were killed by a mob of protesters, the government put the blame on MOSOP and arrested nine of their leaders, including Ken Saro-Wiwa. A special military tribunal found them guilty, and, against all domestic and international pressure, the Abacha regime executed all of them. This unleashed a chain of international protests, even from allies who bought the country's oil. Within the country, it provided yet another reason for building strong social movements against the regime. Ever since 1996 youths in the Niger Delta, notably the Ijo, have resorted to a permanent state of resistance, sometimes in a style similar to guerrilla warfare, to put across their point.

Nigerians entered their worst period of despair. The people lost confidence in their leaders, in politics, in the military, and in virtually all public institutions. The media and the public began to talk of a nation in ruin, one that would require decades to rebuild. Education at all levels virtually collapsed and those who could afford it moved their children to foreign lands. The majority of the population could not afford to eat three daily meals, buy medicine, build or repair their houses, send their children to fee-paying schools, or meet expected cultural obligations. The country was isolated, its infrastructure deteriorated, and the government was unable to check corruption, inequality, and lawlessness. Productivity fell to its lowest level as many workers showed little or no commitment and inflation denied the majority of the population a decent living standard.

While politics consumed the Abacha regime, it was not as if it was silent on the economic front. Early in 1994 the regime abandoned SAP in preference for an ad hoc form of management which produced steady economic disintegration. The official policy was state control of foreign exchange, finance, and trade. External debt servicing was in trouble, running into an annual $3 billion in arrears, in addition to the failure to meet commitments to joint ventures with multinational companies. In 1996 the government created a large commission, Vision 2010, to formulate a development plan for the country. As if an unstable political environment was not important, as if angry and hungry Nigerians did not deserve empowerment, and as if government officials had abandoned their corrupt attitude, Vision 2010 came up with a blueprint that would lift up Nigeria in just a few years. A cynical public rejected both the document and its spirit.

Abacha's vigorous attempt to establish personal rule further injured the economy. Abacha needed to control the economy to attain dictatorship. While technocrats and economists made suggestions, they were either ignored or accommodated within the framework of predatorship. Abacha created a new form of clientelism that subordinated all institutions and their finances to himself. He and his loyalists encroached upon the most lucrative sectors of the economy. Further down the ladder of power, the strategy was the same as theft was the sole aim of macroeconomic management.

POLITICS OF SELF-SUCCESSION

As if to appease the politicians, Abacha announced a new transition program in his maiden speech. He promised to enthrone a true and enduring democracy. He would organize a constitutional conference to allow representatives of all Nigerians to discuss their political future and recommend ways to live together and develop. But the plan was merely a design to consolidate himself in power. As if the previous constitution, political parties, and debates were useless, the country had to embark on another time-wasting venture for an ambitious General.

Not only did Abacha obstruct the transition concluded on June 12, he created new obstacles to a democratic takeover. While previous leaders had used delaying tactics to prolong their rule, Abacha crudely presented his own prolongation as a military disengagement. He initiated a democratic process that would lead to his own appointment as president, not through elections, but by public referendum. He did not plan to relinquish control of the army, he had no political party of his own, and he was not counting on popular opinion or mass support. He revealed his agenda in a slow, but repressive, manner. In the first year, he made it clear that he would not transfer power to Abiola and canceled the previous transition program. After consolidating his power, he dropped many of his cabinet ministers and in subsequent years casually appointed new governors and ministers.

The first step was to pretend that a transition was indeed possible. He did convene a National Constitutional Conference in 1994, which made minor changes to the previous constitution but was prevented from considering the exit of the military or the role of Abiola, now in detention, in politics. On October 1, 1996, the ban on politics was lifted, leading to the emergence of five recognized parties—the United Nigeria Congress Party, the Committee for National Consensus, the National Center Party of Nigeria, the Democratic Party of Nigeria, and the Grassroots Democratic Movement. Soon afterwards, all the parties realized that they must either stay close to the government or risk proscription. Parties with links to Abiola and the pro-democracy forces were refused registration. As with the Babangida transition program, an electoral commission was appointed and a timetable of elections was planned for a two-year period, 1996 to 1998, to elect local government councilors, governors, members of the national assembly, and the president. The process was never brought to any satisfactory conclusion. An anti-democracy decree stipulated that, irrespective of electoral victory, a candidate not acceptable to the military would be disqualified, while the activities of the electoral commission were closely supervised by Abacha himself.

The second step was for Abacha to be the sole source of determining who would participate in any democratic process. He reduced the democratic space by excluding radicals, pro-democracy organizations, and those perceived to be opposed to him. Using a concern for national peace and security as an excuse, he flooded the prisons with his political opponents. By discrediting the military and sponsoring parties without mass appeal, Abacha succeeded in blocking the democratic transition as people lost confidence in the process and in institutions and their leaders. In all the elections conducted during the period, attendance was so low as to embarrass even the government.

As part of controlling the process, Abacha either created chaos or benefited from unresolved issues. The country did not resolve the June 12 crisis and pro-democracy forces insisted that there would be no other elections until Abiola served his term. Abacha wanted to enshrine the principle of zoning into the constitution but without much public debate. Six important offices, president, vice-president, prime minister, deputy prime minister, senate president, and house speaker, would be rotated by different regions—northeast, northwest, middle belt, southwest, east-central, and southern minorities—with each having the opportunity to provide a president once in a thirty-year cycle.

Third, he created a siege mentality. To talk negatively of him or offer a criticism was to incur the wrath of his intelligence and police personnel who were scattered all over the country. He unleashed a reign of terror. Within the army, he created distrust among officers. On two occasions, he made accusations of coups against the government; one he made up and the second he engineered. This enabled him to imprison vocal critics, including Olusegun Obasanjo, a former head of state, and Yar Adua, Obasanjo's deputy, who died in jail. Even Abacha's second in command was incarcerated in December 1997. He descended on opposition forces, jailed or silenced critics, and sent many into exile. The judiciary lost its power as judges took orders from the government on major political cases.

Fourth, Abacha tried to coerce the civil society into silence. Knowing that many were hungry, he imported cheap milk and rice named after him for mass distribution and television sets that bore his name; he even had textiles printed with his photograph. A "support Abacha" button was distributed to civil servants and even army officers, many being forced to wear them. To demonstrate that lack of cooperation would be punished, people were threatened with bombs, some disappeared, and an atmosphere of fear was created. Trade union movements were weakened and the government replaced their leaders with sole administrators who prevented anti-Abacha rallies. As protests failed to cow Abacha, many resigned themselves to fate, praying to God for intervention. Since the hands of Abacha were not long enough to reach outside Nigeria, the opposition became more vocal in the West with protest meetings, anti-Abacha literature, and even a clandestine radio station.

Finally, through the use of force and bribery, all five political parties nominated Abacha as their presidential candidate, although he was not a member of any party. Realizing his unpopularity, he wanted no general election and indeed plans were put in place simply to legitimize him as president. Manipulating the politicians was not difficult as the majority of them were mercenaries in search of money which Abacha was willing to give. Abacha and his predecessors understood the opportunities offered by the state to the political class. Where politics takes the form of a zero-sum competition, to be an outsider brings no reward. For politicians, as a class that is rarely engaged in productive economic enterprises, the offer of involvement in the state is always the best and exclusion from the state must be avoided at all costs. Even if Abacha was arbitrary and erratic, insulting and crude, the political class intent on gaining power could not unite to challenge him. Instead, they would cooperate with him to destroy one of their own in order to reduce the number of competitors.

Opposition forces at home and abroad challenged the Abacha regime. Many were united by a commitment to the June 12 elections, calling for the release of Abiola, a government of national unity, and new election. Among the better known organizations was the National Democratic Coalition (NADECO), a strange gathering of political opportunists and committed democrats, members of the old political parties, minority rights groups, and human rights elements. Another was the Campaign for Democracy, comprising labor leaders, human rights activists, and student organizations. Both demanded a government headed by Abiola and an end to military rule. A series of strikes, violent protests, and demonstrations were organized, especially in 1993 and the annual celebrations of the June 12 election. On a number of occasions, opposition forces were able to detonate bombs in some cities. While a number of opposition groups attained credibility, their activities neither brought down the government nor reduced Abacha's oppressive behavior. Abacha played the old game of buying support, his government presented demands for democracy as an ethnic ploy by the Yoruba seeking to put Abiola in power, and he reached out to the ambitious political notables in other ethnic groups with money and contracts to silence them.

There is always a disconnection between the political class and the civil society. When the poor take to protest, ethnic and political leaders carefully wait to reap the benefits that change will bring. While students and others were protesting the Abacha regime, many losing their lives, members of the political class pursued the alternative of collaboration with the regime, thereby weakening the opposition.

With all the plans in place for self-succession and the repressive agencies of government boasting of their successes at creating a climate of fear, there followed an anti-climax: in the early hours of June 8, 1998, Abacha died in mysterious circumstances. In part ashamed of the circumstances surrounding his death, in part ready to compete for power, the senior military officers rushed to bury him, expelled his loyalists from Aso Rock—the presidential palace—and installed General Abdulsalami Abubakar in power. The public had the last laugh, as many Nigerians openly celebrated Abacha's death, unusual in a culture that forgives the dead.

14

Crisis Management and the Transition to Democracy

General Abubakar presented the image of a temporary caretaker, not bent on major reforms or on initiating fundamental economic and political changes. His government's oft-repeated goal was to prepare the country for a credible civilian government. Because the military was distrusted, doubts were expressed by the public about the integrity of Abubakar himself, in spite of his self-effacing demeanor and reputation for avoiding politics and conflicts. His first speech on June 9, 1998, included a lavish encomium for Abacha—praised for his "innovative leadership, transparent stewardship to the nation, honesty, resoluteness" and total commitment to the country. To those who had seen Abacha's death as an opportunity for change, the speech came as a great disappointment, and the declaration of a one-month mourning period was ignored. Abubakar had to face urgent issues, domestic and international, all geared towards improving the country's battered image, restoring confidence in its leaders and ending international isolation. He himself had no time to mourn!

Abubakar moved quickly to correct a growing perception that he was no different from Abacha by releasing many political prisoners and dropping charges against them, thereby placating a number of opposition forces. Rather than formally apologizing to them, however, he described the decision as a gesture of reconciliation and urged them to cooperate with his government. Meanwhile he rejected a demand either for a Truth and Reconciliation Committee to tackle long-standing grievances and abuses or the release of all political prisoners. He forged a consensus among senior military officers by convening meetings to discuss national issues before policies were announced. He also proclaimed that his regime would be short, with its terminal date fixed initially for October 1998 but later changed to May 29, 1999. The objectives of the government were to achieve "national self-correction and reconciliation." Human rights showed an improvement. No bad decrees were enacted, people were not killed or thrown into prison without just cause, and the government promised to abrogate a law allowing detention without trial. By and large, his administration did not stand in the way of press freedom, political associations, and trade and professional organizations, although many decrees were not eliminated.

However, it cannot be said that the Abubakar administration sincerely addressed all cases of human rights violations. A number of people convicted for instigating coups in 1990, 1995, and 1997 were not released; restrictive trade union laws were not lifted; the government was hostile to public protest; the complaints by the communities in the Niger Delta were not well addressed; and a number of decrees curtailing the power of the judiciary remained in effect. Conditions in the prisons were as bad as ever, raising important issues of human rights and humane treatment. In some states, notably in Lagos, the administrations were opposed to trade union demands. When a union leader demanded increased wages and threatened a strike in Lagos in October 1998, the state governor promptly dismissed him as if he was still in the Abacha era, but the workers went ahead with a strike, benefiting from a changed political climate. Elsewhere, workers threatened to embark on strikes if their wages were not increased.

In his initial months, Abubakar had to consolidate power by getting rid of Abacha's loyalists in the administration, security, and intelligence services, and minimizing their influence in the army. Abacha's Presidential Task Force was dismantled and its officers relocated or retired. A few officers who were very close to Abacha were also retired, notably General Jeremiah Useni, Abacha's personal friend and second-ranking soldier. Abacha's wife and children were kept under surveillance for some months. Politicians loyal to Abacha made public statements of apology to distance themselves from him in order to become part of a new transition. In areas consistently anti-Abacha, those who refused to make peace with the public suffered either public ridicule or even physical attack as in the case of a Yoruba businessman, Alhaji Arisekola Alao, who was chased out of the commencement ceremony at the University of Ibadan after students had destroyed all his cars. The federal cabinet was re-organized, Abacha's core loyalists were dropped from the federal cabinet, and a few new ones were appointed to reflect the so-called "national character." New state governors (now called administrators) were appointed. To curb the restlessness in the army, he appointed a few officers to important political offices, increased military wages across the board, and visited strategic locations to seek the cooperation of his officers.

In the days before Abiola's death, pressure mounted for his release. Pro-democracy groups and a number of national leaders wanted a role for him in the new government. It was clear that Abubakar wanted to release Abiola as long as he had the means to cripple Abiola's ability to constitute a focus of opposition. International pressure was brought to bear upon Abiola to relinquish his mandate. While there were conflicting reports, Abiola himself did not have the opportunity to present his side of the story. He was reported to have told visiting international diplomats that he was no longer interested in the presidency, but his allies denied this and pressured him to demand his mandate. His death in captivity, initially blamed on the government until an autopsy revealed otherwise, followed by widespread riots in many places, ended the political crisis and ensured that the Yoruba politicians had no choice but to support Abubakar's plan for disengagement. The manipulation of ethnicity for power intensified as most groups alleged marginalization, even exploitation by others. While senior members of the army were quiet, not all were convinced that they should relinquish power, primarily because of the lucrative economic gain from their position.

Abubakar also had to obtain public support. By promising to stay in power for only a few months, he was able to please the politicians who had been waiting for so long. By freeing many political detainees and promising to release Abiola (who eventually died while still in captivity), he gained local and international support. By holding consultations with various interest groups, he gave the impression of being a conciliator and an accessible leader. And by making public apperances in different parts of the country, he was able to explain his stand on many burning issues of the day.

CORRUPTION

Even though there was no large-scale investigation of public officers, discoveries revealed the extent of corruption in the Abacha regime, forcing the government to seek the recovery of more stolen loot to assuage public demand. A search of the homes of General Useni, Abacha's right-hand man, was rewarded with millions in local and international currencies along with many cars and trucks. Another search, in the home of the Governor of the Central Bank, produced a hidden store of millions in various foreign currencies, allegedly withdrawn on behalf of Abacha. The same governor had thirty-seven houses in prime locations and a fleet of cars, many of which had to be confiscated. Abacha's security chief was asked to account for over a billion dollars. Abacha's family returned a staggering amount of money, and other details surfaced of accounts in such far-flung places as Brazil, Egypt, and Lebanon of unspecified amounts put at close to $3 billion, all stolen in four years. A few foreign banks cooperated in returning some of the loot to the Nigerian government. Abacha's family and friends had obtained huge contracts in several government agencies, controlled the import of gasoline, and even converted to private use houses belonging to the federal government. This scale of corruption even surprised Abacha's colleagues who themselves had little or no claim to honesty. Some portion of the money was recovered but without prosecuting many of Abacha's associates for criminal activities.

The public was outraged by these discoveries, confirming what they already suspected. Pressure mounted to cast the net wider to include other officers and probe two previous regimes. Not wanting to implicate its allies, the administration was cautious and promised little. However, as more evidence of corruption came to light, it decided to ask ministers, governors, and some army officers to declare their assets. This was not a probe, as such a declaration did not require them to disclose the origins of their wealth or declare again their assets after leaving power. Foreign banks and governments were contacted to identify stolen funds, but only a few people were targeted. Ministers were warned not to see their offices as a license "to [a] goldmine where easy financial fortunes are to be made." As if to warn that he could not win the fight against corruption, Abubakar admitted that

the issue of corruption is not peculiar to Nigeria. There is corruption everywhere. We seem to be pointing fingers at government workers in this country that they are all corrupt. Fighting corruption is the business of Nigerians to make sure that we are sincere in our dealings. And when people go out to look for contracts, we in the civil society should avoid giving bribes. As a step to tackling this problem, we have decreed that contracts should be done by open bidding. . . . The issue of corruption is of serious concern. . . . [1]

The oil industry was corrupted in a variety of ways. Oil concessions and processing leases had been awarded to top junta officials or those with connections to them. As refined oil became scarce, close allies of military leaders became the chief importers from abroad. Those unable to benefit from prestigious deals took to bunkering—smuggling kerosene and petroleum to neighboring countries where they fetched higher prices. Abubakar's administration halted new contracts for oil concessions, but no system of corruption-free bidding was put in place. Abubakar scrapped the oil ministry to reduce corruption and conflicts with the NNPC. The oil ministry and the Central Bank were two problem areas. They were unable to account for $700 million a year in oil royalties, another $954 million was lost yearly in converting oil receipts to the Naira, and many special accounts existed to hide revenue.

Checking criminal behavior was a difficult task, especially with respect to drug trafficking and advance fee fraud, known locally as the "419," against foreigners. Violent crime and robbery continued and even extended to attacks on passenger airliners at the international airport in Lagos and on luxury buses on the highway. With guns available, some even supplied by the police and army, robbery was brutal and spared no regard for human life. Even the police publicly admitted that some of its men were corrupt and supported crime syndicates.[2] Postal theft was so widespread that many letters suspected of containing valuables were opened, tampered with, and dumped. The sale of fake medicine to unsuspecting buyers reached a frightening proportion. In a culture to "get rich quick," some people were willing to kill and gamble.

THE ECONOMY

Abubakar inherited an economy in disarray. Oil prices were falling because of an international glut, reducing federal revenues. The total money in circulation had increased from ₦4.062 billion in 1985 to ₦144 billion in 1997 due to excessive money printing. Prices of all commodities, whether imported or local, were prohibitive; industries lacked spare parts and raw materials; petroleum products were both scarce and expensive, pushing transportation costs to an unbearable level; the electricity supply was unreliable; telephone services were erratic; and the unemployment rate was high. Sustained economic activities were impossible in virtually all sectors owing to the scarcity of raw materials and disruptions of electricity and telephone services. Because of the contraction of manufacturing and agriculture, the income of the majority of the population fell to its lowest level in a century. Food shortages forced the government to resort to massive importation of rice, sugar, and wheat. Food and oil imports further complicated dependence on other countries and on external reserves to acquire basic necessities.

It was hoped that a normalized political atmosphere would attract foreign investors and increase public morality. Regarding his primary task as that of "political re-engineering" and accepting the Vision 2010 project of his predecessor, Abubakar demonstrated from the beginning that the economy would not occupy his prime attention. However, he promised a number of cosmetic changes: the appointment of Boards of Directors for many companies so that they could make decisions on many outstanding problems; and macro-economic measures to reduce inflation, increase domestic output, and stabilize interest rates. Top priority was the importation of petroleum resources, repairs to damaged local refineries, and the provision of fertilizers. The first shipment of gas liquid (propane) by Mobil to the United States of America began in 1998, bringing the expectation of additional revenues.

Attacks on oil companies and their facilities by community protests and workers' strikes continued, causing reductions in production and export. Indeed, belligerent youths and angry peasants in the Delta sought to cause damage to oil flow stations and equipment, attack oil workers, and scare away oil companies in order to call attention to their poverty and marginalization and to demand improved conditions, a greater role in national and local politics, and compensation for damages caused by spillage. The attacks were successful, thereby creating general lawlessness, temporary halts in production, and damage to public property. A government agency, the Oil Minerals Producing Development Commission, set up to alleviate suffering in these areas, was accused of fund mismanagement. In October 1998 the government appointed new board members for the agency in the hope that they would be active in promoting development and thereby minimizing attacks directed at oil companies. A few oil companies publicly called on the government to accelerate the pace of development in the oil-producing communities to prevent more conflicts, while they continued to spend on security to protect themselves. On October 17, 1998 an unprecedented disaster occurred at Jesse, near Warri, an impoverished farming and fishing community in an oil-producing region. Wanting to benefit from a burst delivery pipeline, hundreds of poor people, with small containers, went to scoop fuel they could sell by the roadside. An explosion and fire occurred, destroying the village and killing over seven hundred people. The incident revealed once more how poverty drove poor villagers to theft and protest, how nationalism and patriotism cannot be fostered when citizens are marginalized, how fuel scarcity created opportunity for small vendors to sell oil in any container, how the failure of health services added to the agony of the ill, and how the inefficiency and inadequacy of fire-fighters and the police failed to curb the fire and save lives. The incident added to a growing opposition against the government and multinational companies. Radical organizations among the oil-producing minorities regarded the incident as yet another case of insensitivity to their plight, while some even organized to attack government supporters among them and to vandalize pipelines. The federal government eventually admitted that the oil-producing areas had borne the brunt of environmental degradation and promised to find creative solutions to their problems.

In September the government announced a massive increase in wages for all federal workers, no doubt a popular decision in view of the high cost of living. The result of this and other public spending was that the value of the Naira was depressed while interest rates went down. To meet public expenditures at a time of reduced oil earnings, the government had to draw on foreign reserves. A set of macroeconomic policies was slowly implemented: notably, large-scale expansion of the scope of private operators to compete with public enterprises in transportation, media telecommunications, and energy; the involvement of external partners in a number of joint ventures in fertilizer production and in the oil industry; the allocation of more funds to maintain roads and public universities; and open contract tendering to minimize corruption. Combined with others, they all translated into a set of three economic goals: opening Nigerian borders to greater trade, reducing government spending, and privatizing state-run businesses.

Unlike the political arena, an economy responds more slowly to change. Under the Abubakar administration, the main features of the economy were still largely negative. The country was the thirteenth poorest nation in the world, a fact reflected in the abject poverty of the majority of its population, a GDP of less than $250 billion, a double-digit inflation rate, and an unceasing desire by its youth to migrate elsewhere. Manufacturing and industrial output declined to a twenty-year low. Expenditures continued to rise even when revenues were diminishing, and deficits were financed by borrowing from the Central Bank and drawing on external reserves. The 1998 budget revealed a huge deficit, a failure that may be attributed to increase in domestic public spending, the legacy of massive corruption under Abacha, and decline in prices of crude oil. Domestic inflation combined with downward pressure on the external worth of the Naira. There was no end to mismanagement, especially in the credit markets, while a number of banks were in distress. The level of external debt was still high—at over $30 billion. Off-budget spending continued to enable the executive to divert resources to dubious uses; lack of accountability and fiscal responsibility were the norms. The quality of education was in great decline. Hospitals lacked water supplies, drugs, and uninterrupted access to electricity. The rural areas became almost stagnant. Morale was low as many wage-earners in public enterprises listed for sale anticipated massive labor layoffs, while union leaders attacked the government for wanting to sell these public enterprises without determining the costs and long-term consequences on the economy and society. An anticipated hike in fuel prices created a feeling that the government was insensitive to poverty.

As most countries of the world entered a period of recession in the late 1990s, the strategy to recover has been to expand exports. Nigeria may become a target to dump all sorts of goods, irrespective of quality, and even of such basic ones as soap, cement, toothpaste, safety matches, and candles. However, unlike South Africa and Egypt in the same continent, Nigeria lacks the capacity to reject the goods and expand its own exports to increase external revenues because its manufacturing and industrial sector is degraded and there are too many corrupt officials who will benefit from imports and smuggling. In spite of all these problems, the country occupied the enviable position of being the sixth largest producer of oil.

INTERNATIONAL RELATIONS

Despite its huge population and oil revenues, Nigeria's voice in international politics was subdued. Abubakar's administration received a warm embrace from Western countries and the Commonwealth as ambassadors and diplomats hurried to Nigeria to coax him to embark upon a democratic transition. It was as if a long-awaited wind of change was blowing across Nigeria. Abacha's death provided the West with the opportunity to rebuild relations with Nigeria. Britain, the United States, and other countries called for a stable transition to democracy and a government that would restore and respect human rights. They called for the release of political prisoners and sent delegations to Abuja to discuss future political plans. The United Nations and the Commonwealth Secretariat made similar calls and their Secretary Generals rushed to Lagos to offer suggestions on a new beginning and the "process of reintegrating Nigeria into the international community."[3]

Abubakar traveled to South Africa in August 1998 to mend a sour relationship. Following the execution of Saro-Wiwa in 1995, South Africa had called for the Commonwealth to impose economic sanctions on Nigeria. Not only did Abubakar use the visit to assure the international community of his sincerity in moving the country toward democracy, he also announced a foreign policy agenda, one in which Nigeria and South Africa, as two leading torchbearers and powerful countries, would cooperate as "an axis of power to promote peace and stability on the continent."[4] He was disturbed by the growing perception that African countries were unable to govern themselves and called for a concerted effort to disprove this and the perceptions that the continent was always engaged in violence and warfare. Nelson Mandela also visited Nigeria, a great sign of reconciliation.

Relations within the West African region were also considered important, although long-standing conflicts remained: with Cameroon over the ownership of the mineral-rich Bakassi peninsula, with neighboring countries over smuggling of petroleum resources, and with Cape Verde over the ill-treatment of Nigerian migrant workers. Support for ECOWAS and its military arm, ECOMOG (the ECOWAS Monitoring Group) was high. Nigeria continued to maintain its forces in ECOMOG and participated in bringing about peace in Guinea Bissau. Abubakar visited a number of countries to discuss regional issues and offered continued military and financial support for ensuring peace in Sierra Leone and Guinea Bissau. Nigeria also promised to contribute to the training of the police force in the Democratic Republic of the Congo. In November 1998 Nigeria and Cameroon exchanged war prisoners captured in previous clashes over Bakassi, although the dispute was far from being settled.

In September 1998 Abubakar toured a number of Western countries and addressed the United Nations Assembly where he was warmly received. His mission was to end the country's isolation, restore its image, and attract foreign investments. In addition, he appealed to Nigerian exiles to return home and held meetings with pro-democracy organizations.

The results of the diplomatic efforts were mixed. On the positive side, the country was no longer internationally isolated. Some commercial linkages were revived; notably British Airways and South Africa Airways resumed their flights to Nigeria. British trade missions went to Nigeria to explore opportunities in energy, water, gas, and telecommunications. Sanctions imposed by the United States and the European Economic Community were lifted, the Commonwealth and European Union asked member nations to lift their diplomatic and sporting sanctions, Canada reopened its embassy in Lagos, Japan donated 120 water pumps to fight the problem of guinea worm in the states of Enugu and Ebonyi, India promised to aid in agricultural development, Pakistan showed interest in developing the sugar industry, and South Africa was enthusiastic in investing in telecommunications. The transition program to a democratic government also received international support with such countries as Britain, Spain, and the United States assuring cooperation and India providing training in legislative procedure. The World Bank, the IMF, and other international lending agencies resumed discussions with Nigeria on granting debt relief, in addition to offering suggestions on how to privatize various state enterprises.

On the negative side, respect was slow to follow and Nigeria could not champion the cause of other poor African nations. Continuing economic difficulties, global economic decline, greater attention to South Africa, and increasing consensus in Europe for greater interdependence were among some of the reasons for the failure to fulfill an ambitious foreign policy agenda. Nigeria would like Africa to have a rotating permanent seat in the United Nations Security Council and to be able to nominate a candidate. Domestic problems could hinder the fulfillment of such an ambition. Investments did not reach the expected levels because of the political climate and economic decline, while some countries refused to lift sanctions until the military left power or Nigeria checked drug trafficking. Nigerian travelers were still treated with suspicion in international airports as if they were necessarily drug dealers or carrying forged travel documents, while those seeking asylum were ill-treated. Still regarded as a debtor nation, efforts to seek cancellation and debt rescheduling were not warmly received. Eager to satisfy its various external creditors and also to attract foreign investments, the country pursued a less nationalistic agenda. Calculating multinational companies and smaller foreign firms seized on this weakness to explore those areas amenable to quick exploitation.

THE POLITICS OF TRANSITION

The primary domestic concern was not the damaged economy but rather how the military would exit power. Abacha's death was seen by many as another chance for the country to remake its history. The Abubakar regime accepted the nation's desire for democracy and acknowledged that previous efforts had been marred by the manipulation of political institutions, actors, and structures. Knowing full well that his predecessors had broken their promises, Abubakar used every opportunity to offer assurance that his announcement of democratic transition was sincere. Among the principal suggestions by the members of the media and political class were an extensive dialogue between the military leader and various ethnic groups, and the establishment of a government of national unity. The five political parties set up under Abacha wanted cosmetic changes only, while pro-democracy groups called for the total abolition of these parties. Criticism of the military mounted, as many called for their exit from power. In the early days, many hoped that Abiola would be released and given a role, either as a sort of prime minister or the head of a national government.

Of all the suggestions, the one for a government of national unity to reconcile all ethnic groups received the widest support. However, the military rejected it, arguing that it was undemocratic. To placate the people, the government promised that it would create a federal cabinet that reflected the national character and would transfer power to a democratically elected government within a few months. The government also rejected the call to restore the results of the June 12, 1993, elections that Abiola won, arguing that this would be unjust, unfair, and impractical. With Abiola's death, there was no longer any need to press such a claim, even if the government's argument was unconvincing.

While his words were initially doubted by the critical elite, Abubakar used every opportunity to announce that he would relinquish power in 1999. He even warned fellow officers not to dream of future coups, saying that military rule was not good for Nigeria, but at the same time pleading to aspiring politicians to govern well and resolve not to involve the army in settling their disputes. Unlike his predecessor, he interfered minimally in the process, allowed electoral rules to function, and distanced himself from the key political players. Public opposition to the transition program became rather minimal, the major one coming from the rump of the anti-Abacha coalition led by the Chairman of the Campaign for Democracy, Dr. Beko Ransome-Kuti, who tried to convene a small Conference of Nationalities to discuss the restructuring of the federal system and an alternative constitution. To Beko, Abubakar could not be trusted because he served under Abacha, he was close to Babangida, and he is from the north, the region that has dominated power for many years.

In July 1998 the five existing parties were dissolved and the formation of new parties was allowed. Previous elections to local governments contested by the five parties were declared void and sole administrators were appointed to manage local government affairs. The Independent National Electoral Commission (INEC) was dissolved, and a new one was appointed to register new political parties, compile a voters' list, and conduct elections. A crowded transition timetable was announced:

September 24, 1998: Release of provisionally registered political parties;

October 5–19: Voter registration;

December 5: Local government council elections;

December 23: Submission of names for governorship and state assembly elections;

January 9, 1999: State governorship and assembly elections;

January 20: Release of guidelines for presidential and national assembly elections;

February 12: Submission of names of presidential candidates;

February 13–15: Screening of presidential candidates;

February 19: End of election campaign by presidential candidates;

February 27: Presidential election;

March 6: Run-off elections if needed for national assembly and president;

May 29: Swearing-in of elected president.

Unlike before, the registration of political parties would be provisional for a few months. The real test was performance at the polls in the Local Government Council Elections; a party would become official only if it won 5 percent of the total votes cast in each council in at least twenty-four states and had offices in two-thirds of the country. Also unusual was the fact that the country took a long time to decide on modifications to the constitution made under the Abacha regime, and political contests began before the rules were finalized. The expectation was that a small committee would organize a national debate and suggest changes to the presidential constitution in many areas, including: the suitability of the provision on the zoning, the rotation of the presidency, and multiple vice-presidents; the best way to cultivate a sense of national belonging in diverse ethnic and religious groups against the background of allegations of domination by the north and marginalization by some of the constituent units, notably minority groups; and possible means to prevent military coups. The trouble was that most Nigerians had no access to the revised constitution, and therefore, could not offer meaningful suggestions.

The ensuing political activities revealed great tension in the country. The first strategy was the common game: to revive old parties, as in the case of the United Nigerian Congress that changed its name to the United Nigerian People's Party. This was easy to do because there were political networks and infrastructure in place, and established politicians wanted to retain their influence.

The second was the return to ethnic politics as each ethnic group formed powerful political associations. In the south, the goal was to prevent northern domination of politics. Southern politicians believed that they had been robbed of power for too long and they advocated political decentralization, including the break-up of the army and constitutional changes that would ensure a power shift to the south. Some southern party leaders wanted alliances with the north in order to reach an agreement that the presidency would be zoned to the south. A Yoruba politician established the United People's Alliance as a Yoruba-based political party. Igbo leaders announced the conditions of their participation in politics, which included the zoning of powerful offices to their area, and called for the enthronement of the principles of fairness, equity, and rule of law. In a well-received speech, Ojukwu, one of the Igbo leaders, remarked in his typical combative style, ". . . it is already twenty-eight years since we were said to have been defeated in a war as a result of which they continuously rubbed our nose in the dust. . . . We no longer will ask for pardon or acceptance. We have already suffered for too long."[5]

If the Igbo were angry, the Yoruba leaders were bitter. They had hoped that Abiola would lead and his death threw them into confusion. All along some groups had been campaigning for secession. The Egbe Omo Oduduwa, an association based in the United States, not only made the case for secession, but even came up with a draft constitution. In the north, the goal was either to prevent a power shift to the south, describing any such constitutional provision on this as undemocratic, or to sponsor a southern politician believed to be loyal to the north. A critical voice emerged in the north that blamed the military and a few politicians for the country's ills and called for a competent, rather than a tribal leader, while a minority opinion advocated a diarchy.

The people were enthusiastic about what looked like a fresh beginning. Many among them called for a leadership that would consider the plight of the poor, promote equality, justice, honesty, responsibility, and an inspiration to all. The turn-out for voter registration in October was impressive. However, the exercise revealed the decay in the political system as some politicians bought voters' cards in order to rig future elections, a number of people registered more than once, while the registration process was itself ruined by gross inefficiency and card shortage in many places. In spite of the irregularities, INEC continued with its plans, prescribed the guidelines for aspiring politicians, exercised the right to disqualify candidates, and adopted voting methods that would minimize fraud.

In the same period, twenty-six parties submitted applications for registration and nine were approved: Alliance for Democracy (AD), which called for ethically-driven politics and a welfare program, comprised many anti-Abacha groups, and is left-of-the center; the People's Democratic Party (PDP), a centrist party dominated by rich retired military generals; the All People's Party (APP), a right-of-center party comprising many pro-Abacha individuals; the Movement for Democracy and Social Justice (MDSJ), led by a former police chief, Mohammed Yusuf; the Democratic Advanced Movement (DAM), led by Tunji Braithwaite, a Lagos lawyer who always breaks ranks with other politicians; the People's Redemption Party (PRP), organized by a few leftists; the National Solidarity Movement (NSM); the United Democratic Party (UDP); and the United People's Party (UPP). As was to be expected, those who did not make the list complained of discrimination.

Political parties proliferated, not because their founders expected to win, but because they wanted bargaining power, either in joining a registered party or negotiating amalgamation. Smaller ones fused and six big parties emerged, notably: the People's Democratic Party and the All People's Party, both dominated by veteran politicians. In the discourse on power sharing, many professed "true federalism" in the hope that states and ethnic groups would gain defined rights, obligations, equity, and security. The majority of the politicians pursued personal ambitions, spending more time on "boardroom maneuvering" than on giving serious thought to policies. Neither the military nor the politicians gave consideration to the emergence of a reliable political class, institutions that would help democracy work, or an independent and honest judiciary. The political class can still be described, to borrow words from Frantz Fanon, as a greedy class, avid and voracious, with the mind of a huckster. Strong on rhetoric and weak on actions, many of the parties failed to distinguish themselves by putting forth specific political platforms or reacting favorably to community and worker protests. The campaigns revealed that they had no economic businesses to which to devote valuable time, only the hope that politics would supply the cow that they would milk. In some of the primaries to choose party candidates, the contest degenerated into violence, a bad sign for the future of democracy.

Retired military generals such as Olusegun Obasanjo, established politicians such as Alex Ekwueme, Vice-president in the Second Republic, and Bola Ige, a former state governor, and notable senior civil servants such as Gamaliel Onosode and Olu Falae were among those who made early bids for the presidency in the newly formed political parties. Many other political entrepreneurs were to join, apparently to draw attention to themselves and at least secure political appointments in the future. The competition for power favored either those who had previously served in the government or who had acquired substantial wealth. Retired generals were forced either to compete or collaborate with veteran politicians in a setting that was prone to serious conflicts. Both groups had to spend huge sums of money, as if offices were for sale to the highest bidders. As many had acquired money in previous administrations, money became the lubricant of the corrupt political machine. Rather than sell programs to the masses, they offered material benefits such as textile, bicycles, milk, and cash to buy votes. As each ambitious politician tried to undercut the other, Nigeria appeared to hover in the quiet eye of the storm, preparing for an impending hurricane.

The first in the series of elections took place on December 5 to appoint councillors for 774 local government councils. The election was preceded by fear that many politicians would buy votes or rig in some other ways. In areas where conflicts were ongoing, as in the Niger Delta, a number of communities vowed not to participate. The government tried to prevent possible misconduct. The borders with the four neighboring countries were closed to prevent the recruitment of foreigners to vote for their sponsors. Almost 2,000 foreign observers were allowed to monitor the elections. All the nine parties cooperated as their electoral performance would decide their qualification for parliamentary and presidential elections in 1999. Although some small radical pro-democracy organizations called for a boycott, the parties were able to mobilize many of their followers to vote.

Unlike elections conducted under Abacha's tenure, the turnout was better, an indication that political parties were active. The elections were peaceful, although about fifteen people lost their lives in clashes among rival party loyalists, while the politicians who lost alleged bribery and rigging. Three parties did well in the following ranking: the PDP, AD, and APP. The remaining six parties risked disqualification in future elections and may have to seek mergers with the major ones. The AD had strong support among the Yoruba in the southwest, a strong indication that without a merger with another party it would remain a localized party, even if it received official recognition. The APP was the weakest and its future might depend on forging a strong coalition with another party. The PDP's strong showing bolstered the chances of its candidate winning the presidency, and it was also the most national with strong support in the East and North. It may attempt to weaken the AD to have an impact in the Southwest. If it gets too big and wins power, it may fall on a corrupt patrimonial system to reward many leading members in order to survive as a dominant party. Ethnic bloc-voting, regional alliances, and money would be the three key determinants of victory in the remaining elections. Olusegun Obasanjo, although unpopular among his Yoruba people, stands the best chance of emerging as the president in 1999. He projects the image of a nationalist, his party is well funded, and he has the blessing of many northern leaders who regard him as pro-military, conservative, and efficient.

How long will a civilian republic last? On the one hand, Nigeria has demonstrated that military rule generates authoritarianism and mismanagement, which in turn promote the call for democratization and the withdrawal of the military from politics. On the other hand, the country has equally shown that civilian rule generates anarchy and corruption, which encourage military intervention. This is the great contradiction of a system in search of an enduring stability.

POST-SCRIPT: THE 1999 ELECTIONS

As the book was going to press, the major events were those revolving around the remaining elections, especially with regard to the office of the president. In the first round of elections, the PDP established a clear pattern of victories in the elections to the House of Representatives and Senate, and was able to have the highest number of state governors. In February 1999, attention shifted to the presidential election of February 29. Since Obasanjo had become the strongest candidate, his opponents were forced to make political calculations seeking how to overcome his influence within his own party during the primary or to defeat him in the election. Obasanjo was able to raise substantial funds and obtain the support of fellow retired military officers. The AD and APP entered into an alliance that sponsored a joint presidential candidate, Chief Olu Falae. Both the campaigns and elections generated bitterness among the supporters of both candidates, who happen to be from the same Yoruba ethnic group. Obasanjo failed to overcome the hostility of the majority of his own people, who refused to the very end to vote for him.

Obasanjo won the elections with a wide margin. The irregularities and suspicion of corruption were so great that his opponent launched a court battle, and international observers concluded that the election in fact had been tainted. Since both parties engaged in electoral fraud, it is hard to know the extent to which the outcome reflects a popular mandate or whether the outcome would have been substantially different. The military accepted the result, and Obasanjo promised a government that would be honest and development-oriented. Almost immediately, he embarked upon a world tour to gather friends for Nigeria and build international support for his country. Nigeria's president-elect is a well-known figure. He was once the head of state in the late 1970s, eventually retiring to a life of farming, writing, and mediation in African conflicts. His international stature was high in the 1980s and 1990s, and he was once a leading candidate for the office of the Secretary-General of the United Nations. In 1995, he was sentenced to 15 years in jail, following trumped-up charges of a coup against General Abacha. He was released from jail in June 1998, after which he went into politics.

In the aftermath of the elections, among the questions that continue to plague Nigerians are: Is this a true democracy? For how long will the military stay out of power? Will the economy ever improve? Nigerians are more skeptical than hopeful. The political process, however welcome after military rule, revealed all the ills of the past: the prevalent role of money; the tight control of the political process by established political cliques; rampant electoral fraud; and the still commonplace influence of the military, including the retired generals.

The urgent task now is to rebuild the country after long years of decay, military dictatorship, and corruption. The preoccupation of the Nigerian army is now with politics—without a re-orientation to professionalism, it will continue to destabilize the political system. There is also no indication that there is an end in sight to the mismanagement of oil revenues, or that former corrupt leaders will be called upon to account for their wealth.

NOTES

1. *African News Digest*, September, Third Week, 1998, p. 9.
2. Special Supplement, "Nigeria's Police Force," *Africa Today*, October 4, 1998, p. 43.
3. Emeka Anyaoku, Commonwealth Secretary General, Press Statement, June 30, 1998 (See *The Guardian*, June 31, 1998, p. 1).
4. General Abubakar, Press Statement, Robben Island, South Africa, August 25, 1998. See *The African Herald*, September 9, 1998, p. 11.
5. Emeka Ojukwu, Speech to the Igbo Congress, July 24, 1998, *The African Herald*, Vol. 9, No. 8, August 1998, p. 10.

Epilogue: Problems and Challenges

The modern history of Nigeria is a troubled one, characterized not by success in building a viable nation-state, but by the gross failure to overcome the twin problems of political instability and economic under-development. With enormous natural resources, an enlightened intelligentsia, and a hardworking population, the country has no excuse for being in such a miserable condition.

Nigeria enters the new millennium as a poor country, not much better off than when it obtained its independence in 1960, and its citizens have become disillusioned and hopeless. Millions of its youth see migration out of the country as a solution. An army of jobless people take to crime and gangs; others take to religion as an opiate. Oil wealth has not been carefully managed to reduce the impact of dependence on a single com-modity, generate massive internal capital and foreign investments, and increase overall productive capacity and social capital. A successful class of producers is yet to emerge, as it is always more profitable to gain access to power for prebendalism, or to engage in trade, oil bunkering, smuggling, land speculation, currency changing, drug trafficking, and other fraudulent practices. Local industries, with high import contents, continue to struggle for hard currency while foreign investments remain essentially confined to the oil industry.

Nigeria has not squandered its wealth only on white elephant projects, but also on gross mismanagement and misplaced priorities. It tries to purchase prestige as the giant of Africa and leader of the black race. An expensive foreign policy in the 1970s and 1980s, with limited economic gains in return, a steel plant costing over $9 billion, but proving to be inefficient, six automobile plants that produced few cars, and the building of the new capital city of Abuja are among the drains on revenues. Oil money was not invested in the international capital market to yield high returns, while domestic investments were neither viable nor profitable. The country still has no alternatives to oil income and no backup during downturns in the oil market.

In spite of its abundant resources, including a vibrant and educated population, and the largest oil reserves in Africa, Nigeria has reached this sorry state because of a combination of circumstances: the colonial legacy, bad leadership, political authoritarianism, administrative incompetence, mismanagement of oil revenues, institutionalized corruption, the manipulation of ethnicity by the political class, prolonged military regimes, a zero-sum politics where the winner gets all, and exploitation by external forces. Thus far, the country has failed to devise workable political institutions, especially a mechanism to curb abuse of power and allow a genuine transition from military to democratic rule. Oil revenues have enabled the country to survive and its citizens to think of a better future. Yet, oil money has allowed a tiny political class to enjoy a high degree of political autonomy while trampling on the rights of the majority.

Politics is central to Nigeria's progress. Without a stable political environment, development will be impossible. The aim of the political class is dubious: to gain power is to seek the means to loot the treasury, never to uplift the poor. The military has been discredited, both as a security institution and as a political manager. Democracy, in spite of its problems, offers a path to pursue. However, democracy in Nigeria must put economic issues at its center. Merely transferring power from the military to the civilians without addressing the issues of prebendalism, incorporating the demands of the majority of the rural population, and improving a declining economy will not bring permanent solutions.

UNRESOLVED PROBLEMS

Thus far, the country has yet to solve issues revolving around its continued existence as a nation-state, the protection of human rights, the preservation of the constitution, putting an end to military intervention, and using better economic management to enhance living standards.

To start with the economy, dependence on oil with fluctuating revenues will continue to create problems for planning and development. For many years, a few multinational oil companies controlled the industry and the royalties paid to the country were below par. Since the 1970s the country has renegotiated many contracts, increased its bargaining power, and become involved in most phases of the process. However, it has yet to gain full control of production, decide prices, reduce dependence on the multinational companies, acquire relevant technology, and diversify the economy.

Non-oil revenues from import and excise duties are not large enough to supplement oil revenues in periods of decline. For the greater part of the country's history, agriculture sustained the people and the government. Until the mid-1960s three commodities—cocoa, peanut, and palm oil—contributed the bulk of the export earnings. Nigeria was the second largest producer of cocoa and the leading producer of palm oil and peanut. Since the 1970s agriculture had fallen due to alternative income from oil, poor planning, limited incentives to farmers, and a strategy of food import.

The federal government exercises the power to distribute the proceeds from oil. States and local governments lack the resources to maintain themselves with the result that, in order to share in oil revenues, all of them have to accept control by the federal government. Where a state does not produce oil, access to oil revenues has enabled it to maintain a level of public expenditure beyond available local resources. No state remains satisfied with the revenue-sharing formulae, as each asks for more. In the view of the oil-producing states, a principle of derivation will give them more and create equity. Those lacking oil do talk about the need to use fiscal policy to integrate the country and are unwilling to support any move to redistribute oil revenues. States with oil feel cheated since they do not control the proceeds, and, because they tend to be minorities, they are correct in also complaining about ethnic domination. The power of the center is excessive, used to reward and punish. Understandably, the competition for the center is intense, if only to control oil revenues. The inability to solve economic problems has created many related crises. For instance, inflation is caused by, among other things, low productivity, an unfavorable balance of payments, and external dependence. Inflation has brought social and political unrest and increased the cost of development. There are also the issues of unemployment, smuggling (into and out of the country), and rural-urban migration. All governments have muddled along, deceiving the public with misleading statistics and rhetoric of reassurance that all is well.

For the first half of this century, Nigeria relied on agriculture and was able both to feed its large population and also to export a variety of crops for revenue. A decline in agriculture has set in since the 1960s. The share of agriculture in the GDP has been declining, from 10.5 percent in 1966 to 3.5 percent in 1973. Oil has taken over, accounting for over 90 percent of foreign exchange earnings, over 90 percent of total government revenues, and over 50 percent of the GNP.

To move to the political issues, conditions for secession and civil war remain and political competition is about who gets what, why, how, and when. While the country has adopted a federal system, the center is so powerful as to make state autonomy more of a myth than a reality. While the majority continues to demand a democratic government, the military has refused to disengage. Those who opt for democracy have called for a variety of options ranging from a multi-party system to a one-party or a zero-party, each with its own problems. When the Babangida government legislated a two-party system, it failed to produce a wide enough ideological gap between the parties, and politics virtually degenerated into a south-north, Christian-Muslim dichotomy.

Irrespective of the political model or the constitution, the primary political issue is how wealth is distributed among competing interest groups. The dominant property-owning group has accumulated through access to power and has also gradually moved into insurance, banking, construction, manufacturing, and other sectors previously controlled by foreign interests. This tiny class knows that to lose power is to lose wealth. More predators than producers, their purpose in achieving power is not to benefit the majority of the population but only a few. As the economy declines, the competition for power has intensified. The real power that everybody wants is the power to preside over the allocation of licenses to exploit oil and thrust hands deeply into the federal treasury.

The political actors fall into various groups. The major actor has been the military, which has controlled power since 1965 except for the brief periods (1979–1983). Highly undemocratic and difficult to challenge, the military is a danger to the country: it is opposed to the emergence of a lasting democracy, it is corrupt, and it consumes a large part of the budget. If the politicians are venal and greedy, years of wasteful mismanagement under the military have discredited the army and drawn more and more people to a democratic option. The next group of actors is the politicians who have presided over two failed republics and struggled for power in all the transition programs since 1970. Many among them want money, not the opportunity to serve.

Other groups seek the means for co-optation. The civil servants are always eager to reclaim influence, and some of them favor military rule, which allows them a greater say in management. There are also the intellectuals, generally alienated and bitter about the decline of educational institutions. Many have left the country and many of those who remain behind simply pursue the means to survive. Finally there are the traditional chiefs, some of whom are rich, powerful, and educated. They continue to seek a role in politics, with a few advocating a careful blend of republicanism with monarchy. As many of them enjoy credibility and support among their people, those in power have always felt a need to manipulate them in order to reach the public.

The methods of seeking and retaining power are very destructive and usually set the country on a downward trend. Thus far, the most common has been through force, in coups that displace generals with generals. The ideology has remained the same with changes only in style, extent of honesty, and degree of accountability. When the military was accused of not being intellectual enough, it moved in the 1980s to create its own university, run advanced seminars, and invite guest speakers. The military is not immune from ethnic politics, sometimes following a quota system in recruitment and promotion. Since the mid-1960s it has been dominated by northerners, along the same pattern as civilian politics. Because of its permanent interest in politics, there has been constant debate as to its relevance. Lately, ethnic leaders in the southwest have called for regional armies, apparently to facilitate secession.

The next most important method is the manipulation of ethnicity. Loyalty to the ethno-nations is effective in building alliances, associations, and political parties. It can take the form of a north-south divide or of Igbo against Yoruba. Irrespective of the party arrangement, ethnicity is a problem. The arena of politics is confusing and broad, while cross-cutting ties are difficult to forge. Ethnicity allows leaders to be partial, justify corruption, and tolerate maladministration as long as these are perpetrated by fellow ethnic-group members. The creation of states, now standing at thirty-six and more being demanded, has not solved the problem of ethnic strife as anticipated. If the center allocates money to the states, the thinking is that the surest way to acquire more resources is to keep splitting up existing states in order to increase each one's share of federal revenues. However, ethnic identity cuts across states, and political actions can easily evoke communal and ethnic loyalty.

A third method of seeking and retaining power is the manipulation of religion to accentuate ethnic differences. In the north, Islam has consistently been used to unite the region against the rest of the country. Islam provides the tool to foster northern unity, retain established privileges, and mobilize the people against southern politicians or demands. Since 1978 the demand for the Shari'a and the rejection of the concept of a secular state have been used to create a difference from the rest of the country. The contention is that Muslims should not live in a secular state or that the government should let Muslims be administered under Islamic laws instead of the inherited Judeo-Christian laws. To the Christians, this demand is a ruse to use the Shari'a to rally the Muslims, as a prelude to the conversion of Nigeria to an Islamic state.

Finally, civilian actors are organized into political associations and parties when the military allows them. Political parties manipulate religion and ethnicity and use the media to propagate their views. By and large, all the political parties make similar claims, limiting their differences to personality and campaign style. Political beliefs are fluid, espoused for convenience and without consistency. When a politician is unable to attain power through the ballot, he is quick to support a military regime as long as there is something in it for him.

FUTURE SCENARIO

Political alliances will remain fluctuating and fluid as old and new entrants seek the means to gain power. All tiers of government will continue to struggle over the distribution of oil revenues. The social basis of power will remain crucial, as workers, entrepreneurs, tenants, and landlords make various claims. While the elite will continue to dominate power, it will be challenged by the demands of the poor and marginalized. As the gap between the rich and poor widens and opportunities for upward mobility shrink, the country will witness a spate of riots, some calling for a revolution and others threatening the whole fabric of society.

The threat of the military is constant. The army enjoys influence and power out of proportion to its role in defense. It will continue to demand that its corporate interest be satisfied. It has rejected all suggestions to be active in socially desirable functions, while the politicians have rejected involving it in administration on a permanent basis. Military disengagement from politics is a problem. The military has been known to break its promises. The two republics have been short lived, and future ones may not last long. The army cannot be politically neutral. Divided by ethnicity and religion, and with a corps of officers greedy for money and power, it will remain a danger to political stability. The constitutional provision to prevent coups has been ignored, and the army will continue to tyrannize the civil society. Because its officers have lost respect due to their mismanagement and corruption, the military will continue to be subject to public ridicule. The only way to prevent military intervention is not through the legal system but through courageous massive uprisings against illegal regimes, a successful democratic government that responds to the needs of the people, and international cooperation in withdrawing economic support, including a total boycott of Nigeria's oil and other exports.

Social tension will continue to grow as millions of people lack access to land and jobs and are denied opportunities for adequate housing, education, and leisure. As the rich flaunt their wealth, the poor will demand their own share of the "national cake" and press for a more equitable distribution. Opposition by the poor will find expression in armed robbery, drug trafficking, and other crimes.

As a corollary, the country will be prone to violence. The poor will express their frustration in violence. An insecure state, presided over by illegitimate leaders, will use violence to ensure order and subvert the emergence of democracy. Against the background of the stability of Western democracies, it is appropriate to ask why pro-democracy groups have failed to unite in Nigeria, why politicians continue to succumb to the coercive rule of the military, and why a single general like Babangida or Abacha can hold the fate of 100 million people in his callous hands. The answer is to see Nigeria as a patrimonial state with the following anti-democratic features: whoever controls the state does not tolerate the existence of many centers of opposition or the emergence of other powerful leaders; the state is not shy in using the instruments of coercion and violence to destroy opposition forces; political offices are used to acquire wealth, those who have them will do everything to retain them, and those who lack them consider essential only those principles that will get them to power; elections and coups are the same, both avenues to wealth, not opportunities to pursue policies; and many wealthy people succeed not by their entrepreneurship or economic ingenuity, but through access to state power.

Nigeria will remain a corrupt state for as long as the norms of politics

remain unchanged. When the goal of politics is self-enrichment, klep-
tocracy becomes the political model. When very little can be achieved
without power, citizens demand the privileges and goodwill of power.
When an economy is politicized, participants expect favor and bribes.
The country is yet to obtain the commitment of its citizens to an indi-
visible Nigeria or to build an enduring nationalism. When individuals
refuse to give their allegiance to the government, and the political class
is a group of buccaneers, positive and rapid transformation is difficult,
as the country's abiding creed is: "Everybody to himself and God for us
all."

For as long as oil continues to flow, Nigeria may stay united as a
country, although internally fractionalized. The federal system will be
preserved because it allows those who control power to divert resources
to their region and pocket. A federal Nigeria offers a broad space in
which politicians can operate in, allows foreign countries to manipulate
domestic power holders, and forces weak states to look to the center for
support. Creating a strong, united nation will continue to be a problem
because of religious and ethnic divisions, the rejection of merit as the
yardstick for the distribution of privileges, and the failure of democracy.
The political system will continue to manifest instability for as long as
the country finds it difficult to practice democracy and aggregate the
demands of all the component units in the federation. Given the military's obsession with power, it should be expected that more officers will
stage coups and counter-coups. However, pro-democratic forces, too,
will become further strengthened to address continuous military rule.
The civil society is getting stronger, and, as it surmounts the problems
of ethnic and religious divisions, it will mount a greater force against
authoritarianism.

Nigeria still has enormous resources with which to redeem itself. It
remains a regional power in West Africa and can benefit from improved
operations of the Economic Community of West African States, the main
regional economic union. Nigeria's population remains its major asset, a
hardworking people that will always seek both economic and political
empowerment. Change is inevitable, but it is difficult to anticipate the
form it will take. Positive changes will come when the military retreats
to the barracks once and for all, when the political leadership follows
the rules of the game and respects the constitution, when political competition is free and fair, and when the civil society is radicalized enough
to prevent the subversion of democracy and force political leaders to use
power to transform society.

Notable People in the History of Nigeria

Abacha, Major General Sanni (1943–1998), a veteran of many coups, began his military career in 1962 and served in different command positions. He was promoted to the rank of major-general in 1984 and in 1985 became the Chief of Army Staff. In 1993 he appointed himself the country's president. His era was marked by despotism and economic decline.

Abiola, Chief Moshood (1937–1998), was born at Abeokuta where he attended high school before proceeding to the University of Glasgow, Scotland where he trained as an accountant. He joined International Telephone and Telegraph, Ltd. in 1969, rising to become its Vice President for Africa and the Middle East and its Chairman and Chief Executive in Nigeria. He became wealthy and controversial, and was the country's leading philanthropist. His businesses covered newspaper publishing, baking, air transportation, oil drilling, and the book trade. He was a prominent member of the National Party of Nigeria (NPN) during the Second Republic, but resigned from it in 1982 when he was prevented from contesting in the primary for the Presidential Elections. He staged a comeback in the 1990s on the platform of the Social Democratic Party (SDP), winning the Presidential Election in 1993. The military annulled the election and Abiola spent his last years in detention.

Abubakar, Abdulsalami (1942–   ), born at Minna and enlisted in the Nigerian Air Force in 1963 as a cadet. He transferred to the army in 1966 and was commissioned a Second Lieutenant the following year. After different postings, he became a major general in 1991. Three years later he was appointed to the Chief of Defense Staff, a position he occupied until he became the head of state in 1998.

Achebe, Chinua (1930–   ), author of *Things Fall Apart, A Man of the People, No Longer At Ease, Arrow of God, Anthills of the Savannah*, and many books, is Africa's most celebrated novelist. Born at Ogidi in Eastern Nigeria, he received his degree from University College, Ibadan. Between 1954 and 1967 he worked as a broadcaster, until he joined the University of Nigeria, Nsukka, as a professor. He has received numerous prestigious awards and honorary degrees. Other prominent authors include Buchi Emecheta, Cyprian Ekwensi, Vincent Ike, John Pepper Clark, and Pius Okigbo.

Ade, Sunny (1946–   ), is an international star of Juju music, using a blend of Yoruba and Western instruments. At the age of 17 in 1963 he launched his career which has witnessed profound creativity and constant changes in lyrics, songs, and instruments. Juju music started around 1930 with Tunde Nightingale and a band of five. In the 1940s the electric guitar was introduced and in the 1950s the talking drum. I. K. Dairo dominated the scene in the late 1950s and 1960s with the use of the accordion and a variety of rhythms. Sunny Ade started by imitating I. K. Dairo, but later changed to the style of Nightingale with the use of guitars. By 1967 he had become a star, rivaled only by Ebenezer Obey. One successful hit followed another and in 1974 he began to record under his own label. His music became international with songs recorded in Europe and the United States. He remains both creative and energetic, drawing his ideas from Yoruba culture and contemporary politics.

Adebo, Chief Simeon (1913–   ), was a seasoned administrator, diplomat and lawyer. He was called to the bar in 1948, worked as a senior civil servant, and rose to the post of Head of the Civil Service and Chief Secretary to the Government of the Western Region in 1961. In 1962 he became the country's Permanent Representative to the United Nations. In 1968 he was appointed United Nations Under-Secretary-General and Executive Director of the United Nations Institute for Training and Research. He returned to Nigeria in 1970 and held various appointments as chairman of commissions and the National Institute of Policy and Strategic Studies. Other distinguished Nigerian administrators include Adebayo Adedeji, professor and Executive Secretary of the United Nations Economic Commission for Africa for many years; Akin Mabogunje, a highly acclaimed geographer and recipient of many awards, including two doctorate degrees; and Chukwuemeka Anyaoku, the Secretary General of the Commonwealth.

Aguiyi-Ironsi, Major General Johnson (1924–1966), joined the Nigerian army in 1942, rose through the ranks to become a captain in 1953, served as an equerry to Queen Elizabeth II when she visited Nigeria in 1956 and was promoted to the rank of lieutenant colonel in 1958 and to a brigadier in 1961. In 1965 he was elevated to the rank of major general and General Officer Commanding the Nigerian Army. He became the first military head of state in 1966, but only for a few months.

Akintola, Chief S. L. (1910–1967), controversial politician, was premier of the Western Region from 1959 to 1966 when he was killed in the first coup. A brilliant journalist, administrator, lawyer, and orator, he was one of the early members of the Action Group (AG), served in the Central Legislative Council in the 1950s, and became the Deputy Leader of the AG in 1955. When Awolowo attempted to become Prime Minister, Akintola succeeded him as Premier of the West in 1959. Soon afterwards, he and Awolowo began to disagree on many issues, leading to a major crisis in 1962 and the imposition of a state of emergency in the West in 1963. Akintola's political idea of forging an alliance with the north was one of the sources of trouble, and he had to establish his own political party, the Nigerian National Democratic Party. He was accused of rigging the election in October 1965 that returned him to power. His people of Ogbomoso remained very loyal to him. Today, the state university sited in this city is named after their most illustrious son.

Awolowo, Obafemi (1909–1987), was an enterprising politician, lawyer, author, businessman, nationalist, journalist, and Yoruba hero. He was one of the earliest politicians to give serious thoughts to an appropriate constitution for the country, as he eloquently stated in many books, including *Thoughts on the Nigerian Constitution* (1968). In 1948 he established a cultural organization which became a political party, the Action Group, in 1951. In 1949 he established the *Nigerian Tribune*, a daily newspaper still in circulation which served as the mouthpiece of all his political parties. In 1954 he became the first Premier of the Western Region. During his term of office he introduced a program of free primary education, which made him very popular. In 1959 he lost the election for the federal Prime Ministership but became the leader of opposition in Parliament. Wrongly accused of treason to overthrow the federal government, he was sentenced to jail in 1962 but released by the military in 1966. Thereafter, he played a prominent role in the government until 1971. He again made unsuccessful bids in 1979 and 1983 to become the president. He was awarded many chieftaincy titles and honorary degrees, and the highest national honor of the Grand Commander of the Order of the Federal Republic of Nigeria was conferred on him in 1982. Among Awolowo's followers who became successful politicians were five state governors: Chiefs Ambrose Ali, Bola Ige, Michael Ajasin, Lateef Jakande, and Bisi Onabanjo.

Azikiwe, Nnamdi (1904–1996), was born at Zungeru in the north to Igbo parents. A product of several mission schools, he worked as a clerk for two years before going to the United States in 1925; in the United States of America he obtained two Master's degrees. A successful journalist, publisher, entrepreneur, nationalist, and politician, Azikiwe became one of the most prominent architects of radical nationalism in Nigeria. He mobilized thousands of people to the nationalist cause, used his newspaper for combative anti-colonial campaigns, and rose to become the first Premier of the Eastern Region from 1954 to 1959, President of the federal Senate in 1959 and 1960, and the country's first ceremonial President and Governor General. He never retired from politics, making a bid for the country's presidency in 1979 and 1983. Among his notable works are *Renascent Africa* (1939) and *My Odyssey* (1970). He lived a long and active life with many honorary degrees, chieftaincy titles, and the highest honor of the Grand Commander of the Order of the Federal Republic of Nigeria awarded in 1980. The national airport in Abuja, the country's capital, is named after him.

Babalola, Joseph Ayo (1904–1959), was the founder of the Christ Apostolic Church, one of the independent churches that broke away from the white-dominated missions. Known as the Aladura—"praying bands," a number of others were established with emphasis on prayer and intense worship. He received a vision telling him to preach the gospel. He traveled to various West African cities to preach and heal. He attacked indigenous religions and destroyed their objects. His church grew very rapidly and its members established additional missions outside Nigeria. Other notable Nigerian prophets include Josiah Ositelu, Garrick Brade, and Apostle Obadare.

Babangida, Major General Ibrahim G. (1941–), was born at Minna, Niger State. After his high school education, he enlisted in the army in 1963 and held many positions thereafter. In 1984 he became the Army Chief of Staff and in the following year the country's president after a coup. After his exit from power in 1993, he reasserted himself in national politics with a desire both to be a kingmaker and later a king.

Balewa, Alhaji Sir Abubakar Tafawa (1912–1966), Nigeria's first Prime Minister was born in the town of Tafawa Balewa, Bauchi. He trained as a teacher and worked as an educational administrator until he took to full-time politics in the 1940s. In 1947 he was elected to the Legislative Council in Lagos. Two years later, he and others founded a cultural association which later became the Northern People's Congress. Balewa was the deputy leader of the party. He held various important appointments: Minister of Works (1951–1954), Minister of Transport (1954–1957), and Prime Minister (1957–1966). His friendly manner endeared him to the British who showered him with honors: Officer of the Order of the British Empire in 1952, Commander of the Order of the British Empire in 1955, Knight Commander of Order of the British Empire in 1960, and Privy Councilor in 1961.

Bello, Ahmadu, the *Sardauna* (1910–1966), born in Sokoto, a grandson of Uthman dan Fodio, was the most prominent politician from the north during the twentieth century. He lost a bid to become Sultan of Sokoto in 1938, but was appointed the *Sardauna* (war leader). In 1949 he represented Sokoto in the Northern House of Assembly and was a leading figure in the foundation of the Northern People's Congress. In 1954 he became the Premier of the Northern Region. Although he could have become the Prime Minister of Nigeria, he chose to stay in the north, preferring to send his lieutenant, Tafawa Balewa, to Lagos. He was more or less the effective leader of the country. The first university established in the north by his government was named after him. After his death, his name has become an icon and his followers continue to revere him.

Buhari, Major General Muhammad (1942–   ), head of state, 1983–1985, was born in Daura. After his secondary education he joined the army in 1962 and was commissioned as a second lieutenant the following year. He served in different command and staff positions and was appointed the Military Governor of the Northeastern State in 1975. In the following year, he became the federal minister in charge of petroleum and energy, a post he held until 1979.

Carr, Henry (1863–1945), was born in Lagos of manumitted parents who were originally from England but migrated to Nigeria from Sierra Leone. A distinguished educator, he was one of the earliest Nigerians to receive a Western education and the first honors graduate of Fourah Bay College in Sierra Leone. A great educator and administrator, he served in the Legislative Council and as the Resident of the Lagos Colony from 1918 to 1924. He advocated educational reforms and built a large personal library which outlived him. His quiet criticism of colonial rule displeased a new generation of young nationalists in the 1930s and 1940s who saw him as a friend of the British. He received an honorary doctorate and was appointed Commander of the Order of the British Empire (CBE).

Crowther, Bishop Samuel Ajayi (1809–1891), explorer, missionary, and the first African Bishop of the Anglican Church in the country. He was captured and enslaved around 1821, but his slave ship was seized and he was released. In his temporary home in Sierra Leone, he converted to Christianity, was baptized and educated by the Church Missionary Society (C.M.S.) and later acquired a college diploma. Ordained in 1844 he became a full-time missionary and was posted to Nigeria where he served with great distinction, promoting Christianity and translating the New Testament into the Yoruba language. After clashes with white missionaries over policies, he resigned in 1890. He was a recipient of an honorary doctorate and now is a church icon. Yet another notable clergyman is James Johnson (1836–1917), the second African Bishop of the Anglican Church. Regarded as a pioneer nationalist, he became the leader of the Lagos elite, criticized imperialism, and called for an autonomous African church and the expansion of educational opportunities for Africans.

Dike, Kenneth O. (1917–1983), attended Fourah Bay College in Sierra Leone and later universities in Durham, Aberdeen, and London where he obtained higher degrees. His book, *Trade and Politics in the Niger Delta, 1830–1885*, is one of the pioneer academic books by a new generation of African historians who successfully reclaimed the glory of Africa. He was a professor of history in Nigeria and contributed to the development of the Antiquities Commission and the National Archives. In 1960 he became the first Nigerian to head the University of Ibadan, the premier college. His career was interrupted by the civil war, during which he relocated to Harvard University. The country has produced other prominent historians including Professors Jacob Ade Ajayi, Adiele Afigbo, Bolanle Awe, and Bala Usman. A contemporary of Dike was Eni Njoku (1917–1974), who distinguished himself as a botanist, university administrator, politician, and recipient of three honorary doctorates.

Ekandem, His Eminence Dominic (1917–), was a native of Obio Ibiomo, Itu in Cross River State. He attended Catholic seminaries, was ordained a priest in 1947, became an Auxiliary Bishop in 1954, the first West African Catholic Bishop in 1963, and the first Nigerian Cardinal in 1977. He has received such high honors as Order of the British Empire and Commander and Order of the Niger. The country has produced other prominent clergymen in the twentieth century. Among them are Archbishop Olubunmi Okogie who played a major role in mobilizing Christians in the 1980s and 1990s under the umbrella of the Christian Association of Nigeria and Cardinal Francis Arinze, one of the most prominent candidates to become the next Pope.

Elias, Dr. Taslim O. (1914–), was a distinguished jurist, legal scholar, and administrator. He was called to the bar in 1947 and was the first Nigerian to obtain a Ph.D. in law. He was a legal teacher and fellow in different institutions before serving as the country's Attorney General and Minister of Justice from 1960 to 1972. In 1972 he became the Chief Justice and in 1975 he was appointed to the International Court of Justice at the Hague which he was later to head. He served in other important roles, received many doctorates, and published several influential legal studies. Other distinguished legal luminaries include Sir Adetokunbo Ademola, the Chief Justice from 1958 to 1975; Sir Darnley Alexander, Chief Justice from 1975 to 1979; Nabo Graham-Douglas of Rivers State, the Attorney General from 1972 to 1975; Chief Rotimi Williams, Chairman of the Constitution Drafting Committee in 1975–1976; and Chief Gani Fawehinmi, a celebrated civil rights attorney.

Enahoro, Chief Anthony E. (1923–   ), was born at Uromi, Edo State. After attending the elite King's College, Lagos, he took to journalism and in 1944 became the editor of the *Southern Nigerian Defender*. He worked for other newspapers in editorial positions. He was one of the initial members of the Action Group, winning an election to the Western Regional House of Assembly in 1951. He was later sent to the Federal House of Representatives where he moved the "self-government-in-1956" motion. He was a prominent delegate to all the constitutional conferences from 1953 to 1960. In the 1950s he served as a Minister in the Western Region. When the AG became an opposition party, he was its spokesperson on foreign policy from 1959 to 1963. Together with Awolowo, he was accused of treason and sent to jail until his release in 1966 by the Gowon administration. He became the most prominent leader in the Mid-West and served as a federal minister from 1966 to 1975. He was a leading force in the opposition to the military after the annulment of the 1993 presidential election, conducting most of his activities in exile in Europe and the United States.

Gowon, Yakubu (1934–   ), born in the Pankshin division of the Middle Belt. He enlisted in the army in 1954 and was promoted to the rank of colonel in 1963. Following the first coup, he became the Chief of Staff and the second coup brought him to power as Supreme Commander of the army and head of state from 1966 to 1975. His regime witnessed the Civil War and the oil boom. His state governors were powerful men such as Major General Adeyinka Adebayo who headed the Western Region and later became a civilian politician and businessman. After his overthrow, Gowon went into exile in Britain where he enrolled as a student and eventually obtained a Ph.D. degree in 1984. When he tried to come back to power via the democratic process in the 1990s, Gowon lacked the money, astuteness, and network to compete in a treacherous political arena.

Ibiam, Sir Francis Akanu (1906–1995), was born at Unwana, Imo State. A distinguished physician and statesman, he trained in England and served as a doctor in Calabar from 1936 to 1966. He also participated in politics, serving as a member of the Legislative Council and the Executive Council from 1949 to 1952. In addition, he played a prominent role in the Church, being the President of the Christian Council of Nigeria from 1958 to 1962 and becoming the Co-President of the World Council of Churches in 1961. He was the Governor of Eastern Nigeria during the

First Republic and Special Adviser to Colonel Ojukwu during the Civil War. He received four honorary doctorates, also the national award of Grand Commander of the Order of the Niger and was decorated as a knight both by Britain and the Catholic Church.

Ikoku, Alvan (1900–1971), was born at Arochukwu and trained as a teacher. He was a prominent educator. By correspondence he acquired a University of London degree in Philosophy in 1928. In 1931 he established a private high school, the Aggrey Memorial College. He was active in the Nigerian Union of Teachers (NUT) in addition to serving as a member of the Board of Education for the Southern Provinces, the Eastern Nigeria House of Assembly, and the Legislative Council in the late 1940s. His attempt to enter national politics in the 1950s did not succeed, but he became prominent as President of the NUT. His life was dedicated to education, seeking the means to improve the lot of teachers, founding schools, and establishing private scholarships for needy people. In addition to an honorary doctorate, he has been declared a national hero with his picture engraved on the ₦10 bill.

Ikoli, Ernest (1893–1960), a prominent journalist, was born at Brass, Rivers State. After his high school education, he became an editorial assistant with the *Lagos Weekly Record*. In 1921 he established his own newspaper, the *African Messenger*, and in 1926 became the first editor of the *Daily Times*, for decades the most prominent daily. Two years later he founded the *Daily Mail* while also serving as the editor of the *Daily Telegraph* for another publisher. He was equally active in politics; he won a seat on the Legislative Council in 1941 and 1946 and became President of the Nigerian Youth Movement (NYM) in 1941. Later he served as the Public Relations Adviser to the Nigerian Railway Corporation and as Chairman of the Rediffusion Service. He was awarded the Order of the Member of the British Empire. Among his famous contemporaries were Sir Kofoworola Abayomi, a medical doctor and politician who became the president of the Nigerian Youth Movement in 1938 and Sir Adeyemo Alakija (d. 1952), a successful journalist. Another celebrated journalist is Alhaji Babatunde Jose, who distinguished himself in different positions with the *Daily Times* from 1941 to 1975 and received an honorary doctorate in 1980.

Imoudu, Chief Michael (1902–   ), a front-line trade unionist and politician born at Ora, Edo State. He began his career in 1928 with the Nigerian Railway, starting as a laborer, then becoming a turner. He and others established the Railway Workers' Union in 1932. In 1941 he became the Vice-President of an amalgamated union of workers, The African Civil Servants Technical Workers Union (ACSTWU), including the Nigerian Marine African Workers' Union, the P. & T. Workers Union, and the Public Works Department Workers' Union. His activities upset both his employers and the British government. In 1943 he was dismissed and put in detention. Protests led to his release in 1945. In that same year he led a nationwide strike. He was a member of the NCNC while still leading labor unions as the President of the Nigerian Labour Congress. He was active in many union activities even after independence until he was retired by the military in 1976. Two years later, he received an honorary doctorate. He continued to participate in politics as an executive member of radical political parties in the 1970s and 1980s.

Johnson, Rev. Samuel (1846–1901), was born in Sierra Leone and moved to Lagos with his parents in 1857. He worked as a tireless missionary among his Yoruba people. His fame derives from his book, *The History of the Yorubas*, a manuscript he completed in 1897 but which was not published until 1921. This long book is one of the earliest and best examples of how Africans, now literate in their own and European languages, began to record oral traditions, reconstruct the past, and think of progress for their people.

Kano, Alhaji Aminu (1920–1983), was a teacher, politician, administrator, and founder of two left-wing political parties. His long and distinguished political career as a front-line defender of the poor began in the 1940s. Between 1948 and 1953 he led the Northern Teachers' Association. He broke away from conservative northern politicians to establish the Northern Elements Progressive Union which he led from 1950 to 1966. From 1959 to 1964 he was the federal Deputy Government Chief Whip. His efforts at forging alliances with southern political parties did not succeed in dislodging the NPC. Aminu Kano became a star figure during military rule, serving as a minister from 1967 to 1974. He was a presidential candidate during the Second Republic. The international airport in Kano is named after him. An associate of his who continues the tradition of radical politics in the north is Balarabe Musa, born in 1936 in Kaya, Kaduna State. Musa rose to prominence as a member of the People's Redemption Party and became the Governor of Kaduna State in 1978. With the State Legislative Assembly controlled by a rival party, the

NPN, Musa was embroiled in prolonged ideological and policy clashes that led to his impeachment in 1981.

Lambo, Thomas (1929–   ), born at Abeokuta, trained as a psychiatrist in London and began his active career in 1950 as medical specialist for the Aro Hospital Nervous Diseases. He became a Professor of Psychiatry and Dean of the Medical Faculty at the University of Ibadan in 1966 where he also became the college President in 1968. He was an international figure, serving in various capacities such as the Chairman, West African Examinations Council, founder and President of the Association of Psychiatrists in Africa, Chairman, Scientific Council for Africa (1965–1970), member of the Executive Committee, Council for International Organization for Medical Science (UNESCO) from 1965 to 1968, Chairman, United Nations Advisory Committee for the Prevention of Crime and Treatment of Offenders (1968–1971), Assistant Director General (and later Deputy Director), World Health Organization. Among his many awards are honorary doctorate degrees, memberhip of the Order of the British Empire, and the Selassie African Research Award for 1970.

Lugard, Sir Frederick (1858–1945), was an experienced British colonial administrator posted to Nigeria in 1900 after varied experience as a soldier and treaty-negotiator. He was a leading figure in the conquest of northern Nigeria. After a posting in Hong Kong from 1907 to 1912, he returned to Nigeria. He amalgamated the northern and southern protectorates in 1914 and became a leading ideologue of the policy of indirect rule. He retired in 1919 and published a successful book, *The Dual Mandate in British Tropical Africa* in which he argued that the British were in Africa on a civilizing mission. Among his notable successors in Nigeria were Donald Cameron (1872–1948), the Governor from 1931 to 1935; and Sir Arthur Richards (also known as Lord Milverton), the Governor from 1943 to 1947 who laid the groundwork for the review of the constitution that eventually led to independence.

Macaulay, Herbert (1884–1946), was the founder of the Nigerian National Democratic Party in 1923, the first major political party to contest elections. Macaulay was the grandson of the famous missionary, Samuel Ajayi Crowther. An engineer and a journalist, he was a respected leader who aroused a feeling of national consciousness. He defended the rights of Lagos chiefs to power and land and was active in the opposition to the water-rate bill in Lagos in 1908. His newspaper, the *Lagos Daily News*, served as the organ of his party. To the British and to his critics, Macaulay appeared overbearing and crude. He saw himself as a nationalist but due to two criminal convictions he could not contest elections and had to operate as a "kingmaker." When he died in 1946 delegates came from different parts of the country attesting to his widespread popularity. His activities earned him the description "father of Nigerian nationalism." His portrait is on a currency note.

Mohammed, General Murtala Ramat (1938–1976), was head of state for a few months in 1975 and early in 1976. He enlisted in the army in 1957, was commissioned as a second lieutenant in 1961, served in military and administrative capacities, led a division during the civil war, and became a brigadier in 1971. In 1974 he became a minister and a year later the head of state. He is treated as a hero with places, including the Lagos international airport, and roads named after him, while his portrait is on one of the currency notes.

Monguno, Shettima (1926–   ), born in Monguno, Borno State, was one of the country's longest-serving cabinet ministers. He was trained as a teacher and in the 1940s worked as Education Secretary to the Borno Local Authority. An active member of the Northern People's Congress, he served as a minister during the First Republic and under the government of Gowon. Another prominent Kanuri is the veteran politician, Alhaji Waziri Ibrahim, minister during the First Republic and party leader and presidential candidate during the Second Republic.

Nzeogwu, Major Patrick Chukwuma (1937–1967), was of Igbo parentage but grew up in the northern city of Kaduna where he also went to school. He joined the army as a cadet in 1956 and rose to become a major ten years later. He collaborated with a few others to stage the country's first coup. While the coup succeeded in ending the First Republic, Nzeogwu and his fellow plotters did not secure power. Originally detained by the federal government, he was later released by Colonel Ojukwu. He fought on the side of Biafra during the war. To many he was a hero for removing the politicians of the First Republic. Yet to others in the north he was a villain who had such a notable figure as *Sardauna* Bello killed.

Obasanjo, General Olusegun (1937–   ), was head of state from 1975 to 1979. He joined the army in 1958, moving to the engineering corps in

1963. He later became the Commander of the Engineering Unit. He commanded a division during the war and accepted the surrender of the secessionists in 1970. His fortunes changed rapidly from 1975 onwards: in January of that year he was appointed a federal minister, in July he became the Chief of Staff of the army, and in February 1976 he became the head of state. He retired from the army in 1979 to live a productive life as a farmer, author, and elder statesman. He was honored with the title of Grand Commander of the Order of the Federal Republic of Nigeria in 1980. He has never been shy in criticizing the government, usually in a constructive manner. He was wrongly accused of a coup by the Abacha regime, which sentenced him to a long prison term. He was released in 1998 by the new military leader and he entered politics to run for president.

Ojukwu, Colonel C. Odumegwu (1933–   ), son of a distinguished politician and millionaire businessman, Sir Louis Ojukwu. Odumegwu was one of the first to enter the army with a university degree. He joined the army in 1957, became a lieutenant-colonel in 1963, and was appointed the Military Governor of the Eastern Region in 1967. He was a leading figure in the civil war as the first and only head of state of the Republic of Biafra. He was in exile from 1970 to 1982 when he received a presidential pardon. Since then, he has been active in politics with disappointing results.

Ransome-Kuti, Mrs. Olufunmilayo (1900–1978), was a defender of women's rights and a politician. Born in Abeokuta, she went to school in that city before proceeding to England in 1919, where she studied music and domestic science. She returned to Abeokuta where she worked as a schoolteacher and married the Rev. Israel Ransome-Kuti, son of the distinguished clergyman, Canon Josiah Ransome-Kuti. In 1948 Mrs. Ransome-Kuti mobilized women in Abeokuta to form the Egba Women's Union, which became a powerful political force. One remarkable event organized by the Women's Union was the protest against the *Alake*, the king of the town, for enforcing food trade regulations that made life uncomfortable for the people. The *Alake* had to be deported in 1948 and reforms were introduced into the administration. Ransome-Kuti was active in the National Council of Nigeria and the Cameroons (NCNC), serving as the only woman in the delegation to protest the Richards Constitution in 1947 and holding executive positions in the party. For representing women's interests she became famous and was honored with a doctorate degree, the Order of the Niger, and the Lenin Peace Prize.

Mrs Ransome-Kuti's father-in-law, Canon Ransome-Kuti (1885–1930), was a church leader and respected elder in Abeokuta. Her children, too, were equally famous, the most notable being Fela Anikulapo-Kuti (1937–1997), the "Afro beat" creator and the country's most celebrated musician and international star. For over two decades, Fela was a leading critic of the military who imprisoned him on several occasions. His music is both original and unique, combining African rythms with jazz and blues.With a large band of close to forty musicians and dancers, his club in Lagos was the main venue of his successful concert and talk-show. Yet another famous son is Beko Ransome-Kuti, a medical doctor and political activist. Wrongly accused for participating in a coup in 1994, Abacha sentenced him to prison until his release in 1998.

Shagari, Alhaji Shehu (1924–   ), rose to become President of Nigeria from 1979–1983. He started as a teacher before changing to full-time politics in 1949 as a member of the Northern People's Congress. In 1954 he was elected into the Federal House of Representatives, in 1958 he was appointed a parliamentary secretary, and in 1959 he became a minister. Between 1967 and 1970 he was a commissioner at the state level before being again appointed as a federal minister until 1975. Thereafter he played underground politics and became a prominent member of the National Party of Nigeria on whose ticket he ran for president. His career as a politician has shown him to be more skillful in making deals than in contributing to policies which would uplift the people. His respected Vice President was Chief Alex Ekwueme, an Igbo.

Soyinka, Wole (1934–   ), the first African to win the Nobel Prize for Literature, is a versatile figure. He is a critic, a political activist, and a playwright. He was an important spokesperson of opposition against the Abacha regime. His works include *The Trials of Brother Jero*, *The Road*, *The Interpreters*, and many poems. An author of prodigous energy, he writes in all genres in addition to being an actor and stage director. The Yoruba have also produced other notable writers. One is Amos Tutuola, who popularized Yoruba folklore in many of his creative writings, most especially *The Palm-Wine Drunkard*, in a style that used literary translation from Yoruba to English. Like D. O. Fagunwa, who wrote mainly in the

Yoruba language, Tutola takes his readers to the world of ghosts and spirits.

Tarka, Joseph (1932–1980), was a prominent politician from among the Tiv in the Middle Belt. He was the founder and President of the United Middle Belt Congress (UMBC), which advocated the creation of the Middle Belt State. In 1954 he won a seat in the Federal House of Representatives and he led his party to the constitutional conferences of the period. His efforts to forge alliances with southern political parties met with limited success. In 1967 the Benue Plateau State was created by the military and Tarka became a federal minister. He resigned in 1974 but rejoined politics later as a member of the NPN. He was a senator until his death.

Tinubu, Madam (1805–1887), was a successful businesswoman and leader in the nineteenth century. Born in Abeokuta, she started her lucrative business in salt, tobacco, and slaves in Badagry. When King Akitoye was deposed in 1846, he went to Badagry, where he received assistance from Tinubu. After he regained his throne, Tinubu followed him to Lagos where she became powerful and prominent. Akintoye died in 1853 and was succeeded by Dosumu. Again, the influence of Tinubu grew, leading to accusations that the king was weak. After an unsuccessful fight with wealthy immigrants in Lagos, she was expelled from Lagos and resettled at Abeokuta. She again took to trade and politics, rising to become *Iyalode*, the chief of all women in Abeokuta, in 1864. She is now regarded as a heroine with a square named after her in Lagos and a monument erected in her name in Abeokuta. Other prominent women include Aduni Oluwole, and Omu Oluwei of Osomari and Onitsha.

Fodio, Uthman dan (1754–1817), was born in the northwest Hausa state of Gobir, a Fulani cleric, a missionary, a prolific author, and leader of the social movement that staged the jihad in 1804. Opposition to the persecution of Muslims, excessive taxation and the marginalization of educated Fulani in politics were some of the reasons why dan Fodio organized the rebellion. He was appointed the "Leader of the Faithful" and the jihad began in 1804. By 1812 an Islamic state had emerged. The British used the Sokoto Caliphate to run an indirect rule system, and it provided the basis for northern unity in modern Nigeria. A famous son of dan Fodio was Ahmadu Bello (1797–1837), who succeeded his father as sultan in 1817. A scholar and a warrior, Bello was able to centralize the administration of the caliphate and governed effectively until his death. Two other dominant religious figures of the nineteenth century were Muhammad el-Kanemi (1779?–1835) and Hayatu ibn Said (1840?–1898). Al-Kanemi saved the Borno empire from the invading army of the Sokoto jihadists and established a new dynasty to replace the Sefawa dynasty. Hayatu, a great-grandson of dan Fodio, revived a radical Mahdist movement in the 1880s. In 1881 he proclaimed himself the Mahdi (the Messiah chosen to purify Islam) with the mission of driving away the infidels. He failed to establish a new political kingdom but his ideas became the ideology of resistance against the British.

Selected Bibliography

These bibliographical recommendations are not intended to be exhaustive, but they do suggest additional readings that also contain rich literature on general and specialized subjects. Some useful works are inaccessible to the general audience, while many journal articles are omitted due to limited space.

For a detailed history of the country before independence, with research conducted in the 1960s and 1970s, read the collection edited by O. Ikime, *Groundwork of Nigerian History* (Ibadan: Heinemann, 1980). There is a ten-volume edited work on Nigeria after independence under the general editorship of Tekena Tamuno, *Nigeria Since Independence: The First Twenty-Five Years* (Ibadan: Heinemann, 1989). Now dated, M. Crowder's *The Story of Nigeria* (London: Hutchinson, 1971) and O. Arikpo, *The Development of Modern Nigeria* (Harmondsworth: Penguin, 1967) are still useful for the period before 1945. A book that extends the analysis further is E. Isichei, *A History of Nigeria* (Harlow, England: Longman, 1983). Year-by-year reviews of events are offered in the annual publication, *Africa* (Guildford, England: Dushkin).

Among important bibliographical works on Nigeria are: C. C. Aguolu, *Nigeria: A Comprehensive Bibliography in the Humanities and Social Sciences, 1900–1971* (Boston: C. K. Hall, 1973); E. Baum, ed., *A Comprehensive Pe-*

riodical Bibliography of Nigeria, 1960–1970 (Athens: Ohio University Center for International Studies, 1975); M. W. Delancey and E. L. Normandy, eds., *Nigeria: A Bibliography of Politics, Government, Administration, and International Relations* (Los Angeles: Crossroads Press, 1983); O. G. Tamuno and G. A. Alabi, eds., *Nigerian Publications, 1950–1970* (Ibadan: Ibadan University Press, 1977); and J. Daloz, *Le Nigeria: Société et Politique (Bibliographie)* (Bordeaux 1: Institut D'Etudes Politiques, 1992).

For travelers' guides and basic factual information, see H. D. Nelson, *Area Handbook for Nigeria* (Washington, D.C.: American University, 1972); H. D. Nelson, *Nigeria, A Country Study* (Washington, D.C.: American University, 1982); and A. Oyewole, *Historical Dictionary of Nigeria* (London: Scarecrow, 1987). An essay that reflects on Nigeria and Africa in general is by Toyin Falola, "Africa in Perspective," in Stephen Ellis, ed., *Africa Now: People, Policies and Institutions* (London: James Currey, 1996), pp. 3–19.

CHAPTER 1

Nigerian politics and economy change very rapidly and events are unpredictable. For regular updates, magazines such as *West Africa* and *Africa* are useful. Now dated, an interesting book on the environment is N. P. Iloeje, *A New Geography of Nigeria* (Lagos: Longman, 1965). J. V. Udoh's *Environmental and Economic Dilemmas of Developing Countries* (Westport: Praeger, 1994) reviews various arguments. On infrastructure, see Toyin Falola and S. A. Olanrewaju, eds., *Nigerian Transport Systems* (Syracuse: Maxwell School of Citizenship and Public Affairs, Foreign and Comparative Studies Program, African Series XLII, 1986); and on population and health, see Toyin Falola and D. Ityavyar, eds., *The Political Economy of Health in Africa* (Columbus: Monographs in International Studies, 1992). Studies on cultures are many but are organized around specific ethnic groups. For a summary of cultural practices in many places, see M. U. Okehie-Offoha and M. N. O. Sadiku, eds., *Ethnic and Cultural Diversity in Nigeria* (Trenton: Africa World Press, 1996). For an analysis of contemporary cultures, consult S. Afonja and T. O. Pearce, eds., *Social Change in Nigeria* (Harlow, England: Longman, 1984). For specialized studies of some cities, see for instance, A. B. Aderibigbe, ed., *Lagos: The Development of an African City* (Lagos: Longman, 1976); A. O'Connor, *The African City* (London: Hutchinson, 1983); and W. Ogionwo, ed., *The City of Port-Harcourt: A Symposium of its Growth and Development* (Ibadan: Heinemann, 1979). Among studies on urbanization are: A. L. Mabogunje, *Urbanization in Nigeria* (London: University of London Press, 1968); P. O. Sada and J. S. Oguntoyinbo, eds., *Urbanization Processes and Problems in Nigeria* (Ibadan: Ibadan University Press, 1981); and J. Uyanga, *Towards a Nigerian National Urban Policy* (Ibadan: Ibadan University Press, 1982). For an overview of the development of Nigerian cities, see Toyin Falola, "The Cities," in Y. B. Usman, ed., *Nigeria Since Independence: The Society* (Ibadan: Heinemann, 1989), pp. 213–49. On the country's population consult *Population Data Assessment in Nigeria* (Benin City: Population Association of Nigeria, 1980). On the problems of internal boundaries the most valuable study is O. Adejuyigbe, *Boundary Problems in Western Nigeria: A Geographical Analysis* (Ile-Ife: University of Ife Press, 1973).

CHAPTER 2

For an overview, see Toyin Falola and Biodun Adediran, eds., *Nigeria before 1800 AD* (Lagos: John West, 1986) and Toyin Falola et al., *History of Nigeria: Before A.D. 1800s* Vol. 1 (Lagos: Longman, 1989). There are many highly specialized studies and journal essays on different communities. See the bibliography in Toyin Falola, *The Political Economy of a Pre-colonial African State, Ibadan, ca. 1830–1900* (Ile-Ife: University of Ife Press, 1984). On the history of some cultural groups, see, D. Forde, *The Yoruba-Speaking Peoples of South-Western Nigeria* (London: I.A.I., 1969); M. A. Onwuejeogwu, *An Igbo Civilization: Nri Kingdom and Hegemony* (London: Ethnographica, 1981); and D. C. Ohadike, *Anioma: A Social History of the Western Igbo People* (Athens: Ohio University Press, 1994). On indigenous religions among the most useful sources are: J. S. Mbiti, *African Religions and Philosophies* (New York: Praeger, 1970); and E. B. Idowu, *Olodumare: God in Yoruba Belief* (London: Longman, 1962). Books on gender include: N. Mba, *Nigerian Women Mobilized: Women's Political Activity in Southern Nigeria, 1900–1945* (Berkeley: University of California Press, 1982); David Sweetman, *Women Leaders in African History* (London: Heinemann, 1984); O. W. Ogbomo, *When Men and Women Mattered: A History of Gender Relations Among the Owan of Nigeria* (Rochester: University of Rochester Press, 1997); and C. Johnson-Odim and N. E. Mba, *For Women and the Nation: Funmilayo Ransome-Kuti of Nigeria* (Urbana and Chicago: University of Illinois Press, 1997).

The nineteenth century is well documented including monographs on the Yoruba wars, Islamic revolutions, trade in the Niger Delta, and other topics. Toyin Falola and Dare Oguntomisin, eds., *Nigeria in the Nineteenth Century* (Lagos: John West, forthcoming) is an update on the research findings on different issues. An accessible overview is Toyin Falola, et al., *History of Nigeria; Nigeria in the Nineteenth Century*, Vol. 11 (Lagos: Longman, 1991). On Islam and Christianity, see Toyin Falola and Biodun Adediran, *Islam and Christianity in West Africa* (Ile-Ife: University of Ife Press, 1983).

CHAPTER 3

Background reading on the expansion of Europe to Africa include M. Crowder, *West Africa Under Colonial Rule* (London: Hutchinson, 1968). A valuable book of sources is T. Hodgkin, *Nigerian Perspectives: An Historical Anthology* (London: Oxford University Press, 1975). On the spread of Christianity important works include: E. A. Ayandele, *The Missionary Impact on Modern Nigeria, 1842–1914: A Political and Social Analysis* (London: Longman, 1966); J. F. A. Ajayi, *Christian Missions in Nigeria 1841–1891: The Making of a New Elite* (London: Longman, 1965); and F. K. Ekechi, *Missionary Enterprise and Rivalry in Igboland 1850–1914* (London: Frank Cass, 1971). J. H. Kopytoff, *A Preface to Modern Nigeria: The "Sierra Leonians" in Yoruba 1830–1890* (Madison: University of Wisconsin Press, 1965) is a fascinating study on the role of a new elite. Accounts of the activities of some explorers include E. W. Bovill, *Missions to the Niger* (London: Hakluyt Society, 1966). On trade and trade rivalries important studies include: K. O. Dike, *Trade and Politics in the Niger Delta, 1830–1885* (Oxford: Oxford University Press, 1959); and R. O. Ekundare, *An Economic History of Nigeria, 1860–1960* (London: Methuen, 1973). A good summary of events in eastern Nigeria can be found in C. C. Ifemesia, *Nigeria in the Nineteenth Century: An Introductory Analysis* (New York: Nok, 1978).

CHAPTER 4

This is a fertile area of research with hundreds of books and essays on different aspects of the partition and the response by Africans from a variety of perspectives. A short overview is O. Ikime, *The Fall of Nigeria: The British Conquest* (London: Heinemann, 1977). A useful source on the nature of colonial boundaries is A. I. Asiwaju, *Partitioned Africans: Ethnic Relations Across Africa's International Boundaries, 1884–1984* (London: C. Hurst, 1985). For a biographical work on Lord Lugard, see M. Perham, *Lugard* (London: Collins, 1960) and for Nigerian heroes of the period a recent study is by D. C. Ohadike, *The Ekumeku Movement: Western Igbo Resistance to the British Conquest of Nigeria, 1883–1914* (Athens: Ohio University Press, 1991). On the cultural dimension of resistance, see J. B. Webster, *The African Churches Among the Yoruba, 1888–1922* (Oxford: Clarendon Press, 1964). For an overview of this period, see Toyin Falola, et al., *History of Nigeria: Nigeria in the Twentieth Century*, Vol. 3 (Lagos: Longman, 1992).

CHAPTER 5

Among important general works on the colonial administration are F. Lugard, *The Dual Mandate in British Tropical Africa* (London: Frank Cass, 1922 and 1965); H. A. Gailey, *The Road to Aba: A Study of British Administration Policy in Eastern Nigeria* (New York: New York University Press, 1970); and I. F. Nicolson, *The Administration of Nigeria 1900–1960: Men, Methods and Myths* (Oxford: Clarendon Press, 1975). For comparative studies consult C. Young, *The African Colonial State in Comparative Perspectives* (New Haven: Yale University Press, 1994). Education, especially higher institutions, was of concern to a growing indigenous elite. Educational trends have received elaboration in A. Fafunwa, *History of Education in Nigeria* (London: George Allen and Unwin, 1974), O. Nduka, *Western Education and the Nigerian Cultural Background* (Oxford: Oxford University Press, 1964), and N. Okafor, *The Development of Universities in Nigeria* (London: Longman, 1971). For the evaluation of colonial policies on Nigeria, see Toyin Falola, ed., *Nigeria and Britain: Exploitation or Development?* (London: Zed, 1987).

CHAPTER 6

On nationalism, the following are highly recommended: J. S. Coleman, *Nigeria: Background to Nationalism* (Berkeley and Los Angeles: University of California Press, 1958); R. L. Sklar, *Nigerian Political Parties: Power in an Emergent African Nation* (Princeton: Princeton University Press, 1963); B. J. Dudley, *Parties and Politics in Northern Nigeria* (London: Frank Cass, 1968); H. I. Bretton, *Power and Stability in Nigeria: The Politics of Decolonization* (New York: Praeger, 1962); K. W. J. Post, *The Nigerian General Election of 1959* (Oxford: Oxford University Press, 1963); K. W. J. Post and G. Jenkins, *The Price of Liberty* (Cambridge: Cambridge University Press, 1973); and C. S. Whitaker, Jr., *The Politics of Tradition: Continuity and Change in Northern Nigeria, 1946–1966* (Princeton: Princeton University Press, 1970). For attempts to reform the colonial rule at the time of decolonization consult: P. Kilby, *Industrialization in an Open Economy: Ni-*

geria 1945–1966 (Cambridge: Cambridge University Press, 1969); and Toyin Falola, *Development Planning and Decolonization in Nigeria* (Gainesville: University Press of Florida, 1996). For autobiographical accounts of some of the nationalists, see: O. Awolowo, *Awo: The Autobiography of Chief Obafemi Awolowo* (Cambridge: Cambridge University Press, 1960); N. Azikiwe, *My Odyssey: An Autobiography* (London: C. Hurst, 1970); and A. Bello, *My Life* (Cambridge: Cambridge University Press, 1962). Wogu Anababa's *The Trade Union Movement in Africa: Promise and Performance* (London: C. Hurst, 1979) analyzes the role of trade unions in their early days in relation to British rule.

CHAPTER 7

Recommended works for this chapter include: B. J. Dudley, *Instability and Political Order: Politics and Crisis in Nigeria* (Ibadan: Ibadan University Press, 1973); B. J. Dudley, *Nigeria 1965: Crisis and Criticism* (Ibadan: Ibadan University Press, 1966); E. O. Awa, *Federal Government in Nigeria* (Los Angeles: University of California Press, 1964); L. Diamond, *Class, Ethnicity and Democracy in Nigeria: The Failure of the First Republic* (London: Macmillan, 1988); A. Adedeji, *Nigerian Federal Finance: Its Development, Problems and Prospects* (New York: Hutchinson, 1969); K. Ezera, *Constitutional Development in Nigeria* (Cambridge: Cambridge University Press, 1964); J. P. Mackintosh, *Nigerian Government and Politics* (London: George Allen and Unwin, 1966); H. A. Oluwasanmi, *Agriculture and Nigerian Economic Development* (Oxford: Oxford University Press, 1966); O. Aboyade, *Foundations of an African Economy* (New York: Praeger, 1966); G. K. Helleiner, *Peasant Agriculture, Government and Economic Growth in Nigeria* (Homewood, Ill.: R. D. Irwin, 1966); R. Anifowose, *Violence and Politics in Nigeria: The Tiv and Yoruba Experience, 1960–66* (New York: Nok, 1980); and, I. A. Gambari, *Party Politics and Foreign Policy: Nigeria During the First Republic* (Zaria: A.B.U. Press, 1979).

CHAPTER 8

The civil war era has generated a wide array of studies from a variety of perspectives. Some studies express emotions rather than providing objective analyses. Among others, see: O. Eze, *Nigeria-Biafra Conflict: Social and Economic Background* (Basel: University of Basel, 1971); E. W. Nafziger, *The Politics of Economic Instability—The Nigerian-Biafran War* (Colorado: Westview, 1983); G. A. Affia, *Nigerian Crisis 1966–1970: A Preliminary Bibliography* (Lagos: Lagos University Press, 1971); J. De St.

Jorre, *The Nigerian Civil War* (London: Hodder and Stoughton, 1972); O. Ojukwu, *Biafra*, 2 vols. (New York: Harper and Row, 1969); A. Ademoyega, *Why We Struck: The Story of the First Nigerian Coup* (Ibadan: Evans Brothers, 1981); Africa Research Group, *The Other Side of Nigeria's Civil War* (Boston: Africa Research Group, 1970); N. Akpan, *The Struggle for Secession, 1966–70* (London: Frank Cass, 1971); S. Cronje, *The World and Nigeria: The Diplomatic History of the Nigerian Civil War 1967–70* (London: Sidgwick and Jackson, 1972); F. Forsyth, *The Biafran Story* (London: Penguin, 1969); A. H. M. Kirk-Greene, ed., *Crisis and Conflict in Nigeria: A Documentary Source Book 1966–69* 2 vols. (Oxford: Oxford University Press, 1971); A. A. Madiebo, *The Nigerian Revolution and the Biafran War* (Enugu: Fourth Dimension, 1980); N. J. Miners, *The Nigerian Army, 1955–66* (London: Methuen, 1971); A. A. Nwakwo, *Nigeria: The Challenge of Biafra* (London: Rex Collins, 1972); O. Obasanjo, *My Command* (Ibadan: Heinemann, 1980); I. Nzimiro, *The Nigerian Civil War: A Study in Class Conflict* (Enugu: Fourth Dimension, 1978); and J. J. Stremlau, *The International Politics of the Nigerian Civil War, 1967–70* (Princeton: Princeton University Press, 1977).

CHAPTER 9

The literature on oil is now impressive, but only a few can be mentioned here. L. Schatzl, *Petroleum in Nigeria* (Ibadan: Oxford University Press, 1969); K. Panter-Brick, ed., *Soldiers and Oil: The Political Transformation of Nigeria* (London: Frank Cass, 1978); A. A. Ikein, *The Impact of Oil on a Developing Country* (New York: Praeger, 1990). On educational changes, see M. Bray, *Universal Primary Education in Nigeria* (London: Routledge and Kegan Paul, 1981). B. Labanji, *Anatomy of Corruption in Nigeria* (Ibadan: Daystar, 1970) captures the concerns with corruption during the 1970s. Among other useful works are G. Williams, *State and Society in Nigeria* (Idanre: Afrografika, 1980); G. Williams, ed., *Nigeria: Economy and Society* (London: Rex Collins, 1976); G. J. Apeldoorn, *Perspectives on Drought and Famine in Nigeria* (London: Allen & Unwin, 1981); A. D. Ayida and H. M. A. Onitiri, eds., *Reconstruction and Development in Nigeria* (Ibadan: Oxford University Press, 1971); and Dupe Olatunbosun, *Nigeria's Neglected Rural Majority* (Ibadan: Oxford University Press, 1975).

CHAPTER 10

The most detailed work is O. Oyediran, ed., *Nigerian Government and Politics Under Military Rule, 1966–79* (London: Macmillan, 1979). Other useful books are: W. I. Ofonagoro and A. Ojo, eds., *The Great Debate: Nigerian Viewpoints on the Draft Constitution 1976/77* (Lagos: *Daily Times*, n.d.); and T. O. Odetola, *Military Politics in Nigeria: Economic Development and Political Stability* (New Brunswick, NJ: Transaction Books, 1978). Toyin Falola and Julius O. Ihonvbere, eds., *Nigeria and the International Capitalist System* (Boulder: Lynne Rienner, 1988) offers a more cautious analysis than many pro-military books. For a summary of different issues, one useful source is H. Bienen, *Political Conflict and Economic Change in Nigeria* (London: Frank Cass, 1985).

CHAPTER 11

Two authoritative accounts of the period are R. Joseph, *Democracy and Prebendal Politics in Nigeria: The Rise and Fall of the Second Republic* (Cambridge: Cambridge University Press, 1987); and Toyin Falola and Julius Ihonvbere, *The Rise and Fall of Nigeria's Second Republic, 1979–84* (London: Zed, 1985). For two essays on the subject see L. Adamolekun, *The Fall of the Second Republic* (Ibadan: Spectrum Books, 1985). Other notable sources covering both this and the preceding period include: W. Graf, *The Nigerian State* (London: James Currey, 1988); P. Lubeck, *Islam and Urban Labour in Northern Nigeria* (Cambridge: Cambridge University Press, 1986); A. Kirk-Greene and D. Rimmer, *Nigeria Since 1970* (London: Hodder and Stoughton 1981); P. N. C. Okigbo, *National Development Planning in Nigeria* (Enugu: Fourth Dimension, 1981); T. Forrest, *Politics and Economic Development in Nigeria* (Boulder: Westview, 1995); and Toyin Falola, ed., *Modern Nigeria* (Lagos: Modelor, 1990).

CHAPTER 12

A leading book on the oil industry in the 1980s is P. O. Olayiwola, *Petroleum and Structural Change in a Developing Country: The Case of Nigeria* (New York: Praeger, 1987); but see also J. K. Onah, *The Nigerian Oil Industry* (New York: St. Martins, 1983) and G. Etikerentse, *Nigerian Petroleum Law* (London: Macmillan, 1985). For the anticipation of future crises, refer to C. Stevens, *Nigeria: Economic Prospects to 1985, After the Oil Glut* (London: The Economist Intelligence Unit, 1982). On the role of the World Bank and the IMF in African economies, see among others, B. Onimode, *The IMF, the World Bank, and the African Debt: The Economic Impact* (London: Zed, 1989); and M. B. Brown and P. Tiffen, *Short Changed: Africa and World Trade* (Boulder: Lynne Reiner, 1992). A few sources exist on escalating criminality: see A. U. Kalu and Y. Osinbajajo, eds., *Narcotics: Law and Policy in Nigeria* (Lagos: Federal Ministry of Justice, 1990); and S. Ekpeyong, "Social Inequalities, Collusion, and Armed Robbery in Nigerian Cities," *British Journal of Criminology*, 29: 1 (1989), pp. 21–34.

CHAPTER 13

From the growing body of literature on Nigeria since 1993, the following are recommended: P. Williams and Toyin Falola, *Religious Impact on the Nation State* (Aldershot, England: Avebury, 1995); M. H. Kukah and Toyin Falola, *Religious Militancy and Self-Assertion: Islam in Northern Nigeria* (Aldershot, England: Avebury, 1996); and Toyin Falola, et. al., *The Military Factor in Nigeria* (New York: Edwin Mellen, 1994).

CHAPTER 14

The nature of the contemporary crisis is examined in C. Ake, *Democracy and Development in Africa* (Washington D.C., 1996). Stimulating perspectives are offered in O. Obasanjo and Hans D'Orville, *Challenges of Leadership in African Development* (New York: Crane Russak, 1990) and Toyin Falola, *Violence in Nigeria* (Rochester: University of Rochester Press, 1998).

Index

About the Author

TOYIN FALOLA is Professor of History at the University of Texas at Austin. A leading historian of Nigeria and a distinguished Africanist, he serves on the editorial board of many journals, co-edits the *Journal of African Economic History*, and serves as series editor for Studies in African History and the Diaspora. His publications include many essays and books on Nigeria, including *Decolonization and Development Planning* (1996) and *Violence in Nigeria: The Crisis of Religious Politics and Secular Ideologies* (1998). He is currently working on a book called *The African Intelligentsia*.

Other Titles in the
Greenwood Histories of the Modern Nations
Frank W. Thackeray and John E. Findling, Series Editors

The History of Japan
Louis G. Perez

The History of Israel
Arnold Blumberg

The History of Spain
Peter Pierson

The History of Germany
Eleanor L. Turk

The History of Holland
Mark T. Hooker